The Waiting Womb

To order additional copies, please contact us.
BookSurge, LLC
www.booksurge.com
1-866-308-6235
orders@booksurge.com

JILL SAYRE

THE WAITING WOMB

2006

The Waiting Womb

ACKNOWLEDGEMENTS

The following people deserve special thanks: My husband, Brian, who tolerates my "ADD" and challenges me to be a better person—always. Thank you to my initial proofreaders, Joy Ward and Wendy Cornell. To Isabella Dayton and Amy Bruns for your faith and support. To Zach for being a good big brother. To Danielle Meyer for modeling. And to Lily for inspiring this story.

"Your children are not your children. They are the sons and daughters of Life's longing for itself. They come through you but not from you, And though they are with you, yet they belong not to you.

Kahlil Gibran, The Prophet

Welcome House Adoption Program, mentioned in the novel, is a real agency associated with the Pearl S. Buck Foundation. They have provided quality service for over fifty years and are still going strong. They are thorough, professional and highly reputable. If you are considering adoption or know someone who is, you can access information from the Internet at www.pearl.s.buck.org.

While some situations were borrowed from personal experience, the characters in this novel are fictitious. Any resemblance to real people is purely coincidental.

CHAPTER ONE

The ladies' room at Macy's was as good a place as any to have an emotional breakdown. The bloated, crampy feeling in my abdomen was not, after all, a sign of lactose intolerance triggered by the chocolate ice cream I'd had for breakfast just an hour earlier. Even though I was overcome by the usual sinful chocolate cravings, I had been in denial, refusing to accept that I might be getting my period once again. Without the appropriate feminine supplies at hand, I improvised a makeshift maxi-pad out of neat little squares of toilet paper.

When I turned to flush the toilet, the reality hit hard. Yet another month had passed by without any signs of a pregnancy. It had been well over two years since I'd been trying to conceive a second child. All that tedious mid-cycle sex, month after month—for nothing. After going through six cycles of Clomid to stimulate ovulation, I realized that a more serious fertility problem lay ahead. On these drug-enhanced cycles, my period always seemed to be just late enough to create an illusion of hope.

I was not conscious of sliding down the cold steel wall of the restroom to the floor. Thirty years of conditioning myself not to touch anything in a public restroom without using my elbows or my sleeve as a germ barrier, went out the window. With the onslaught of that day's merciless menses, I found myself propped up on the floor with my knees tucked under my chin and sobbing over what I knew lay ahead for my husband and me. I had known far too many couples with fertility problems. My womb had become useless and barren. I pictured my eggs lounging back, smoking a cigarette, and mocking my efforts by saying, "Who does she think she is, trying to force us into procreation? It's too damn much work, I tell ya! We gave her one baby, didn't we? Leave us alone, lady! Get a hobby! Get a life!"

Yes, I did have a beautiful and healthy four-year-old son. I dared not forget to be grateful for that, because everyone seemed to feel at liberty to keep reminding me about it. "I *am* grateful!" I wanted to scream at them. Truly, I *was* grateful. But having tasted the sweet experience of being a mother, I wanted more. Those who had never found themselves in this maddening situation had no understanding of what it was like. Secondary infertility was just as painful as not being able to conceive the first time. In some ways, it was actually worse the second time, because you knew what you were missing.

I ached for my son to have siblings. The last thing I wanted was a spoiled only child. Jake was conceived two months after my going off the pill. That had required no work at all. The second time, I desperately tried retracing my steps, by going on the pill again for three months, then off it. No go. Now my body seemed to be done. I began pleading with God for understanding. How did we get to this place, I asked myself. How could I conceive and give birth to one child without a hitch and fail to conceive another? What was the big mystery?

I had been patient. Having faith meant believing, and I believed the medication I was on would be the ticket. Why, then, was I being punished? The only response to my question was the sound of a toilet flushing.

To be overcome by despair so early on might have seemed premature, but deep inside, I had expected something like this. Being a pessimist by nature could do that to you. Well, I was more like a hopeful pessimist. I knew I would never win the lottery, but bought tickets, anyway. Still, you imagined you could plan your life. And this was so far from my plans of having four children in stair-step sequence. I couldn't help thinking that all I had been taught in life was just one magnificent lie.

"Wait until your late twenties before you have children," people advised me. "Build a career first."

"Staying on the pill preserves your eggs," claimed others.

I, like millions of women, was sold on the idea that we could actually "plan" our children.

"Ma'am?" said a faint female voice. "Ma'am, are you all right?"

Darn! I was caught. From under the stall door, I saw a pair of stocking-clad legs supported on three-inch designer heels. Lovely shoes, I thought, but I was betting that this woman did not have children. A woman with children would probably not be mall shopping in those shoes. After childbirth, it was almost a strategic impossibility.

"I'm fine...fine," I croaked. "Just having a bad day. Thank you." I swiped at my wet face. There was no way I could bring myself to tell a woman wearing designer heels why I was so upset. If only she had been wearing sport clogs, the kind that looked like house slippers, I would have invited her into my steel fortress and unloaded my sorrows. I needed to make someone understand how hard it was trying to make a baby.

I waited until my "savior" was locked away in her own stall before I made a hasty exit. I bolted from the store, my purpose for visiting it unfulfilled. I'd left my four-year-old son with his grandparents so that I could do some Christmas shopping and find myself a casual outfit to wear for a dinner date that my husband, Ryan, and I had that evening with Dave and Alexandria Martin. Dave was a new friend that my husband had recently met through work. Since I was meeting the couple for the first time, I wanted to make a good impression. New clothes usually boosted my confidence level, like that sexy red number I'd worn without anything under it at a cousin's wedding last month. Watching my husband drool, made me feel beyond sexy that night.

I could not possibly go tonight. Doing the commando dash through Macy's and ineffectively hiding my mascara-smudged face, I felt as though every patron there were reading a sign; the one in boldface red ink that I imagined plastered on the front of my coat with the message: *Julia Leary got her period again!* During my sprint out the door, I spotted three pregnant bellies belonging to miserably

3

uncomfortable-looking women. My gut-wrenching reaction was that if only I were pregnant, I would be glowing and contented-looking, not haggard and unhappy like them. I made it to the refuge of my minivan, a presumptuous purchase made when we thought we would easily have four babies to cart around. I called Ryan at work. I dreaded going though the song and dance routine with the school secretary to reach him. But since this was supposed to be his prep period, I took the risk.

"I can't go tonight," I pleaded, when he finally came to the office phone, "you'll have to cancel." Besides, I thought I had more than fulfilled my quota of public outings for the month. Against my better judgment, I had already attended two holiday parties for friends and a work party for Ryan. All the while scanning the crowds for pregnant women and fielding intrusive questions about our plans to have a second baby.

He paused. I was not sure if he was trying to place my voice or thinking of the right thing to say. "We can't cancel again. It will make us look unstable," he whispered.

He was an extremely private person and did not want the whole school knowing about his personal business.

"I *am* unstable!"

"No, you're not. You're just having a moment."

"Some woman found me sobbing on the bathroom floor at Macy's."

"Oh! Okay," he said, intuitively summing up the situation. My husband was not one of those quiet types with little to say. But he simply could not bring himself to engage in revealing conversation within earshot of the school secretary. "Listen," he suggested, "we'll talk later. I'll leave early today. Go home and make that phone call, will you?"

This was code for "Call the fertility specialist for an appointment."

Ryan had been pestering me to do so for several months now, but I was not ready to admit that I needed a specialist to get the job done.

"I will...I will," I responded, cringing at the thought. "But I'm still not going tonight. I want to cuddle with Jake and eat chocolate until I puke."

"Chocolate has caffeine," Ryan warned.

"I have to have *something*," I pretended that chocolate did not contain caffeine, one of the forbidden pregnancy toxins. I refused to be convinced that a little caffeine could do so much damage to a developing egg cell. But when you did not have the answers to your fertility problem, you succumbed to any snake-oil remedy offered.

My husband should have known that I would, in fact, head directly home and have myself a nauseating food binge. I could teach him a thing or two about feeding your soul. There was Hershey's syrup in the refrigerator with my name on it. Forget the ice cream to go with it. I'd spoon it straight from the can. And Jake would be right there beside me, cheering me on as I set an unacceptable example of food abuse. We'd gorge together and call it a Mommy and Jake party. We'd play Uno and Go Fish. We'd toss M & M's in the air and catch them in our mouths.

A bell rang in the background. "I gotta go," my husband said. "Make that call." Eager little students were waiting.

Ryan was a middle-school history teacher and football coach. He seemed to like his chosen career. One of the things I admired about him was his way with children. He was the kind of man who should have a large family. He could keep six little kids in line. The idea that I was limiting him because I could not provide something so basic gnawed at my soul.

Ryan would be completing his guidance degree at Villanova University in the spring. The decision to move into school guidance was based more on financial compulsions than on calling. Since our son, Jake, was born, we had been living on a single income. We needed the hike in salary to reach our financial comfort zone. Often, I toyed with the idea of going back to work full-time, but the thought of missing out on a large chunk of my son's formative years stopped me from following through. Being teachers, we tended to obsess over things like that. Children were little only for a short while. I did not want to miss a day of his blossoming growth in fear that I would never have the chance of experiencing it again. Besides, this was the time in my life I had set aside for having babies. My self-imposed sabbatical had been spent taking the occasional continuing-education courses and preparing my body for fertilization. Mainly attempted by trying to relax and lead a healthy life. And by enduring intercourse methodically every month on cycle days twelve, fourteen and sixteen.

CHAPTER TWO

At 7:00 p.m. on that same cold, dreary day, Ryan rang the doorbell of Dave and Alexandria Martin's home, cradling a bottle of Merlot in one arm and me with the other. I was miffed with him. Our sixteen-year-old babysitter must have thought we were nuts. I had cancelled with her when I got home from the mall. Then, after work, Ryan had called her back and told her it was a mistake, that we needed her, after all.

Everything within me rebelled at the idea of being at the Martins'. Ryan had absolutely no understanding of how unbearable these forced gatherings were for me. When it came to getting his way, my husband could, sometimes, be the proverbial bull in the china shop. Like when he took last year's tax refund to purchase a new ride-on lawnmower he "needed", because it cost him too much in time to use a push mower. Never mind that pushing the lawnmower constituted his only form of exercise. The choosing of our fixer-upper house, several years ago, was his most triumphant moment ever. I felt it required too much reconstruction to make it habitable. I had wanted something more modern, but he was smitten with the neighborhood and insisted that the location of the house was more important than its condition. Basically, I doubted his ability to undertake and complete all the needed repairs. But he pleaded his case and pitched his ideas. Eventually, he wore me down with his arguments. He got his project house and became quite the Harry Homeowner, spending summers and weekends with a tool belt strapped to his hips. I did not get my dream house, but I'll have to admit that it has evolved into a beautiful piece of property.

We were one of those quintessentially opposite couples. If music had symbolized our contrasting personalities, he would have been the Rolling Stones and I, the Bee Gees. Trying as he could be, I had to humbly admit that he was exactly what I needed—someone to give this procrastinator a little nudge now and then. Did I make that phone call he'd mentioned earlier? It was either do it or deal with the lecture I would get from Mr. Get-It-Done-Now.

"You okay?" he asked, looking down at me on the Martins' doorstep.

"No," I replied flatly, "But I'll get through it. I always do."

In the December darkness, I saw him shake his head.

The door opened and we diverted our attention to our hosts.

"Hello, come in...come in," said Dave Martin in a gravelly voice achieved from too many cigarettes. He wore that pained look on his face some smokers get, and he looked more like a weathered construction worker than a math teacher. I smelled cigarette smoke residue diffusing through the air as we crossed the threshold of their home, and my sinuses started to clog.

When I met Alexandria Martin, I was befuddled. She was not a smoker. How could a svelte, neatly-dressed non-smoker live with a smoker? It must have been like trying to diet, while your partner enjoyed chips and ice cream right in front of you. This mismatched couple intrigued me, perhaps, because I was still trying to figure out the nature of my own mismatch with Ryan. There is always that one thing that brings a couple together, even if they have nothing in common. What was their story? She was tailored, while he was...well, let's just say less well-groomed. From the background information Ryan had provided me, I knew the Martins were both raised in Philadelphia. But it was only in Dave that I detected the city. My focus for the "brief" evening I vowed to spend with them was to figure out these two people. It would help me pass the time. Ryan and I had agreed to leave early by conjuring some excuse involving the sitter.

After we had shed our coats, I felt twenty pounds lighter. Drinks were offered. I would have loved a glass of red wine, but opted for bottled water instead. I was still abiding by Dr. Harold's advice, which was to detoxify my body as much as possible. Dr.

Mark Harold was the ob-gyn who had delivered my son and started me on the Clomid regimen to help induce ovulation. He had offered me a long list of lifestyle changes that I should follow: I was to drink lots of bottled water, eat organic food whenever possible, take daily vitamins, no alcohol, no caffeine, no unnecessary medication, no hot tubs and last, but not the least, no smoking. The only prohibitions that really affected my husband had to do with abstinence from caffeine and alcohol. And there was, of course, the matter of letting his "boys" breathe better by switching from briefs to boxers. As was par for the course, it was the female of the species who had to make most of the sacrifices. Dr. Harold claimed that certain toxins decreased sperm count and motility and caused egg cells to mature too quickly, resulting in hardening of the egg's outer membrane and causing implantation problems. Of course, I challenged all of it. "Then how did the world become so overpopulated? If it were not for alcohol, many of us would not be here, now would we?" I reasoned. I was pretty sure I was conceived under the influence.

With a bottle of water in my hand, I concentrated on Alexandria, engaging in that uncomfortable small talk that marked the beginning of every new acquaintance. While she prepared the salad, we analyzed the weather. Would it snow for Christmas? Would we really get three inches of snow that night? You couldn't trust the weatherman. Frankly, it could hail buckets of golf balls for all I cared at the moment. I wished that I were home, in the comfort and safety of my bed. I was so tense, my shoulders ached.

Alexandria had a sign over the stove that read: Menu: Take It or Leave It. I wondered if it was indicative of her culinary skills. A prolonged silence hung over the kitchen. Darn, say something, I thought to myself. I did not know what to say. Think, think, I urged myself.

"I love your kitchen, it's very homey," I offered. It was warm and cozy with soft under-lighting reflecting off the neutral counter and cinnamon-wood floor. My nervous tension started to subside. The men were in the garage, coveting some new piece of machinery while we women got to know each other.

"Thank you. We just remodeled," she explained.

"Really? We need a kitchen make-over as well. We bought a real fixer-upper a few years ago, but the kitchen is the only room we haven't tackled. It seems too overwhelming a project. How did you manage without being able to use your kitchen for so long?"

"Well, it is a big job. But since we don't have kids, we eat out a lot, anyway. I had thought that with a new kitchen, I would like to cook more. But I really don't," she said casually.

I chuckled, "Should I 'take it or leave it?'"

Alexandria glanced over her shoulder at the sign and smiled. "I'm not a bad cook actually...when I do cook." Then she switched gears. "So, Dave says you have a son. You could have brought him along, you know."

I liked people who were not afraid to have their guests' children over as well, but since the Martins did not have any children, we had thought that Jake would be bored. And when our son got bored, trouble usually followed.

"We rarely ever go anywhere without him," I said, longing to be near him.

"How old is he?"

"Four and three quarters, as he would say."

"Are you planning on having more children?" she asked.

And there it was. The question everyone always wanted answered. I seemed to be perennially holding my breath for that question, because it required an explanation. It was the reason I begged off socializing, broke down in public restrooms and declined baby-shower invitations. I felt people asked the question, not just to make conversation, but because it seemed so unnatural to see someone with just one child. Certainly, by now, another should have been on the way. Almost everyone had at least two children: an heir and a spare, as they put it. To have two or three offspring usually involved a choice, but no one, it seemed, chose to have only one child. Such a predicament could only be the outcome of unfortunate circumstances.

"Planning," I replied, peeling the label off the bottle.

"How long have you been trying?" She had stopped chopping the vegetables, her knife suspended in the grip of those long elegant fingers, and was giving me her full attention, indicating that we were no longer having a casual conversation. I sensed an energy emanating from her that told me she knew my secrets. Just the way she looked at me with those trusting brown eyes made me want to reveal my life's story. What was this strange feeling? I didn't usually feel so comfortable with anyone right away. Normally, I was cautious with new people.

The only reason I hesitated was because Ryan and I had an agreement to keep this thing private. "Since Jake turned one," I blurted out.

"Secondary infertility?"

"The beast has a name," I confirmed.

She tucked her brown hair behind her ears and took a deep breath, "We've been through twelve years of fertility treatment…on and off. I've had three miscarriages, a cystic ovary that had to be removed, a near divorce, a reconciliation, a cancer scare and hundreds of intrauterine inseminations. Thirty thousand dollars down the drain. The whole nine yards. And a laundry list of stupid, yet well-meaning advice from family and friends."

Did I hear that right? Thirty thousand dollars? Twelve years? In twelve years, I'd be forty-two! I'd really be put out to pasture then. Alexandria knew my pain. Before me was the first person I'd come across in my adult life who did not require me to explain the exhausting details.

It was corny, but I felt a sense of sisterhood between us. Here was someone, at last, for whom I didn't have to try in vain to describe what I'd been through. Nor would I have to justify the anger and frustration I felt toward those who merely had to snap their fingers to get pregnant.

"How old are you now?" Oops. "I'm sorry."

She smiled at my embarrassment. "Thirty-five."

We were quiet for a moment as she wiped the countertop.

"Alexandria?"

"Call me Alex."

Thank goodness. I could barely pronounce three-syllable names, let alone five. "I hear it's awful. When do you give up...the treatments, I mean?"

"When your one good ovary finally explodes from all the over-stimulation!"

I liked her.

It began to flurry on the ride home at one o'clock in the morning. Ryan was yawning so much that tears were creeping out of his eyes. "So much for an early evening. How did that happen?"

It had happened because Alex and I had spoken for hours, sharing intimacies and infertility experiences. I had so many questions and she had provided knowledgeable answers to them. I was a sponge soaking up information.

With my head resting back on the seat, I responded groggily, "It seems Alex and I have a lot in common." Unlike everyone else who pretended to understand my feelings, she knew from personal experience.

"Such as?" he yawned.

I yawned in reaction. "Did you know they have been trying to have a child for twelve years? And I thought we had it bad! She's been through so much torture and financial stress. She recommended some books I should read. She's very well-informed."

"So you told her about us?" Suddenly, Ryan was wide awake. He was not comfortable about being exposed. No one in his immediate family knew of my conception problems as of yet. And it was not a topic I was comfortable discussing with my father.

"It was kinda hard not to. It just poured out of me." I could feel him tensing over the way I had confided in Alex. "I'm sorry, Ryan. I need to talk to someone other than you. It was enlightening. I feel better about seeing Dr. Castlebloom next week. I told her what happened today. You should hear her stories."

"Like what?" he asked.

Oh, he was so curious about other people's dirt, but no one could hear about his own.

"I'm not sure I should tell you."

"I'm your husband. What can't you tell me?"

There was plenty I would not tell you, I thought. "I can't remember any details right now," I fibbed, because when it came to girlfriends, my husband was on a need-to-know basis. I wasn't convinced that he was entitled to our private conversations. Girl talk was sacred. On the flip side, I kept most of the intimacies relating to my marriage to myself. Well most of them, anyway. There may have been one or two husband anecdotes that I simply had to pass along. You know, just to see if everyone else went through the same things. Though I had just met Alexandria, I had experienced near-instant chemistry, like connecting with a long-lost friend.

"Do you have money for the sitter?" I asked, attempting to change the subject.

"I thought you had it?"

"Why would I have it?"

"I asked you to stop at the teller machine today," he said with more than a hint of exasperation in his voice.

"If you don't write it down, I can't be expected to remember what you say to me at six o'clock in the morning. And how many machines did you pass by on your way to work? You couldn't stop?"

"You never do anything I ask of you any more." His voice was raised as he gripped the steering wheel tightly.

"So not true and you know it. And maybe, if I could just have a little coffee or tea once in a while, my brain would work better."

I wouldn't mention the chocolate I sneaked like a thief. When I married him, I thought, I never signed on to be his secretary/ Girl Friday. Some days, my whole existence seemed to be defined by doing things for him like scheduling doctor appointments, car appointments, fetching his dry cleaning and buying, washing and ironing his clothes...When had he ever ironed my clothes? When had he ever bought a work shirt for me? I too used to leave the house for work and needed the same services as he did, didn't I? And now, he had the gumption to claim I didn't do anything for him!

Defensively, I added, "I do complete all the things you ask me to do."

"No, you don't."

"Yes, I do."

Obviously, he had developed premature senile dementia. This bantering denial was setting my blood to boil.

"Do not," he persisted.

"Pull over, there's a machine." Our verbal showdown could go on forever. Just about the only thing we had in common was the fact that we were both last-word people. Earlier in our marriage, it had posed a much bigger problem, but after Jake came along, my energy for arguing dwindled and I became more passive than aggressive in dealing with Ryan. I knew I was right. Knowing that I was right had to be enough satisfaction sometimes.

Naturally, I was the one who had to get out in the cold and dark to tap Mac, because I had screwed up! Other women just adored my husband. It was true. I heard it all the time. The general consensus was that I was so lucky. They thought him so charming and chivalrous. But at way past one in the morning, who was standing out in the cold while he sat all cozy and warm in the car?

We arrived home in blissful silence. Then Ryan left to drive the sitter home. As the grandfather clock downstairs bonged on the half-hour, I quickly snuggled into bed. My mind lingered on the irony of the day's events. That morning, I was so sure there had been a sign that I should crawl into the cocoon of my bed and stay there. Instead, I had made a new friend. More than a friend, actually. A confidante. So much for signs! Ryan stumbled into the dimly-lit bedroom and tripped, almost falling over our dog, Taco. Disturbed, the little white Chihuahua yipped in protest.

"I thought you were going to call the carpet guy?" Ryan asked in that tone he adopted when I hadn't done something within the time frame he had set me. Our newly-laid carpet was getting lumps in places and needed to be re-stretched. They were so numerous, it was almost as though we had moles in the bedroom.

"I'll call tomorrow."

He mumbled something more, but I had my head sandwiched between two pillows, so that he could have the last word—again.

Dr. Aaron Castlebloom, MD FACOG
Reproductive and Endocrinology Specialist

Patient History Date: January 9

Name: <u>Julia Leary</u>

Address: <u>1400 Hampton Ave., Attleboro, PA 19040</u>

Date of Birth: <u>5-16-72</u> Height: <u>5'6"</u>

Weight: <u>Too much!</u>

Date of Last Menstrual Cycle: <u>Dec. 18</u>

Description of Flow: <u>Awful!</u>

List Any Previous Abdominal Surgeries: <u>None</u>

Number of Successful Pregnancies: <u>1</u>

Number of Miscarriages: <u>0</u>

Number of Abortions: <u>0</u>

Any Known Drug Allergies: <u>None</u>

History of STDs, Gonorrhea, Syphilis, etc.: <u>None</u>

Current Prescribed Medications: <u>Claritin</u>

List Any Herbal Treatments: <u>Herbal Essence shampoo</u>

Check Any Symptoms That Apply: Pain During Intercourse:_____

Abnormal Flow: <u>x</u>

Skipped Periods: <u>I wish</u> Severe Bloating and Cramping with Period:_
<u>Yes</u>_____

Breast-hair Development: <u>What the F*%#</u> Sexual Dysfunction in
Either Partner:__<u>Yes</u>__If so, describe:_____<u>Don't want to do it!</u>

Vaginal Dryness:_____ Night Sweats:_____

Any other information that may be helpful: _____

How did you hear about our office? Friend:_____ Phone Book: <u>X</u>

Newspaper:_____Doctor Referral:_____ Other:_____

_____

CHAPTER THREE

Loud, whining children were arguing over the rules of a game. One of them seemed to be bullying the others. The screaming and wailing just would not stop. Who was raising these kids? What were they doing in my bedroom?

I opened one eye and realized, thank God, that the awful noise came from The Rugrats blasting on the television. My own little carpet mongrel, Jake, was sitting Indian-style at the end of the bed and munching on dry cereal. Taco was close by, snorting and salivating for some crumbs. What a beautiful child we had made! He had his father's thin blond hair and my blue eyes and dimples. It was absolutely fascinating to see how the genes manifested themselves. It truly was a miracle, creating a life. For everything else, we went to the store and selected what we wanted off the shelf. But a child came from your body cells. Each day, a child's features changed, ever so slightly, revealing ancestral genes. One day you saw Dad in him or her. The next day, it was Mom. The following day, it could be Grandma's eyes shining out of your child's face or Uncle Joe's off-centered smile.

On days that I did not wake up before Jake, this was his routine: to get his own cereal and juice and sit "quietly", until I got up. My little man. He could be quite independent when he wanted to be. However, if you wanted him to clean his room, you could forget it!

The downstairs clock bonged annoyingly for the eighth time.

"Hey you." I managed with a dry mouth.

"Morning!" he sang out, not looking back at me.

"Could you turn that down a little?"

He complied and climbed up closer to me for a cuddle. Wrapping my arms around him was the purest feeling in the world.

"Thanks for letting me sleep," I said, as I stroked the softness of his hair. He smelled of sleep and fabric softener. There was more wailing from the television. "Angelica is not very nice, is she?" I asked.

"She's mean, Mommy. What are we doing today?"

"Well, Grandpop is going to pick you up from school, because Daddy and I have an appointment."

"What kind?"

"A doctor's visit."

"Are you sick?"

"No, it's just a check-up," I assured him.

"What kind of a check-up?"

"When the doctor looks you over to make sure you're healthy. You know, like the one you had when you turned three?" I explained.

"Why can't I come?" he begged.

"Because we'll be gone a long time. Besides, Grandpop is going to take you out to lunch."

My father loved to hang out with Jake. Their relationship was phenomenal. Having my son around seemed to have given my father a new lease of life. He was always taking Jake fishing and to ball games. Together, they had quite a hectic social life. Soon, they would be hanging out at the mall together and scoring women.

"Where is he taking me?" Jake asked.

"Anywhere you want."

"I like McDonalds," he declared emphatically.

"Are you sure? There are other places to eat, you know."

"They have the best fries," said the connoisseur.

With him, it was all about the fries. Like many kids, he was extremely particular about his food. He ate nothing green, except olives and pickles. On occasion, I would put plastic servings of vegetables on his plate, just to balance out the color.

We lay there cuddling for a while. I could have gone back to sleep, but I forced myself to get up. There was so much to do. "Okay, time to make myself beautiful."

"You're already bootiful, Mommy."

Of course I wasn't, but my heart melted. You have to love a child who thinks his mommy is "bootiful" at eight in the morning, fresh from bed. I could not tell him the real reason why I needed to freshen up. Ryan and I were scheduled for a post-coital test with Dr. Castlebloom. This was the first test in determining the nature of our fertility problem. The exam was meant to determine the relationship between the cervical mucus and the sperm. The goal was to observe how well the "boys" were swimming and how they responded to the mucus. It was possible that I had hostile mucus that was killing the sperm. The test would also determine if I was making antibodies against Ryan's sperm. I would not be surprised if that were the case. My recent psychological aversion to sex had probably manifested itself into a physical "kill all sperm" response. This must be the answer. It was probably as simple as that. I desperately hoped it was as simple as that. Simple and curable.

What was really happening while our son was at pre-school and then with his grandparents, was that Ryan was coming home from work so that we could copulate in the middle of the day. I would then rush off to the doctor's office to be poked and prodded. Having sex on demand was like eating ice cream for every meal and snack for about a week. After a while, the deliciously decadent treat lost its taste and your body repelled it.

"Work with me a little," Ryan pleaded, as if verbal pressure would suddenly get me in the mood.

"It's all wrong. We never do this in the daylight. I can't relax." Even though I knew that I had to do this by 11 a.m., I still grasped for the excuse not to.

Ryan expelled a heavy sigh and pulled me by the wrist into Jake's room. It was the darkest room in the house because of the darkening blinds we installed to get him to sleep past 6 a.m. "How's this?" he asked, pulling me down on top of him for the marital kiss. There had been a time, long, long ago, when a simple kiss would have had me begging for more.

How was it? We were in my son's room surrounded by fifteen pairs of stuffed-animal eyes. It was inappropriate. But we were running out of time. I cleared my head by thinking of a young Nick Nolte. Ryan used to look like Nick Nolte...used to look—thirty years ago. There did not seem to be any ruggedly blond men who were currently popular icons to compare him with. Young Nick was an image worth revisiting. The long, wild blond hair and the tanned summer skin that first captured my attention nine years ago were gone. I was now married to a well-groomed, upstanding, law-abiding pillar of the community without a tan. Not as hot.

Ryan tucked my hair behind my ears. "You're so beautiful," he whispered immediately afterwards, waiting for his heartbeat to slow down.

His eyes were clouded over with the warmth of sex. Even cheap, quick sex was satisfying for him. My heartbeat did not soar.

"We're gonna be late," I said, as I struggled off the floor and bit at an uneven nail. Making love was so much more fun when we feared getting pregnant, like during those stolen moments before we were married. To think that a late period used to cause so much anxiety and alarm. Now sex had become like punching the time clock at the salt mine. Work, work, work.

Following my meltdown at Macy's, I'd scheduled a meeting with an infertility specialist, and we had now arrived for that first invasive test of many to come. The consultation with Dr. Castlebloom actually went off fairly well, except for a few odd quirks of behavior that could, hopefully, be attributed to genius. He was thin and youthful-looking and resembled Ryan's college roommate. He wore his tousled brown hair in a stubborn cowlick at the front. His youth surprised me a bit. I'd pictured someone more advanced in years with the weight of experience behind him. The doctor's office lacked décor. The only items on his desk were a box of tissues, a phone and an odd-looking egg-shaped figurine with legs on it. There were a couple of posters on the wall displaying the female reproductive organs. I wondered if the posters were there for patients to refer to or for the doctor himself. As a woman—if I were treating men—

I could not begin to name all the parts of the male body. I was thankful that Ryan had accompanied me, because I tended to lose focus on the technical issues. With him there, the pressure to pay attention was not exclusively on me. I knew I could rely on Ryan's phenomenal memory for all the statistical and concrete details. Besides, I could not get my mind off that ugly, smiley-faced egg person on the desk. Was it supposed to be Humpty-Dumpty or just an ordinary personified egg?

After the introductions were made, Dr. Castlebloom looked past us and said, "So, tell me about your situation."

My "situation" was that I could not seem to get pregnant despite all the effort we were making. My "situation" was that I had grown weary from trying. I had become obsessed by the years that might lapse between my first-born and the next child. I wanted at least three more children, not just one. I had invented horrible diseases for both of us as an explanation for my inability to conceive. I was sure that in the process, the doctors would detect uterine or ovarian cancer. And so far, I had failed to fulfill my husband's desire for a large family. We commissioned my father or my in-laws to look after our son during appointments like this one and lied about what we were really up to. I took a cleansing breath. Wanting to appear calm and rational before our new doctor, I recounted our struggle and the few tests that we had done so far.

"Was your sperm count normal?" the doctor asked Ryan.

"Yes," he said tightly. I could feel his pain at revealing such intimate details.

"I'll need those results faxed over from your gynecologist. Any pain during intercourse or painful periods?" he asked Ryan again.

Shouldn't that question have been addressed to me? And all periods were painful, because they meant I was not pregnant. "No, none," I answered.

"Have you tried the basal body temperature method?"

"That could not possibly work for anyone," I replied.

Taking your temperature at the same time every morning before you got out of bed was tedious work. I lasted about three days before I gave up, mainly because my urge to pee preceded the need to take a temperature. Once I had gotten out of bed, I figured I had already screwed up my temperature. Besides, Dr. Harold had explained the mucus test and that seemed so much easier. You should know approximately when you were about to ovulate by examining the consistency of your mucus. It was supposed to change at the onset of ovulation from thick and cloudy to clear, thin and stretchy, like egg whites. Just give yourself a little feel and examine your bodily signals. No problem!

I admit that I am slightly sexually inhibited and did not much like the idea of fingering myself so often to check for mucus consistency. But it had to be done.

"Well, no need to worry," Dr. Castlebloom now reassured me. "We won't put you through that."

He then went into a long description of his credentials and his clinic's success rates. This was where I tuned out. Numbers boggled my mind. I must have some sort of number dyslexia, I told myself.

"...so if you decide to work with us, we will want to do a series of tests. Have you had a post-coital?"

Ryan and I both looked at each other. "No."

No way!

We left Castlebloom's office feeling hopeful and relieved. He strongly felt that the answer to this dilemma was simple. His diagnosis was leaning towards endometriosis. But I did not really suffer from any of the symptoms such as painful intercourse or heightened menstrual pain that was caused by abnormal cell growth outside the uterus. The nasty cells even attached themselves to the bowels causing complications. Only laparoscopic surgery could completely rule it out. Since I had already borne a child, the doctor figured he would have me pregnant in six to nine months. In fact, he almost promised it. It sounded so wonderful. He was so confident. Six to nine months was nothing. Jake would only be five by then. It was perfect! We would have one kid out of college before the next one started. We would need to move the office downstairs to the overflow room we had gained from the addition to the house. Assemble the crib!

While going into the consultation, we already knew that we would work with this doctor. In September, Dr. Castlebloom had made the cover of Philadelphia Magazine as one of the top docs in the area. His fertility-specialist rating placed him in the top three. He was only twenty minutes from our home in Attleboro. Some people commuted all the way to New York City to see top specialists. That kind of traveling would only have added to the stress.

After we had settled in at home from the post-coital test, I called my new friend and confidante, Alex, to ask her about the next test: the hystero-salpinogram. She promised that this test would have me jumping off the table while they shot dye through my fallopian tubes to make sure there were no blockages. I wouldn't have the pleasure of anesthetized tranquility for this one. And the cramping would feel like labor contractions. With her nursing degree, Alex was a wealth of information. Sometimes too much, but still, I had asked. I called on her as much for the emotional support she offered, as for the inside scoop on what really went on in this or that process. She'd been there, done that.

"It seems I don't have a hostile vagina after all. I was so sure that was it," I said, when she asked how it went. Then I told her about a disturbing scene we had witnessed while waiting in the outer office. A woman had stormed out of a patient room and slammed the exit door so hard, it had rebounded and swung open again. The receptionist had to come out from her glass fortress to close the door.

"What do you suppose happened?" I asked Alex

"Maybe, she did not get pregnant," she offered.

"Maybe, she did and found out they used the wrong sperm."

I'd clearly seen too many soap operas. I worried about sloppy mishaps.

"It was probably just drug-induced rage. They may have told her she did something wrong or cancelled a cycle on her."

That had been Alex's experience with fertility drugs. When

she was on Pergonal, she had gone through what she described as a chronic state of road rage, despising every pregnant woman she saw. Naturally, there tended to be an enormous amount of pregnant bellies around when yours was empty and waiting. On one occasion, Alex flipped out at the bank over their excessive fees and had to be escorted out the door. In her Pergonal rage, she chastised grocery clerks for bagging sloppily. She confronted the neighbor, the guy everyone else was afraid of, for taking up two street-parking spaces— and won. Her husband thought she was evil. Her family just avoided her. For years, she had been a patient of Dr. Chambers, the top doctor in Philadelphia who was brimming with self-love. During a point of frustration, Alex had questioned the doctor's methods, causing him to puff up his chest and respond imperiously, "If I can't get you pregnant, no one can."

The omnipotent statement told Alex that it was time to leave. Soon, she started isolating herself and avoiding people. Her nursing job caused her too much stress, so she ended up taking a job with a health insurance company. Occasionally, she subbed as a nurse when the local hospital had a shortage, but she did not want to do it full-time any more.

"Whatever it was that caused the woman to storm out," I confessed to Alex, turning on the stove for tea, "it made me very uncomfortable to be going in next. Maybe I should reconsider doctors."

"It's just a highly emotional area of health care, not much different than dealing with crack addicts." I was hoping against hope that I did not have to take the injections. I could not even think about needles without breaking into a sweat.

Pergonal Addicts: now there was a title for a novel!

"Besides," Alex consoled, "he has a terrific record. You'll be fine. You know…you've gotten me motivated again," she announced.

"Oh?" I asked, as I searched for the vanilla cream in the refrigerator.

"I think we are going to start another round, with a new doctor," Alex volunteered. "I think he's in the same hospital as yours…Dr. Rosen."

"Wow, that's great! I think, or maybe, it isn't. How do you feel about it?"

"Hopeful, actually. He promised that he would cut to the chase and be aggressive."

"Meaning?"

"Meaning, if all goes well, we may do an in-vitro within the year."

"That's great, Alex! You sound really calm about it. I hope it goes well for you."

It truly was great to hear Alex sound positive about giving it another try. Although finances were one of the biggest hurdles in her baby quest, the many disappointments she had encountered were what had caused her to pull the plug.

"Alex, I never asked you about adoption. Have you ever considered it?" I asked cautiously, because I always feared that I would hit a nerve and send her into a three-day depressive binge. That was what we did. It was one of our commonalties. We had too many commitments just to check out from the world, but we could hold on until Friday and hide under the covers in a fetal position until Monday, all the while, cathartically eating and crying and purging the pain.

She let out a heavy sigh. "I have...but...I just don't feel that I have exhausted all of my medical options. I know it's silly, but I have to try. I have to experience a life growing in me. I feel like I won't be...complete...if I can't do that basic thing. And we have already invested so much financially, I don't think we could afford an adoption."

"It's not silly, not at all. Why shouldn't you have that experience? It's biological. It's genetically preprogrammed into our cells. It's what we as women are supposed to do: find the right guy who's a good provider and make babies. Be fruitful and multiply."

"Thanks," she said. "It's so nice to finally have someone who unconditionally understands."

"I know. Me too." That was an understatement. I had felt isolated for so long among family and friends of the fertile world.

They simply did not know how to behave with someone desperately trying to conceive, especially, the second time around. It was as though, if you never conceived again, you were not allowed to have feelings. You started to feel as if you were making everyone else uncomfortable and it might just be best to go away. Of course, the road could have been a little easier without the onslaught of baby showers that had come my way lately. I began to make up lame excuses, like I had another shower to attend on the same day or that I'd be away that weekend. I always made the cowardly weekday call when people were at work, so that I would get the answering machine. By doing so, I avoided the endless idiotic advice that came my way, like "Get drunk and relax."

Tried it.

"Go away for a romantic weekend."

Tried that too.

"Put your feet up above your head for one half hour after intercourse."

Tried that 50,000 times!

And "Don't try so hard."

Yeah, right!

The most overused piece of advice was: "Be grateful for what you have."

Hello! Did I ever say I was ungrateful? Does wanting more imply ingratitude?

The most crack-pot advice ever thrown my way came from a book on natural fertility. It claimed that when women were in the presence of other pregnant women or newborn babies, it stimulated ovulation. This theory was based on the fact that some women experienced spontaneous lactation when hearing a baby cry. And, on the hypothesis that women living in the same household tended to be on the same menstruating cycle. The author obviously did not do his research on the emotional and psychological aspects of surrounding yourself with babies and pregnant women when you yourself were unable to conceive. Idiot! That was the last thing I could bear to do. If I did that, I'd truly be suicidal. Alex had never thrown those words of "wisdom" my way. Her restraint was just one of the many things I appreciated about her.

"So, what about you? Have you and Ryan talked about adoption?"

"Not so much. I think he would be okay with it," I said, sitting at the kitchen island with my milky tea. "It would just be nice if we could have one more, though." After a pause I added, "You know what's ironic?"

"Hmmm?"

"My own words are echoing in my head from when I was a teenager. I remember having this conversation with an adopted acquaintance and I told her I would adopt if I couldn't have kids. In fact, I've said it many times to people over the years. It's almost like I'm being called to eat my words or something. But I don't know, Alex. Now that I'm faced with the reality of it, it scares me. For one, it's so expensive! And look at all those situations where the child is reclaimed by the birth mother. Could you bear that?" The news footage of the Michigan toddler being taken away from her adoptive parents because of a loophole in the law, the claim that the biological father did not know of the birth, still haunted me.

"You mean give the child up?" Alex asked. "No. It seems like biological mothers have all the rights. They choose the parents they want and demand any amount they can get. It's scary. I think people who adopt are extremely brave."

"You think that pumping your body full of artificial hormones and risking ovarian cancer isn't brave?" I challenged. Ultimately, cancer was the risk that women took after years of unsuccessful treatments. They said that if you got pregnant from the process, it evened out the risk factors for female cancers, because pregnancy caused the ovaries to be dormant from nine months of not ovulating.

"Well, it's a different kind of bravery," Alex decided.

With that, Alex, as usual, left me with much to ponder. Was it bravery that compelled people to adopt? No, it couldn't be. It surely was so much more than that. I mean, why did we adopt that ugly rat of a dog, Taco, who was now curled up like a king in my best chair? Not because of courage, surely. It was because I needed someone or something else to love. Taco was meant to pacify my baby pangs.

It worked for all of two days.

I thought of my friend, Lauren LaRosa, who was so busy being the area's most successful realtor that I did not get to visit with her as often as I used to. She had two adopted children, but not because of fertility problems. She carried the gene for Huntington's disease and after watching two immediate family members suffer horribly, she had opted out of playing genetic roulette. Of course, she was divorced now, but that was another matter altogether. After the kids came, her husband had become a control freak. Then when he lost his job, he began drinking excessively. He felt threatened by her ability to support them. The marriage had crumbled from the pressure of too many external forces.

I sat there for a while, alone in the quiet. I used to love the solitude of being home alone. But now, at the dull gray end of a winter's day, the silence was maddening. In the quiet, my thoughts were more audible and not too entertaining. I hopped off the counter stool and put on a Jimmy Buffet CD. Nothing like "Margaritaville" to make you forget the winter blahs. I took out some nail polish and began painting my nails ruby red. I did not bother with the prep work of filing and buffing. So like me. I went immediately for the glory jobs.

Paint. Hmm. I could use new wall paint in the bedroom. Fresh paint would feel like a new beginning, like early spring. Maybe, I'd redecorate. Yes! That was exactly what I needed to lift my spirits. A satisfying project. But I might need to finish the nine other projects I had already started, like the curtains I began three months ago and got bored with. Or the stenciling in the bathroom that had seemed, initially, as though it would be so much fun. Or that old dresser I started stripping until I realized that it was more than I'd bargained for. It was now on my list to take to the dip-and-strip shop, where, for a gross fee, professionals would do it for you. I yawned widely, forcing tears out of the corners of my eyes. Ah, forget the new project, I told myself. A nap sounded divine.

CHAPTER FOUR

Jake was another satisfied five-year-old today. Chuck E. Cheese had suckered another pair of gullible parents out of $200 for the birthday-party package. Half the kids were afraid of Chucky and the other half wanted to climb on him. Three kids had to be rescued from the climbing tunnels. One frail little boy regurgitated his cake in the ball pit. Three temper tantrums had to be addressed, and one couple neglected to pick up their child. Apparently, they had assumed that the invitation stood for free child-sitting and transportation. But all in all, it was a good party and the mess was gloriously not mine to clean.

Jake was exhausted and we had just finished reading *The Lorax* by Dr. Suess. What a clever environmental lesson for children!

"Say your prayers," I said, as I tucked him under the covers.

He went through his usual routine, but added a new twist to it tonight. "I know I just got a lot of nice things for my birthday, God, but I really wanted a baby brother or sister. Amen."

Ugh, went my heart. "Jake, when the time is right, God will give us one." I said, not really believing my own words.

"Andrew's mom is having a baby."

"I know."

"Caitlyn's mom is having another. That makes four."

"I know."

"Why can't we have one? It's not fair when some people have three and four."

"Not every kid gets to have a dog," I said, looking at Taco licking his privates at Jake's feet. And they say a dog's mouth is cleaner than a human's! "You keep praying and God will hear us."

"Can I have bunk beds when I get a brother?"

"You bet!" I said with an aching throat, "but right now, you need to get some sleep. Happy Birthday. I love you." I kissed him goodnight.

"Mommy?" he asked, as I braced for the last-minute request for water.

"Yes?"

"How does God put a baby in your tummy?"

"Uh...well...," I stammered, "it's like a seed that grows into a baby. When two people who love each other want a baby, God makes it happen. It's like those sea monkeys we grew last summer."

It was lame, I knew, but I was just not ready for the birds and bees with a five-year-old.

"Oh, goodnight," he said acceptingly.

"Sleep tight."

Oh, I felt like such a fraud telling him to have faith when I had none. I needed a glass of wine. But I couldn't have one. There loomed the surgery tomorrow. With the pressure on, both from Dr. Castlebloom and Ryan, I had agreed to go through the laparoscopic surgery to rule out endometriosis. I had protested, because I did not have any symptoms. Yet, apparently, the parasitic cells could still be there, thriving and feeding voraciously on my body. I was promised that it would be a simple outpatient procedure and that it would provide some concrete answers to our problem.

I trudged back downstairs for a piece of toast and ginger ale to calm my nervous stomach. Ryan was feeding Taco who was about to jump out of his hide from starvation. I opened the refrigerator and not finding the bread, asked, "Do we have any bread?"

"How should I know? You're the curator of the house," Ryan replied in one of those fight-picking tones.

Immediately, my back stiffened at his tone. "What is that suppose to mean?"

"It's your job, isn't it?" he retorted. "You're the one who does the shopping."

"Am I also supposed to keep track of what everyone eats? How do I know you didn't come home and make yourself three sandwiches?" *Like you did with the cheese last week, polishing off the main ingredient for the casserole I had planned.*

"Well, you're always saying the house is your job, that's all." I looked at him like he had three heads because I had no clue where his semantics were coming from. At first it seemed as though he were about to back-pedal, and soften his tone but he swept his arm in a wide gesture, turned his back on me and mumbled, "Although it seems you've been on vacation for a while."

I slammed the can of ginger ale on the counter and reached for a glass. "If you don't like the way the house is kept, *you* clean it!"

"I work all day. You're home all day," he said lamely. Despite all his lofty intelligence, there existed a tiny, chauvinistic section of brain tissue that believed "being home" was not work.

"First of all, this house is a big job. Secondly, we live here. It's lived in. If you wanted a perfect house, you should have married your mother."

I thought I was going to end it by walking away, but he lured me back in and said, "It's just that...what's with these projects you've got going, there's crap everywhere."

I quickly scanned the dining and family rooms he was referring to and saw the unfinished curtains I'd started two months ago. Also lining the hallway were the paint supplies I had not put away, because, well, I had not finished. Then there were Jake's matchbox garage towers and Power Ranger gear lying about. On top of it all were the recent birthday gifts, just piled in and stuffed everywhere.

"I'm going to put Jake's stuff away," I said, rolling my eyes. "Jeez, we just got home."

As though trying heroically to keep calm, Ryan said through tight lips, "It's not the new stuff that's bothering me. It's the old stuff. *Your* stuff. The stuff you never finish."

That was it! It had hit a nerve. Those were not *my* newspapers all over the place! Those were not *my* shoes by the back door! And his shoes were so huge, anyway, that one of his made *two* of mine. And not one single coat lying across the bench was mine!

"Oh, why don't you just exaggerate? I *finish* things." With that, he started to walk away.

But wait. I was not done. Now I wanted to get to the root of the problem. "Don't you walk away! We are not finished!" I hollered. "Let's finish this."

The phone rang and Ryan grabbed it to escape my wrath, as Taco raced frantically from the back door to me in a fearful plea to be let out. Can't you ever go to someone else, you weasel, I thought. Taco was a five-pound drama queen. Whatever need he had always seemed to be at crisis level. After letting the dog out, I sensed that Ryan was in a serious conversation with someone from work. There was no room for me. So I gave up and retreated upstairs to our bedroom. I noticed that the bed was made and everything was neat and tidy, except for his ties lying haphazardly on his side of the dresser, along with about a thousand receipts that he seemed terrified of throwing out. He used his dresser as his filing cabinet.

A half hour later, I was nestled in bed, surfing channels on "mute" and looking for something interesting to watch. Ryan came into our bedroom, tripped over a bump in the carpet and muttered telepathically, *I thought you were going to call the carpet guy.*

"I called," I replied, "They haven't called me back yet." Okay, not true. I was just trying to diffuse his anger toward me, but I would call tomorrow. No, I'd be in surgery tomorrow. Okay, on Friday, then.

Ryan sat on the edge of the bed and began taking off his shoes and socks. His hair was tousled, wild from frustration. "I'm sorry," he said with a loaded sigh. "I'm just worked up about tomorrow."

"Why? You're not the one who's going to be stabbed with needles and cut open."

"I just worry about you, is all," he said, crawling up the bed to force a make-up hug and cuddle. "I just worry about your health. I wish this thing was over."

"What does that have to do with the bread?" I asked, wondering how this whole argument got started. "And why, if you're so worried, do you pick on my shortcomings?"

"Stop…stop it. I'm sorry," he moaned in defeat.

You started it.

Accepting his apology, I "unmuted" the television, because Marie Osmond was on *Larry King Live*. There was a short list of women I admired whose lives I had chronicled in a fashion over the years, like Jackie O., Princess Diana and Marie. I had come of age with their tabloid stories and trend-setting styles. I had written essays on each one of them at one time or another during my academic career. Each of these women represented a quality, which, in another life, with a different set of parents, I might have had. When I was nine years old and my mother left home, I looked outward for ideals to live up to: the grace of Jackie O., the humanity of Lady Di and the beauty of Marie. I had none of their qualities. I still received mothering from both my grandmothers and my aunt, but I wanted to evolve into more of a fantasy character. Only an old-fashioned finishing school could have saved me from the likes of my father and my brother. Not that they did a bad job, but it was hard to be feminine in a testosterone-filled environment. Instead of learning about the proper placement of china when setting the table for a meal or the art of sitting like a lady, I learned about self-defense and football strategies. It was a bit like being raised by wolves. My father refused to send me off to college until I completed self-defense classes. Thankfully, I never needed to prove my ability, but I did feel confident that no perpetrator could get the better of me.

We lay there in a cuddle, as Ryan groped my breast for a therapeutic feel. Marie Osmond and Valerie Harper were speaking about their respective adoption experiences. I became engrossed in the show, as Ryan fell asleep. Their revealing stories emanated with love and happiness. Marie's story, especially, captivated me, because her family was a mix of biological and adopted children. There was something eerily appropriate about the timing of the show. I made a mental note to tell Alex about it. And I pondered whether or not I could adopt a child. It was not that the idea hadn't crossed my mind. Yet, something in me needed to keep trying the old-fashioned way, however torturous it might be.

CHAPTER FIVE

Oooooh...Oww! The pain...The unbearable pain. Something was moaning like a cow in heat and it was a good while before I realized that it was me. Why did it hurt so badly? Thank God I was alive, but all I wanted to do now was die. A gravelly female voice called out my name. "Julia? Wake up, hon. Julia, c'mon, time to wake up." The distant voice belonged to someone who was rubbing my arm as I continued to moan and writhe in pain. Something was stuck in my ear, then removed. There were other voices I could not quite decipher, apart from beeps and bleeps and scrapes. It was hell. I must have made it to hell for not being a more doting wife or a better housecleaner or, possibly, for not being fertile enough.

"She's in a lot of pain and her temp's elevated."

"Increase the morphine. We're going to have to admit her."

I heard people around me, but could not open my eyes or make my mouth move to speak.

"Who's her doctor?" asked the female voice.

I heard Dr. Castlebloom's name and things began to fall into place, offering me an idea of where I was.

"Can someone bring her husband back?" After a lull, voices began mumbling again. It sounded as though they were all speaking a foreign language, punctuated with technical and official terms.

Again, I heard, "Julia, wake up. Your husband is here."

I opened my eyes just enough to see Ryan standing to my right, looking disheveled and helpless, but I could not speak to him. My throat was raw and felt like it was stuffed with cotton. I made several futile attempts to swallow down the lump in my throat.

Later, I woke in a dimly-lit hospital room with wires and tubes coming out of me from unmentionable places. Ryan was there. He was wiping my forehead with a cold cloth. "Hey," he said in a soft voice.

"What happened?" I asked hoarsely.

"Your doctor fucked up." His tone was angry, yet tempered with weariness. He had one hand on my arm and was running the other through his hair which looked as though it had been taking some abuse. "You lost a lot of blood during the surgery. They zapped a main artery by mistake and it took hours to clean up their mess."

A nurse walked in and said, "Ah, you're awake. I'll tell your doctor." She pointed to some ice chips and suggested to Ryan that I might like some to soothe my throat.

As the cold ice slid down my raw throat, Dr. Castlebloom strolled in. He looked different to me: less confident, less capable and less trustworthy. But he had retained his habit of not making eye contact. He began to explain why I was there. I hoped that Ryan was absorbing the information, because my mind was more focused on the cramping in my gut which made me feel, strangely enough, as though I were about to give birth—to an alien.

Explanations were floating around in the room about them hitting a main uterine artery, having to call a specialist to clamp off the bleeder and my losing close to two pints of blood. My hemoglobin levels were down to six. Apparently, an acceptable low would be around ten. Meaning, that if I'd lost two pints of blood, my pre-surgery hemoglobin levels were at the anemic stage. Since I was running a fever, they feared infection. I bet if they re-counted their surgical supplies, they would find a missing sponge or a forgotten clamp. Hey, it happened all the time on medical shows, didn't it? It was because of my pain and fever that I had been admitted.

A while later, the intense grogginess wore off. As I lay there attached to tubes and wires, I thought of what a frightening, sterile environment it was to wake up in. You immediately sensed something was wrong. I was thinking that, maybe, this was an area where hospitals could improve patient recovery and healing.

Perhaps, they should create a more Feng Shui-friendly environment. Paint the walls taupe. Adorn the bedding in warm-colored linens like cranberry, navy or green. Light butter-cream pillar candles of varying height. Choose a warm-patterned rug in muted shades for the floor to tie all the colors together. Now *that* would be a room to recover in. Heck, it was better than my own bedroom at home. One trip to Pottery Barn would do it. Maybe, I could market this idea? We could call them "healing rooms," instead of patient rooms. I must have been feeling better, now that I had mentally redecorated my surroundings. Good to know that I was not in a coma.

My husband was asking questions and taking mental notes, while I kept thinking how I had been assured that all I would have to go through was a simple outpatient procedure. Then a phlebotomist came in to draw blood.

"No," I said emphatically, shooing her away. "No, no, no."

"We need samples for testing," explained Castlebloom.

"Haven't you taken enough?" I protested.

"We need to keep checking your hemoglobin and creatine levels."

It was just the damn needle that worried me. I held my breath and closed my eyes as the phlebotomist went to work on my arm. At the moment of entry, I let out a cry for help to my husband.

"It's almost over," he reassured. Surely, though, he had to be thinking, don't be such a baby! Then he asked Dr. Castlebloom, "So, how much endometriosis did you find?"

"All in all, there was only a moderate amount of endometrial cells," he replied. "However, there was considerable scar tissue on the right ovary. Bands of tissue were wrapped around it, pulling it downwards and crippling its ability to function. You may have noticed that you were ovulating only from one side. We removed the scar tissue and freed the ovary. Luckily, it looks very healthy and viable. It should return to normal function, now that it's no longer restricted."

"So did you staple or clamp the bleeding arteries? And what will happen to them?" asked Ryan.

Dr. Castlebloom's chin edged up a little. "Staples. We had to use metal, so they stay."

Hold on a minute. "Will I be setting off security alarms at the airport?" I asked.

"No."

"Won't scar tissue develop around the staples in time?" I added.

With a look of unmitigated guilt on his face, Dr. Castlebloom defended his honor. "That won't affect your ability to get pregnant. Your right ovary should resume working order now, doubling your ability to produce eggs. I firmly believe that once you get back on your feet again, we'll have you pregnant in no time. You're young and healthy. You've borne a child successfully. That should clear the way to everything working as it should."

Promises, promises. My grandma, Meg, who was a very wise woman, always claimed that doctors were not to be trusted. I was beginning to think she was even wiser than I'd thought.

Later, after Castlebloom had retreated to the care of other patients, Ryan and I compared notes. "I noticed," said my husband, "that he did not admit to having made any mistakes."

"Of course not. Would you?" I said.

"You could have died," he said in a tired voice.

"I wanted to, earlier." It was frightening how easily I would have accepted death that morning. I just wanted the pain to go away. They say that when you feel pain, at least you know you're alive. Still, when it had peaked, there were no thoughts of Jake or Ryan, the two people in my life I loved the most. "So, I guess your parents have been officially informed?" I asked him, referring to our entire infertility nightmare.

"Yeah, they said they suspected it."

Of course, they did.

"The whole time?" I asked him.

"I don't know. They just sensed it, I guess. They're concerned. Jake is going to sleep there tonight."

Perhaps, it had not been fair to leave Ryan's parents in the dark. But I suppose that I had always been a little intimidated by them. George and Lois Leary had been terrific grandparents and very supportive in-laws. I did love them like my own family, but they had an air of know-it-all superiority about them. George was a consummate actual-factual intellectual who always knew everything there was to know about any given experience. That is to say, other people's experiences were never exclusively their own or unique to them. He'd been there, done that. So I learned early on to filter the information they received. You could not tell George anything new. He wouldn't believe you. He was the kind of person who shot the messenger if the news was not what he wanted to hear. Okay, perhaps I was exaggerating a little. But there was no way he would admit to being proved wrong.

So we had learned to operate around my in-laws, as we did recently, when they planned to take us out for Ryan's birthday. They had wanted to go to the Crab Claw, a new place they insisted was fabulous. We had heard from our crew of friends that it was not so great. Besides, Ryan preferred steak. The day before we were due to go, we had heard on the grapevine that the place had been shut down by the board of health, but decided to keep it to ourselves and let his father discover it on his own. We duly arrived at the place at 6 p.m. for dinner and walked to the door to witness George's face droop at reading the *Closed* sign. He scratched his belly while processing in his mind the fact that his beloved restaurant had been permanently shut down, and because of health reasons, no less. This way, we were at least spared the blame for his disappointment. It was a beautiful moment, one I would not forget.

Without getting involved in a direct confrontation with his father, Ryan had won. He got to choose the restaurant and we all had fat, juicy steaks for dinner.

Feeling sleepy again, I suggested that Ryan go home and get some sleep. I couldn't keep up a conversation. Later in the night, I woke up again feeling intense heat and an uncomfortable fullness in my abdomen. My stomach was rock hard and bloated. I rang for a nurse by pushing the magic button on the side of the bed.

No response. I waited. And waited. I pressed the button again. Finally, a nurse the size of a ten-year-old child appeared. How awful to be that...short. I mean, could you even eat anything when you were so short? Taller people definitely held the advantage, over the whole food-for-pleasure verses food-for-survival thing. I was just in-between, which meant that if I wanted to look decent, I still had to watch my food consumption.

"Something's wrong," I said, pointing to my distended abdomen.

She flipped back the covers to investigate, then walked around to other side of the bed to examine the urine bag which, I noticed, was empty.

"I'll be right back," she promised, not commenting on her discovery.

Soon, three medical personnel were tending to me, greatly displacing my sense of dignity. My legs were spread apart in the birthing position, while three individuals tried to replace the catheter that had somehow slipped out of place, causing urine to overfill my bladder. Since everything was so swollen inside, they could not manage to reinsert the catheter. Further and further apart went my legs, until my feet seemed to be in my throat! Alzheimer's would not have been such a bad thing at that moment. I was so mortified by my predicament that I had to crack a joke to ease my own nerves.

"It's a pissy job, eh?" I offered. Not one of the people present acknowledged my attempt at humor. "I guess you hear that a lot," I mumbled.

One of the male nurses in the trio said to Nurse Shorty, "Let's try a pediatric cath."

With that brilliant suggestion, a catheter was properly inserted and I was finally able to urinate with celebrated relief. As the pressure on my bladder eased, I drifted off to sleep again, only to be awakened sometime in the pre-dawn of the following day by the blood lady. On and on went the routine. Sleep. Needles. Sleep. Needles. Yes, it was a living nightmare. The numbing morphine was the only thing keeping me from having panic attacks about the needles.

A beam of sunlight pierced my closed eyelids through a narrow gap in the window blinds, when the phone rang, arousing me from restless slumber. I recognized the voice immediately.

"I think you have the worst luck," said Alex. "That kind of screw-up is extremely rare."

"I beat the odds for once." I debriefed her on my laparoscopic misadventure and the pee situation.

"I'm sure they were comparing you to everyone else," she chided. "'Look at this woman, her labia majoras are so uneven'."

On and on she went with the jokes.

I started laughing, only to be seized by pain. "Stop, stop," I pleaded and gripped my sore abdomen with the pillow for padding. "I can't laugh. It hurts too much. I know I ripped out stitches when I sneezed earlier. Remind me to never have a tummy tuck. This is awful!"

Alex continued on to inform me that my husband had called her late last night, because he was upset over the situation. She was apparently helpful in calming his nerves. I was grateful that he had someone to talk to. He was so intensely private about these matters. Alex signed off, but not without warning me to ask for the Operation Report, which would provide the details of what exactly had happened during the surgery.

Sometime during my second night I received a roommate—a moaning, groaning, flatulating roommate with a seemingly low tolerance for pain. I thought *I* was bad. It was hard enough enduring your own pain, without being forced to listen to someone else going through hers. I could feel myself growing increasingly warm with fever, as I kicked off the covers and struggled with consciousness. Later, I woke in a panic as I felt myself literally levitating off the bed. I grabbed the bed rails for support. The room was spinning. Overcome with fear, I violently pressed the nurse pager.

The same short nurse who had come in earlier responded only to tell me that I was just having nightmares from the fever and, possibly, from the cocktail of antibiotics and painkillers flowing through my veins.

I groaned and winced. "This is more than a fever. I think I have a migraine. My head is pounding."

The nurse insisted that there was nothing she could do, apart from administering more Tylenol for the fever. Bang, bang, went my head, as though someone were pounding my skull with an iron skillet. Bang! Bang! Bang! My vision was blurred. I was nauseous and choking back vomit. I decided I wanted my husband to rescue me from this place and take me home. So I called home, oblivious to the fact that it was 1:30 a.m.

"Get me out of here, please," I pleaded with Ryan, "I want to come home." Of course I knew I could not leave without being formally released, but I was beginning to feel a bit like a neglected prisoner. I described the floating feeling that had overtaken me and told him of the migraine I suspected I was suffering from. I felt so isolated and alone.

Since Jake was missing me and had chosen to sleep next to his father, Ryan whispered his reply into the phone. "I'll call the front desk and make sure they take care of you," he promised. "I'll be over in the morning. Think happy thoughts." It was what we always said to Jake, when he was upset about a bad dream.

Ryan seemed to understand that I just needed to connect with someone from my real life. I needed the comfort of a familiar voice. Besides, who else was I going to wake up at one-thirty in the morning? I knew that he would not have hesitated to wake me up if he were in need of comforting, though it usually involved another, more physical sort of solace. Shortly after I hung up, a female intern came into the room to talk to me.

"How painful is your headache?" she asked, as the patient next to me moaned.

"Like slamming pots colliding with my head. It's migraine level." I knew that doctors just hated it, when patients self-diagnosed.

"Do you normally get migraines?" she asked.

I winced again from the horrendous pain, "I've only suffered from a couple of them. My husband gets them." I was implying that I was able to recognize one.

"We've already given you Tylenol. Perhaps, you need to give it some time to work."

I did not have time to debate the severity of my head trauma. Apparently, she had never had a migraine or she would not have been quibbling with me. I was familiar with the debilitating agony, even if I had experienced it only twice. The first time, I had had no clue as to what I was going through, until Ryan diagnosed it for me. He was the real sufferer, being afflicted by migraines on an average of five times a year and had to take Maxalt, the medication prescribed for him. I knew it worked wonders for him, because before he started on prescription medication, he used to be confined to bed for days on end. Now, he could at least get through the day.

Holding up two fingers before me, the intern asked, "How many fingers do you see?"

Now, while my vision was blurred to the point where I would not be able to read anything, I was not blind. Besides, double vision was not always a symptom of a migraine. I gritted my teeth through another slamming sensation in my head before saying, "I see two fingers on one hand. And one stalling intern who needs to give me 10 mg of Maxalt!"

She stared at me in disbelief for a moment. The suffering woman in the bed next to mine cried out in pain again.

"Oh, and that poor woman is in extreme pain," I continued. "If you can't give her more pain medicine, at least give her something to help her sleep. Why are you so stingy with your medication around here? I want Maxalt! Give it to me! Give it to me *now*!"

The intern bolted from the room. Not so cocky now, eh, I thought. Soon a nurse returned with the blessed migraine relief.

On the third day following my "outpatient surgery", my temperature had dropped. I felt grungy and scummy. Ryan strolled in with my favorite potted pink tulips and kissed me on the lips. I thanked him and said humorously, "Does this mean I have to put out tonight?"

"Like I would climb into bed with you right now," he quipped, referring to my decomposing appearance.

"I hear the grunge look is still hot. I read somewhere that one of the Motley Crue members went for a month without bathing and still got laid every night by crazed fans. Gross, huh?"

Ryan shivered from the thought. "Sick."

"Help me get a shower."

I started to get up and he panicked, mostly because he is a rule-oriented person and wouldn't dare do anything unless the nurses approved of it. Ryan looked around nervously as though we were about to break the law. "Are you allowed to?" he asked.

"Oh, I'm getting a shower. I don't need their permission to shower."

After Ryan got clearance with the attending nurse, she worked the logistics of the IV fastened to my arm. With Ryan's help in the shower, I finally felt human again, though very faint and exhausted.

I realized that during our nine years together, this was the first major health crisis we had been forced to tackle. It was a testimony to the overall strength of our marriage and a foreshadowing of our elderly future. I wondered how long it would be before he cracked under the pressure. He was generally very caring during my viral illnesses. But, after a while, the pressure of "doing it all" caused him to snap. That, usually, was the point where I knew it was time for me to get out of bed. Then I was overcome by guilt. For whenever he was in bed with the flu, I tended to just stay away and let him sleep it off. Being germ-phobic, I sprayed Lysol on all surfaces and in the air. For that, I had, on occasion, been accused of insensitivity, but why get everyone infected. I resolved, there and then, that the next time he was ill, I would pull out all the stops to repay him for all that he was doing for me. I would fluff his pillows and rub his feet. I would serve him breakfast in bed with a freshly-cut flower in a vase. I would butter all four corners of his toast, just the way he liked it.

I was not a vain person, but I confess that after my refreshing shower, I did apply some make-up. Three days of going *au natural* was enough for me. Satisfied with my appearance, I winked at Ryan.

"So, do you wanna, now?" I offered facetiously.

"Tempting. You can make it up to me when we get home, gorgeous," he retorted. Of course, my offer was in vain. Never, ever would I do it in a hospital room with only a thin curtain blocking off my moaning roommate. But in healthier days, in our younger days, we used to have a fairly spontaneous sex life.

The very first time we consummated our relationship turned out to be the proverbial hook, line and sinker for Ryan. It was preceded by a month of dating in college. Then the time had come for the big moment, the coupling of us. We had been teasing each other about having discovery fantasies. So one cold October night, when he was studying for an exam in his private study room at the library, I knocked on the door. Equipped with a bottle of champagne and a candle and dressed in nothing but a red teddy under my long wool coat, I seduced him. He was smitten from that moment on, lured by the delusion that our entire sex life would forever be as spontaneous and hot as it was on that one night. Then we got married and life seemed to rule our libidos.

There were other satisfying copulations during our marriage, like the ones we enjoyed during the year we were trying to conceive Jake. Atop the picnic table at Reed's Park was memorable. Bare-assed in the moonlight, one summer night, to christen the new deck was one of Ryan's favorites. We even established a sort of a tradition, christening every newly-redecorated room in our house. Yes, we could be creative, but having to do it on scheduled drug cycles often seemed like a horrible chore. Oh, to have the library days back! Our library rendezvous was apparently not all that original. I heard that a year after we graduated, someone was caught in flagrante delicto in one of the study rooms, whereupon the authorities removed all the doors.

That third day in the hospital was a rare time of new bonding for us. Ryan lay on the bed with me and we talked all afternoon. He comforted me while the blood lady came and took her vile little specimens, and helped me to the bathroom. In a way, I was almost thankful to be there as a patient. I couldn't recall a time when we had just lounged in bed all day and talked.

But he did not leave without unburdening his heavy thoughts. He took a deep breath and said, "I want you to know something. You don't have to do this for me, you know."

"What?" I asked.

"You don't have to go through all this pain just to have a child. We could adopt. I could love any child. Or I could be happy with just Jake."

"You really could do that? Adopt?"

"Absolutely. It wasn't what I had planned, but I'll be okay," he said affirmatively.

I sank deep into my pillow. "I'm not ready to quit," I whispered.

"I know. But when you are, don't forget there are other options."

I contemplated what he said. I was relieved that he had been the first to bring up the idea of adoption. I had been afraid to mention it to him. My husband could truly be Mr. Wonderful at times.

"I love you," I said. "I don't tell you that often enough, but I do."

CHAPTER SIX

Now that spring was promising to assert itself, a walk into town seemed like the perfect idea. The intoxicating scent of freshly-cut grass drew me outdoors to absorb the warmth of the day. The sun's heat was nature's therapy, as Jake and I headed to the local drugstore for a few supplies and a taste of the season's first ice-cream cone.

Attleboro, was an original Bucks County, Pennsylvania, village. Originally settled by Quakers, it spanned only five miles in diameter. Modern suburbia and cookie-cutter houses surrounded the town. But when you passed through or took a leisurely stroll, you could forget about modern excesses for a moment and almost feel as if you had stepped back in time. It was one of those intimate communities where everyone knew everyone else, and if you were not in the mood for pleasantries and local gossip, you could easily drive to the larger chain grocery store just outside of town. Still, the place had an unmistakable charm that other neighborhoods couldn't boast of. There was a measure of comfort in knowing the local business owners and shopkeepers by name. The local barbershop, where Jake got his "Princeton" cuts, had not been refurbished since the turn of the century.

Attleboro was a town where all the old homes had names like Middleton, Buckley and Deveraux. As Jake and I walked past the eighteenth and nineteenth-century stone and Victorian homes, I waved to neighbors I had not seen all winter. I had been cooped up for too long. Even people seemed to thaw out in the springtime, becoming more visible and colorful.

It had been eleven days since my "outpatient" debacle. Five of which were spent in the hospital fighting spiking fevers and enduring antibiotic cocktails. After lying around the house, recuperating and watching too many infomercials on TV, I felt a sudden burst of energy. I had to move, to get outdoors and walk. My legs were wobbly, the muscles weak from a long period of inactivity.

At Murray's drugstore, we bought toothpaste, shampoo, M & M's and dish soap, then headed over to the ice-cream shop. Jake's eyes were bigger than his stomach as he ordered the large chocolate-chip cup. Feeling generous, I splurged. If he could have a large order, so could I. As I was savoring the decadence of my chocolate-almond ice cream, my friend, Ally, and her son, David, approached. Ally seemed to color her hair to match her outfits. One day, her hair was auburn; the next day, it was blonde. Our boys had once played together often, but since they now attended different pre-schools, their friendship seemed to have tapered off.

Ally and David ordered their ice creams and joined us. It was a nice, spontaneous chat session, as she was my source for the latest town gossip. The nail shop was going out of business. The Market, our little family-owned grocery store or glorified 7-Eleven, might go under too. The Thompsons who lived next door to her were moving, thank God. And her mother-in-law was having reconstructive bladder surgery the following Tuesday. If you were exhausted, as I was, Ally was the perfect companion, because she didn't really expect you to reciprocate. When excited, she had a habit of speaking in one, long-drawn breath. And while she devoted her attention to me, she remained oblivious to the fact that David was teaching Jake how to spit ice cream on ants.

Ally was one of the first friends I had made when we moved to Attleboro. We had become pregnant around the same time. We exercised together, colored each other's hair, gave birth and nursed our sons at the same time. David, however, was her third son. She was the person I'd leaned on, when I was sleep-deprived and exasperated from the New Mom game. Ally was a "chain" person, the kind who sent email chain letters predicting dire consequences, like a tree falling on your house, if you failed to send them on to nine other people. I was not a very good friend, because I invariably broke the chain. Before I went into surgery, she had given me a Tupperware cup full of yeast goop to make Friendship bread. I was supposed to make the bread and pass a cup of yeast goop on. Well, I still hadn't made it. It had probably turned green by now.

My appetite had not returned. I could only finish half of the ice cream. Nothing usually affected my ability to consume food, especially sugar-laden delights like ice cream. I always wished I were one of those women who couldn't eat when sad or upset—or even when happy. But I just never seemed to lack an appetite. Yet, with the surgery, I had lost nine pounds! Clearly, I should have gone under the knife sooner.

As I stood to head home, the shopping center swirled around me. I fell right back into my chair.

"Are you all right?" Ally asked in alarm. "What's wrong?"

I was short of breath and suddenly felt very weak.

"I can't walk home. Could you drive us back?" I asked breathlessly.

"Sure...sure," she agreed, reaching for my arm to help me up. Without looking at her son, she commanded, "David, knock it off! Throw that cone away!"

Wow! I thought. Some people really did have eyes at the back of their head.

"Are you sure you're okay, Julia?" Ally asked anxiously.

"I'll be fine, really. I overestimated my stamina. I'm still making red blood cells, ya know."

"My sister once passed out cold in a restaurant when she was anemic. They got a free meal out of it," she said while helping me to her car.

"Maybe I'll give it a try tonight. We *are* a little low on cash right now."

Once Ally had escorted me home, she insisted on taking Jake home with her to play with David. It wasn't difficult to sway Jake. I was proud to have an independently spirited child, but given the choice, Jake would always go off with someone else rather than be with us. I suspected there was not enough action at home. He thrived in Ally's house full of boys. I didn't even know anyone who had daughters. It seemed as if most of my friends had evolved out of the fact that we had sons who played together.

Ally promised me a girl's night out when I was feeling better and lectured me on how it had been too long since we had any fun. I collapsed on the couch and into one of those deep naps I used to take when pregnant with Jake.

When Ryan came home from work, my siesta was over. Another take-out meal and another credit card purchase later, Ryan suggested, "I think we should sue Castlebloom."

He looked quite handsome in his blue oxford and tan khakis. He had a bit of sun on his face, lending it a nice glow. Suddenly, I was overcome by a need for orgasmic lovemaking. But I was on medically induced abstinence. That was how it always happened with me. The rare, sudden urge consumed me whenever I was physically not able to act on it. Sometimes, desire flooded me in the grocery store or in the middle of the day, while folding laundry and Ryan was at work. By the time he came home, forget it. Nada. The feeling had passed. Or by then, I was just too tired.

Would suing the doctor get me pregnant? I thought.

"Why should we sue?" I asked.

"Look what he did to you! What if they screwed up more than he admitted and you're really unable to have more children?" he said hotly.

"How could you prove that? And the whole process could take years."

"I just think...you know...he should pay for his mistake."

"Alex said it wouldn't be much of a claim, especially after the lawyer's fee," I explained. "They did, after all, save my life."

"But they would not have had to save you, if they had not fucked up," he reasoned. "Still, maybe it would be enough to pay for an IVF."

IVF or in-vitro fertilization was the test-tube process whereby the egg and sperm were placed together in a Petri dish for fertilization. Once that happened and it had multiplied to at least eight cells, the blastocyst was transferred back to the woman's uterus through a catheter. For many women, making the embryo was the problem and this laboratory process relieved the body of doing the job, thus greatly increasing fertility. The abbreviation, IVF, was beginning to sound like something from outer space. In fact, the whole infertility world was alphabet soup.

"I'm hoping not to have to go that far," I replied. "Besides, I thought you wanted to adopt."

"Well, it could pay for that then."

Ryan just wanted someone to blame. Moreover, I suspected he was getting anxious about where all the money was going to come from, once we plunged deep into drug therapy. Our health-insurance carrier only covered half of my prescription costs and completely excluded coverage of in-vitro fertilization procedures.

I, on the other hand, felt that I had been getting the royal treatment from Dr. Castlebloom since I'd been home. He was nervous. He had, so far, called personally, each day, to check on my progress. So I surmised that it would be best to stay with him rather than change doctors or start a lawsuit. I sensed he wanted to redeem himself and do his best to get me pregnant and thus, out of his life. It was a gamble. But what in life wasn't? Besides, the past three years had been overshadowed by utter negativity. A lawsuit would be an insalubrious assault on both my mental and physical stamina. So the oddball doctor and I were in a bit of a showdown.

You give me quality care, and I won't sue your ass!

CHAPTER SEVEN

Ah...July. I loved summer. Flip-flops, cut-offs, less cumbersome clothes, less laundry, ice cream, extra daylight and sunshine! It was my happy time of year. Ryan and Jake were taking in a Phillies game with friends. Alex and I were shopping in Peddler's Village.

We were different shoppers. She was focused and determined to hit every shop, determined to find that one great bargain. I only wanted to go into shops that seemed unique or carried clothes. I was doubtful that there were any real bargains in this trendy village. But I would never pass up the fudge shop, even if everything in it was overpriced.

Exhausted, we sat down at an outdoor café to order lunch. Alex was a walking advertisement for Ann Taylor in her cream Capri outfit. I was clad in Old Navy cargo pants and tee shirt, an attempt at looking youthful. I was a little envious at how she always looked so put together. She had that Jackie O. quality.

There was a tabloid magazine left behind on the table next to us that caught my eye. I reached for it, because there was a picture of Jennifer Aniston and Vince Vaughn happily strolling hand in hand on a Malibu beach. "They look happy, don't they?" I commented.

When our salads came, Alex dropped the bomb. "Dave wants a divorce."

Choking on a cucumber slice, I said, "What?"

She had seemed quieter than usual.

"He says he's done. Says he can't jerk off one more time." Alex gnawed off a piece of bread. She had started her IUI's—intrauterine insemination. In this process, the husband or "lover" slips into a dim backroom full of girlie magazines and produces a sperm sample. It is then "washed" and placed directly in the woman's uterus through a catheter. The idea is to make less work for the millions of sperm vying for the attention of that one languishing egg.

"What does he mean, he's done? He doesn't want you to have a child?"

"Remember last week, when I told you my cycle was bad and it had to be cancelled?"

"Yes," I responded with baited breath.

"The truth is…Dave pulled the rug out. He said he just couldn't do it any more…the trying, the money, the jerking-off…me…" Her tone seemed disturbingly flat. "We nearly split up several years ago. This time, it's for real."

I was flabbergasted. I was obviously a bad judge of character. It seemed to me that they had a strong marriage, although they were mismatched. Divorce was often a sad consequence of fertility treatments. It eroded the best of relationships.

"Alex…I don't know what to say…I'm so sorry."

She released a breath as if she had been considering a thought and said, "I'm not."

"What do you mean?"

She pushed her plate aside and leaned in on her elbows. "It was over long ago. Starting up the treatments again was just a catalyst to get him to make a move."

"You seemed like you got along so well."

"Appearances can be deceiving," she said, while nodding in the direction of Jen and Vince on the magazine cover. We haven't had a real marriage in two years." Well, mine hadn't been so great either. But still.

"Do you think he has a girlfriend?"

"Probably."

"You don't care?" I couldn't get over how disinterested she seemed.

"If he does, it only makes my case better."

"But...what about your baby dreams? How can he do that to you?"

"I don't need him to have a baby."

This was big.

"You have been plotting, haven't you?" I challenged.

"A little." She shrugged. "Look, we got along okay living together, but there was no real marriage, no desire to be together physically. At first, I thought it would pass. But it hasn't, and the fact that he wants out when called to action, just validates how I feel."

"How do you feel?"

I was feeling terribly sad for them.

"I'm done with him," she said on a note of finality. "We've outgrown each other. He's not my soul mate. And I cannot stand the thought of him sleeping in my bed any longer." She paused awhile. I just sat numb. "I want to move on with my life."

"What will you do?"

"First, I am going to buy a new house and then, maybe...have a baby."

Shocked, I said, "Oh Alex. Are you talking about donor sperm...like from a total stranger?"

I didn't know if I could personally handle having a stranger's sperm swimming around in me.

"Unless that hot young waiter over there wants to have a quick fling, yes."

"Don't romanticize what it's like raising a child. It's hard work, even with a father around. Much as you might love your child, some days you just want to be off-duty," I cautioned.

Alex rolled her eyes, "If it works, it will be hard...I know. Hell, even if Dave were the father, I would be doing ninety percent of the work anyway, plus cleaning the house and working full-time."

"That's true." I was starting to get sucked in by her rationalizations. "Forgive me for being the devil's advocate here, but how will you finance all of this?"

"I'll downsize. Besides, when I'm done with him, money won't be a problem."

"Well, if you need a realtor, let me introduce you to my friend, Lauren. I know you'll like her. And she happens to be newly divorced. You may find you have a lot in common."

Maybe, money wasn't an issue for her, but divorce was such an emotionally painful process, even when both sides agreed to it. I had seen too many couples torn apart by it. Even my own father who, in the end, was better off without my mother, had suffered. He battled with trust issues and heartbreaking loneliness. He never married again. At least I never had to deal with a stepmother.

For all of Alex's apparent confidence, I saw the cracks of doubt in her posture. I suspected the uncertainty lay more in her ability to get pregnant than in surviving a divorce. I was also unofficially sworn to secrecy about her life from then on. The fact that our husbands were friends complicated matters. How would I be able to skirt this subject with Ryan? He would have to be dealt with very carefully. We'd had our share of arguments from siding with friends. Another one was brewing.

CHAPTER EIGHT

It had been a week since my lunch with Alex, and I was teetering on eggshells for two reasons: one because it was time for my first IUI cycle and second because Ryan had been asking me all week, "How's Alex? What's new with her?"

Each time he did so, I twitched a little and said, "Nothing," which, of course, in female lingo, really meant "a very big something". I knew he knew that I knew something, but he wouldn't divulge what. So we had been throwing the verbal volleyball back and forth. The last time we had gone through something like this with friends, we had such a nasty argument, that we agreed not to talk to each other about our friends' problems. So much for that agreement. He was needling me because he was nosy. But I wouldn't budge. I was loyal and true. I would not rat out a friend.

However, after several days of Ryan hounding me, I caved. "Okay," I said. "I know you know they're getting divorced. So knock it off."

"Did she tell you how she's screwing him?"

This was our problem. He always unquestionably took the man's side, while I took the woman's and there we were, fighting over their issues.

"What? Ryan. Just stop. Don't even go there."

"Just don't you go getting any ideas. I don't need you to be influenced by her," he said, revealing his insecurities about us.

But I was so mad at him for taking sides without knowing the facts, that I couldn't bring myself to reassure him at the moment. Before I could stop the words from leaving my mouth, I said, "What makes you so sure that *I* didn't influence her?"

Yeah, that would comfort him all right.

He shot me a withering glance and shook his head.

"Julia?"

Finally! I was being called back to the patient room to see Dr. Castlebloom. It had been forty minutes of waiting. Honestly, did they think we had nothing more pressing to do? True, *I* didn't exactly, but other people did. Other people had jobs to get back to. I just had painting to finish, and curtains to sew and bathrooms to clean. No need to rush back for that.

The nurse handed me a tissue-paper robe and asked me to get undressed from the waist down. The exam table was one of those stirrup contraptions with booties. I refused to position my feet there for one minute longer than necessary, so I sat waiting with my feet dangling. But this only served to expose my buttocks that were aimed right at the door. I made a mental note to always wear longer shirts to these visits.

Alex had *not* warned me that the ultrasound device was really a dildo with a camera attached to it! I was expecting a scan from atop my abdomen, not one rammed inside my vagina! It was all so vile. Afraid of emitting offensive foot odor, I had worn fresh white socks. They also helped to disguise my pedicure-neglected feet. I wondered whether my efforts at hygiene were wasted on the doctor. He probably didn't even notice that I had shaved and lotioned my legs before thrusting them near his face. Even my husband didn't get that consideration.

After Dr. Castlebloom completed his exam, he left me with the nurse to review instructions on taking the medication. He offered a rehearsed-sounding, "Good luck," before leaving. Nurse Jayne took over. She reminded me of Patty Duke in her late forties. As she came closer, I smelled her perfume: Victoria's Secret no. 33.

Nurse Jayne pulled out a box of Pergonal and a needle. Oh, boy. I started to get sweaty and anxious. Then she proceeded to tell me how to prepare the injection. Wait a minute! Me? Prepare my own injections? There must me some mistake. Didn't they have that needle incident from the hospital on file? I didn't do needles!

"Okay," Nurse Jayne said. "You just flip the top off the ampoule like this." She swiftly snapped it off with her thumb. "First make sure there is no air in the syringe by pushing the chamber flat. Insert the needle into the saline first, withdraw, inject the saline into the powder, swirl, withdraw and inject into the second powder and withdraw. Then slowly push the chamber up to the edge and tap out any air bubbles like so." She did a quick, skilled flick on the syringe. "There, you try."

Oh Jayne, you don't know me very well. Reluctantly, I took the syringe and copied her technique, only not as gracefully.

"Good," she praised. Then she demonstrated with an orange how to inject the magic solution that would make me ovulate. She threw the syringe into the orange in one swift motion. Then she handed me a prescription for the Pergonal and wished me good luck.

Now, I may have missed something in my anticipation of receiving a shot in the ass. But apparently, I was to do this *myself* at home by ten o'clock the following night. Sacrificing my claims to intelligence, I said, "I thought you would be giving me the shots."

"No, they're done at night. Your husband can do it for you. Sometimes, it's better than doing it yourself," she said casually. "Make sure he practices on an orange first."

Myself, huh. Could you pull out your own tooth? Could you reset your own broken bone? Could you stand at the edge of a tall building, if you were afraid of heights? Defeated, I trudged downstairs to the hospital pharmacy to fill my first Pergonal prescription. This was it. This was the big time.

When the pharmacist took my prescription, I gasped. Oh. My. God. Please don't notice me, I thought. It seemed that Eddington Hospital had employed my former college boyfriend, Greg Magats, pronounced Ma-gatz. Or so he liked to claim. It never stuck, though. His fraternity brothers forever called him Maggots, anyway. Honestly, why didn't people with horrible names legally change them? It reminded me of my high school math teacher, Ms. Dilda. We sexually-obsessed adolescents only knew her as Ms. Dildo. Sometimes, from saying it so often in jest behind her back, I feared that I would have a Freudian slip and embarrass us both. I fantasized about slipping her an anonymous note asking if she would consider getting married and changing her hideous name.

Unfortunate name aside, Greg really was a great guy. Very ambitious. Very focused. Very predictable and steady. Just the kind of guy a girl should marry. But look at him now, flirting with obesity and thinning hair at only thirty. You never could tell how a person would age!

When we dated, he had a nice tight body, not too muscular. He had always been a gentleman, but to the point of suspicious restraint. Marriage had come up between us, but I just could not see myself married to such predictability. Well that, and no way in hell would I go through life with fly larvae as my last name.

Greg the Pharmacist turned around slowly, recognizing me. "Julia?"

"Greg! It is you. I wasn't sure." *Because you've gained eighty pounds.*

"How are you?" I asked.

"Good, great! You?"

"I'm good." *Please don't notice what my script says.*

"So, Leary," he said reading my name off the script. "You married that Ryan guy."

"Yes." He knew that. He had warned me that I was making a big mistake. Greg did not think I should marry Ryan because he was too reckless, too much of a partygoer and not focused enough on goals. So not true...now. While it was true that my husband had drunk his way through undergraduate school, he had matured and was clean and sober in graduate school. Straight A's all the way, which, coincidentally, was when we started dating. I finished my Bachelor's degree the same time he finished his first Master's. He claimed he had stayed on at school to meet me. Right. He wasn't yet ready for the real world.

"So, what do you do now?" he asked, still holding my script in his hand.

"Oh, well. I'm home full-time with my son. He's five. You know...life. Are you married?"

"No, couldn't replace you."

Ugh! "That's sweet, but you're wrong about that. You just haven't met her yet." *And if you don't lay off the pastries, you might never.*

"Hey, do you have a few minutes? I'm on lunch in ten minutes. We could talk. Catch up?" he asked hopefully.

"Oh, I can't today. I promised my sitter I'd be home by twelve. She has a...thing...an appointment," I stammered.

Jake was gleefully swimming at the neighborhood pool with Ryan. "Can I get that filled? I really have to rush."

"Sure," he said, dejectedly. He assembled my prescription and added up the bill. "That's three thousand twenty-five."

My heart palpitated in response. And that was only a month's supply! I could tell already that we were on our way to credit-card hell. I suddenly felt faint. Never in my life had I paid so much for medication. I mean, three thousand dollars was a trip to Disney World! Having no choice and on the verge of tears, I relinquished my Visa card. Sure, I would get $1600 back on a reimbursement, but it seemed so...unjust.

During the drive home, I kept replaying the odd-chance encounter with Greg "Maggots". I did feel really awful for not giving him a little of my time. But what was the point in dredging up a past I did not want to revisit? So I left, leading him to believe that I'd see him next time. There wouldn't be a next time. I had already planned to get my prescription filled nearer home. At least, he had not questioned my drug purchase. Of course, it was self-explanatory. Needing Pergonal was fairly specific, compared to needing say, Darvon for pain. Oh, you're in pain? What kind of pain? Ruptured disc, kidney stone, migraine?

If I had ever doubted marrying Ryan, I was sure, right then, without a doubt, that he was the one—well, at least between the two of them anyway. If John F. Kennedy Jr. were one of my options, I surely would have gone with him. But then, I'd be dead now. Odd, how I'd thought I was marrying the guy who would be full of adventure. Ryan had turned out to be more like Greg than Greg himself. I might feel differently about Ryan after he flipped out over the prescription bill. The other Ryan would undoubtedly surface to rant about the cost, as if I were in charge of deciding the pricing plan. It was like that in a marriage. People have dual personalities and the less attractive of the two often emerged in a marriage. Intimacy did that to you. You did not allow yourself the same outbursts in public that you did in your own home. Wouldn't it be great if you could yell at your co-workers, the way you yelled at your spouse, and never get fired? I say it's all backward. We should be on our best behavior with our loved ones and be grumpy at work. We ought to save the serpent's tongue for the lazy co-worker who never refilled the paper in the copy machine. All kidding aside, it was when times were tough that Ryan proved his salt and I realized that God had sent me a gem. And Leary was certainly a better surname.

CHAPTER NINE

Now, let's see. Was that mix two saline ampoules and one powder or two powders and one saline? What did Nurse Victoria's Secret instruct? I was contemplating the task before me and beginning to feel so confused. Where had my brain been lately? I needed Alex.

"Hello?" answered a sleepy voice.

"Alex, did I wake you? I'm so sorry, but I'm freaking out. I can't remember the mixture," I explained, balancing the phone between chin and shoulder while I held the packages in my hands.

"Two powders and one saline," she assured.

"Are you sure? Because you sound like you're sleeping."

"I'm sure. Get the needle in straight. It will hurt less."

"I'm sorry, I'm just nervous, I guess."

I felt bad about waking her, but Alex was kind of like my after-hours nurse/ therapist. Still, she was not a nocturnal person like me. "Go back to sleep."

Finally, I made a perfect solution and set the syringe aside. With a sigh, I took a gulp of wine. Now that I was on the high-octane meds, I figured I could relax a little on all those other restrictions. Wine was definitely back on the list.

Ryan entered the bedroom after an evening shower and tripped over that damn lump in the carpet.

"Jesus, Julia!"

"Have you noticed that you're the only one who trips on them? Maybe, you should pick up your feet when you walk."

"I know you're waiting for me to take care of it, aren't you? Well, I won't. I can outlast you sometimes," he challenged.

I just rolled my eyes at him, because, he could *not* outlast me on anything, actually. I had far more endurance when it came to a showdown.

"Are you ready there?" he asked, indicating to the loaded syringe.

"As ready I'll ever be, I suppose," I groaned in misery.

We had been over the procedure, practicing not on an orange, but on a grapefruit. I had him repeat the procedure over and over again, so that his technique would achieve some level of perfection and not bruise me. With another gulp, I downed the wine, dropped my sleep shorts and fell face first into a pillow on the bed. The challenge for me was to not clench my butt cheeks in cowardly apprehension. I needed to remain relaxed, so that the needle went in smoothly.

Ryan started rubbing my butt and smacked on a kiss. "You have a lovely ass, you know."

I lifted my face out of the pillow. "Shut up."

Then bam! He rammed the syringe so hard into my resistant flesh that I let out a scream, deep into the pillow. A burning sensation flowed through the muscle mass at the injection site. His method was, at least, swift, and it was done in an instant.

"Ryan!" I yelled.

In a perfect impersonation of Vinny Barbarino from *Welcome Back, Carter*, he responded, "What?"

"You suck."

"How about you suck me?" he asked, kissing my butt again and flopping back on the pillows, ready and waiting.

"Pig." I huffed out of the room.

"You know you want me," he called after me.

What I want is for you to take a needle in the ass, also!

That was pretty much how it went for the next four nights. Ryan slammed needles into my ass and I stormed out, angry at his insensitivity. I was at his mercy and I suspected he was enjoying it a little. I also had five dime-sized blue dots on my behind.

Today was payback time. Ryan was being subjected to the most unpleasant task of producing a sperm sample for the IUI. He was being called back to the "porn" room and turned to look at me. "Aren't you coming?" he asked, under the delusion that I would help with the insipid task. A private hand job was lewd enough; to do it in a specialized sterile office room bordered on impropriety. The beads of sweat dancing on his brow suggested he felt the same way.

The non-verbal approach was really the best. With a smile, I merely shook my head. No. I couldn't help but feel empowered by the fact that he was being subjected to some humiliation as well. Up to this point, the burden had been entirely mine. I had weathered most of this experience alone. My theory was that *he* needed to experience some discomfort in order to feel more involved in the whole process. Why did it always have to be me?

While Ryan was perusing *Playboy* centerfolds, my thoughts drifted back to a time when we were in college and I had requested a "sample" from him. It was scavenger-hunt night for my sorority and each of us elders had supplied a request for the list that the pledges were to retrieve. Of course, the idea was to make it as difficult as possible, so that the pledges would fear retribution. Really, in the end there was no actual reprisal. It was just fun to make them sweat it out. We all went through it. On that night in early May, I sent our pledges to Ryan's apartment to bring back some "protein lotion", a.k.a. semen. It was a gross thing to covet, but the point was to embarrass him. Did he play along? Couldn't he just humor me and whip up some mayonnaise concoction? Of course not. It was then that I knew he was extremely private about the matter of sexuality. He sent a note to me via the pledges that he was "all tapped out at the moment, but perhaps in three hours, you could come provide assistance."

This time around, more was riding on his ability to produce. He was at least efficient, because before long, I was in the birthing position with feet in stirrups and my legs freshly shaved and glossed. Castlebloom inserted his magic dildo, looking for ripe eggs and found two that were mature enough for fertilization. Every time I went through the process, my mind latched onto something in the room to divert my attention. Usually, it was the perforated ceiling tiles. Sometimes, I counted them. Sometimes, I connected the dots and envisioned crazy shapes. This time, the perforations looked like constellations as I separated my mind from my body. Among the dots, I saw the shape of a piece of cake with a candle on top. Or was that a phallic symbol? Finally, the cold and sterile tube slid past my cervix to the high point of the uterus. Like an army of soldiers, the "boys" were sent to the front line to battle with an unwilling egg.

"All done," announced Castlebloom after the insemination. If conception occurred, there would have been four of us at the party.

"I think I need a cigarette," I joked, when Ryan and I were left alone in the room. "Was it as good for you as it was for me?" I asked, with my knees pulled up to my chin for the ten-minute pause, a technique practiced a thousand times at home to no avail.

"Most certainly."

"We could do it for real, right here, right now. Then if we conceived, we would never know the difference."

I recalled a romantic story I had recently heard about my friend Cathy's sister, Corinne. Corrine suspected that she was pregnant. In sharing the suspicion with her boyfriend, he suggested that they get married anyway before they actually took the pregnancy test to confirm it. So they did and she was, in fact, pregnant. But they would always look back and be able to claim that they got married because they wanted to and not because they had to.

Ryan looked at me as though I were deranged. "I'm all tapped out right now. Let's get some lunch," he said, handing me my clothes. He was still irritated because I had not helped with the collection process. If he only knew about his buddy Dave's most embarrassing moment in the sperm collection room. I'm sure Dave would have been mortified to know that his soon-to-be-ex-wife was spilling intimate stories such as the one where a nurse walked into the wrong room while Dave was going to work. There he was with his pants down to his ankles and the *Playboy* centerfold stretched out before him. Poor guy! No wonder he felt he couldn't do it any more.

I was three days into the second round of injections and $6,000 in debt with Visa. Alex and I were on a pre-scheduled day trip to Atlantic City, NJ. I tried vainly to cancel so that I could stay home and watch the E Channel to catch up on the latest celebrity gossip, but Alex wouldn't let me weasel out. Her lead foot was propelling us down the AC Expressway toward our fate, she claimed. She had come across an exhibit that was on display for a short time at Ripley's Museum. Apparently, there were African fertility statues which, when touched, had blessed thousands of women with pregnancies. Alex was drawn to this kind of unexplained mystery. She would not accept that I did not buy into voodoo.

"It'll be good for you," she claimed.

"It's a hoax, Alex...like Area 54 and the Loch Ness Monster," I said, while scratching viciously at my arms. It wasn't that I did not believe in the supernatural world, because I completely did. It was just that whenever there was a fee attached, I was suspicious. I was proud of the fact that I had yet to be suckered by garden-variety scam artists or telemarketers.

"Shh! Don't say that. Area 54 is real. Have you never watched the Discovery Channel? Your skepticism is part of the problem. If you can't believe in the unexplained, it really won't work for you."

"Oh, come on!" I couldn't stop scratching my arms. "My skin is horrible!" I exclaimed in frustration. I itched all the time lately. My skin felt like it was on fire. I had mentioned it to my father and he had suggested that, maybe, I was allergic to our dog. But I'd had dogs all my life. Why would I suddenly be sensitive to one now? "Do you have any lotion in here?"

"In the glove box, where no one keeps gloves," she answered. "So, what about God? You believe in God, don't you?"

"That's different," I argued, as I generously applied Aveeno to my arms.

"But can you explain God? Can you see God?'

"No, but I feel His presence, sometimes. Granted, not much lately. And you aren't still serious about having a child on your own, are you?"

I had hoped that after further thought, she would see the enormous challenge it posed.

"I don't know. I guess it's a silly notion." She sighed wistfully. "Maybe, I'm kidding myself."

This made me sad for her. Just as her peak fertility years were coming to an end, her husband had left her. He'd been gone three weeks and true to the ultimate cliché, had moved in with his mother.

"Any word from Dave?"

"No." An uncomfortable silence lingered.

"What is it?"

"His new girlfriend has two kids. A nine-year-old boy and a six-year-old girl."

I thought for a moment about how painful this news was for her.

"Do you want me to egg his car?" Then in an attempt to be rational, I added, "I know you aren't thinking along those lines right now, but you could also hook up, one day, with someone who already has kids."

"I really do not want to be married again. Ever. If I find someone, I'll just use him for sex. I will never give up my freedom again."

"So, I guess your only option then is to be a single parent?"

"Exactly."

"Well, okay...," I said, trying to think of the positives. "At least, if you got pregnant alone, you would never have to fight for custody."

"Now you're talking my language."

"Is it that important to you? Having your freedom, as you say?"

She thought for a moment and sighed, "I don't ever want to wash another man's laundry or cook his meals or be the secretary or report in when I'm out or ask permission to purchase something with my own money!"

I tried to interject, but she was on a roll.

"And, that whole fart-whenever-you-please thing. They don't do that when you're dating, you know. It's like they get married and all the gross stuff oozes out. It kills the romance."

"But so do infertility treatments."

"That too!"

All the way to the door of Ripley's Museum, I suffered Alex's litany of negative male characteristics. Sure, part of me agreed with her. Part of me also understood that she was going through a life change and was just venting her anger about her husband. Either way, we were still going to touch those damn statues.

And there they were, ugly as hell, right inside the main entrance. They were approximately four feet tall and carved from dark wood. A small crowd, with us in its midst, stood around reading the testimonials to their powers. Story after story detailed how women had become mysteriously pregnant. One article told of how seven out of ten of the female office workers who had handled the statues, were found to be with child. Some stories were from women who thought they were done having their children. Others were from women beyond their fertile years. So okay, what the hell, we touched them, groped them, and had our photos taken for posterity. Then there were postcards to take home that the curators wanted us to complete and return if we found ourselves pregnant within the next year. For this, they would send us a free gift.

Naturally, we went gambling next. You cannot go to Atlantic City and not indulge in the sin of throwing away your hard-earned money. We strolled through the opulent-looking Taj Mahal and tried our cosmic luck on the slot machines. On a ten-dollar investment, I won thirty-five dollars and considered myself lucky. Alex lost forty dollars and considered herself done.

We had a fabulous crab-cake lunch at the casino, compliments of Alex's mother who gambled once a month with her retirement-home cronies. Mrs. Plavinski was one of those senior citizen gambling mini-addicts that the casinos continually lured back with offers of free hotel rooms and lavish meals.

We strolled along the boardwalk, taking in the freak shows and panhandlers while savoring ice-cream cones. I stopped at an electronics store, drawn by the E Channel's news coverage of Brad and Jen, Vince and Jen, and Brad and Angelina saga. "It's so awful," I said, wiping at a tear. "What is it with celebrities anyway?" Maybe I was dwelling on this too much. Why should I care about them? Obviously, I did not know all the sordid details. But I just felt so bothered still by the break-up of Brad and Jen. You always rooted for good couples to succeed. They were our role models. When they failed, it seemed to confirm that Happy Ever After did not exist. A tear slipped from my eye. Get a grip, Julia, said a voice of reason. You would not be this emotional, if it were not for those horrid fertility injections. It's like being pregnant a hundred times over. I would to have to stop watching the news. I couldn't stop crying. And itching. Maybe I had fleas! Did Taco have fleas? Could people get fleas?

We moved on and came to Maria's Palm Readings. For only twenty-five dollars, you could have a reading done.

"Let's go in," Alex urged.

"No. Not here. You can't trust these people. The neighborhood is a little seedy, don't you think?"

"Would you go to one if you thought they were more reputable?"

"I guess. Why, do you know someone?"

By now, I had to sit down on a bench outside Maria's. My knees and ankles were throbbing and stiff.

"I do. I went to a lady three years ago and it was amazing, the stuff she said that was true."

"Did you ask if she saw a baby in your future?"

"She said yes, but that I would have a lot of disappointments first."

"Hmm," I said in reply, considering the prospect. It would be nice to have some insights into the future. It sure would be a relief to know if I was wasting my time or not.

"She also said that my husband was my soul mate,"

"It could be true. Just because you're getting divorced doesn't mean that your time together was not meant to be."

"Whatever," Alex said, her disgust over having wasted fourteen years obvious in her tone. "You can't really take psychics too seriously. If you go, you do it mainly for fun. You can't make life-altering decisions based on it."

"Okay, sign me up," I said, trying not to sound too eager to swallow some more snake oil.

CHAPTER TEN

Every three months or so, Ryan decided that it might be a good idea to balance the checkbook. This time, six months had gone by and our attention was drawn to the matter by an insufficient-funds notice from the bank. In truth, neither of us was very good at record-keeping. Those ATM withdrawals were dauntingly evil. I always seemed to lose the annoying slips of paper. He, at least, brought them home, only to tack them on the refrigerator for me to record. Obviously, I hadn't. Three hours into the overwhelming task, I heard a lion's roar coming from the office.

"Julia!"

I twitched. After nine years together, I had learned that his tone was a different language altogether. I was in for it. He had unearthed some fault that was, no doubt, mine. I was being summoned, the way a child would be, to receive my punishment. It mattered little that I just might have been in the middle of something crucial.

For two months, I had been dealing with aching muscles and inflamed, burning skin. The mildly annoying itching had turned into full-blown hives. I was covered with red welts all over my body, especially, my torso and arms. So far, they had not crept up to my face, thank God. I was in the process of applying cortisone cream that only mildly alleviated the discomfort. Last month, when my feet were in the stirrups, exposing the burning rash on my legs, I asked about the skin irritation, wondering if it could be from the medication.

"I've never known it to happen before," Castlebloom insisted. "Besides, this medication leaves your system within twenty-four hours, anyway."

"Oh? Then why is one always advised to wait three months after going off the pill before trying to conceive?"

"Just a precaution. To be sure the hormones have left the system. Too much floating estrogen has been linked to breast development in males and genital abnormalities."

"What? Isn't this the same thing, in a way?"

"It just has not been documented. Perhaps, it is stress-induced."

According to Dr. Castlebloom, the rash and hives should have disappeared after each cycle. Well, they hadn't! To assuage my anxiety, I was sent to an allergist and completed a full round of testing. The allergist found nothing obvious that could cause the hives, other than stress. "Relieve yourself of stress," he advised me. But infertility treatments caused their own stress, with mood swings, endless, invasive doctor's appointments, sex on demand and money down the drain with each failure.

"Julia!" came another roar.

"What?" I snapped from the bathroom that was one door away from the office.

"I need you in here."

"I'm busy," I sang.

"Well *I'm* busy trying to straighten out *your* mess, and I haven't had anything to eat yet today."

Right. Now it was my fault that he did not have time to eat. No one had held a gun to his head and forced him to hole up in the office all day. Next, I'd be blamed for the federal deficit.

"So, go eat!" I yelled back. "I'm tending to my hives."

He then barged into the bathroom with evidence in his hands. I was standing precariously in my underwear with one leg on the sink counter applying cortisone cream.

"Jeez, can't it wait until I get dressed?"

"You have $300 worth of cash withdrawals you did not record," he said, waving the statement in front of me, marked with six red circles. Meaning: we had a deficit of $300 and it would come out of *my* savings.

I pleaded in self-defense, "You're talking three months' time, though. Maybe, you should balance the checkbook more often."

"And this," he thrust the Visa bill in front of me. "What are all these purchases at Gap, Macy's, Old Navy and Target? The only thing that is supposed to be on this card is your medicine!"

"It's true that I've been doing a little extra shopping lately. I bought some Christmas gifts." Actually, I'd only bought one gift, earrings for his mother, but he did not need to know that. "And, I've gained weight from the drugs, Ryan. I needed some new clothes." Actually, I was guilty of using shopping as therapy. What woman didn't?

It was like genetic or something. In fact, I was confident that in the future, scientists would discover that women carried a gene for shopping. And when they did, we would all be absolved of what was now regarded as a near-crime. It was just such a rush to find the right outfit or a great bargain. Every failed IUI sent me to the retail world, looking for comfort. To date, I had gained twelve pounds in three months and I didn't just hate all my old clothes; none fit. At five feet six, I had gone from a size nine/ ten to a twelve. I loved junk food way too much to obsess about being less than a size nine/ten, but twelve was beyond my threshold. And now we were pushing toward a size fourteen.

"It has to stop. We can't afford this," he lectured.

"Oh, I should just go around in moo-moos and stretch pants, then?"

Ryan did not pay much attention to female fashion, but if there was one thing he hated, it was stretch-pant leggings on women, especially when paired with the big oversized tee shirts. Never mind that they had been officially out of style for years, but darn if you didn't see women still wearing them. Why did I even bother discussing fashion with him? Arguing with a man about needing clothes that fit was a losing battle. When they gained weight, they simply dropped their pants lower and let their gut hang over their belts. They had no need for larger sizes.

"All I'm saying is that we cannot afford it. If you keep spending frivolously, we'll soon be living on welfare. We can't even afford the medication. It's killing us. When this is done, I'll have to sell some stock to pay these bills."

"Isn't that why we have that stock, for rainy days?" That wasn't good. We had a measly 100 shares of Smithkline stock inherited from his grandfather. It was only worth about $3,000. I kept praying for a huge pharmacological breakthrough on their part. A cure for diabetes would be most excellent in more ways than one.

"It's not for your damn clothes!" he shouted with a red face and a bulging carotid artery.

Okay, okay, I got it already. But as usual, nothing would be resolved. I always ended up promising to do better, but how could I not buy new clothes? I did not think that a few extra purchases would make that much of a difference. But then, 'twas the season; he was obviously feeling the holiday stress. It did not help that our son was holding us hostage for retail toys. Ryan wanted to give Jake the moon. He was driven by a great desire to spoil his only child, which was yet another solid reason for every child to have a sibling. I ended the "financial discussion" somewhat gaining the upper hand by saying, "Fine, don't buy me anything for Christmas, then." I began to sniffle back tears. "My new fat clothes will be my Christmas. And by the way, I know all about your deal with Jake regarding my catalogs!"

I had been saving this information for the right moment to expose him and the shady deal he had made with our son. I had noticed Jake taking an unusual interest in collecting the mail lately. One day, I caught him leafing through and pulling out my Chadwick's catalog.

"What are you doing, Jake?" I inquired.

"Nothing," he said, hiding the magazine behind his back.

"Jake. What's up? Why are you hiding Mommy's magazine?"

Reluctantly, he confessed, "Daddy told me to."

"Why would Daddy tell you to hide Mommy's magazine?"

Jake looked down at his feet, afraid to make eye contact with me. "He said I couldn't tell you."

"Well, you better tell me or Santa won't be happy with you." That's the ticket. Find the child's weakness.

Hesitantly, he said, "He said he would give me five dollars for every clothes book I found in the mail. He said it would save him money, and we could buy more toys."

"What? He told you that?" The nerve of him! "Give me the magazine."

Slowly, Jake handed it over.

"And how much money *have* you made?"

"Twenty bucks!" he claimed proudly.

"Daddy was wrong to tell you to hide my catalogs and now Santa will be bringing him a load of coal for Christmas. Go play now. I'll take care of Daddy." And maybe, I'll steal his mail. Maybe, I'll tear out all the good pages in *This Old House*! I could just picture him sitting on the toilet reading an article on installing skylights and then discovering that the instructions page was missing!

Naturally, Ryan brushed it off as a silly prank, but I felt violated that he had plotted behind my back with my son.

The following week, my friend, Ally, and I went to the much-anticipated psychic reading. Since Alex was too busy with her divorce issues, Ally was the next obvious choice to accompany me to the supernatural world. There were always a few important things that forged bonds between friends. For Ally and me, our bond was our boys, John Travolta and anything to do with the supernatural.

We arrived at a row house in North-East Philadelphia, about twenty minutes from my home. Christmas decorations overtook the tiny yard. The psychic's husband greeted us. One at a time, we were led back to the kitchen to meet Luanne. I was first up, leaving a then blond-streaked Ally to chat with the lady's husband. What I saw was not what I had conjured in my head. I had visions of a crystal ball atop a table covered in a cloth of purple and gold. I had expected soft music, candles and incense. Instead, the backdrop to my first psychic flirtation was just an ordinary, dimly-lit kitchen with a simple white candle burning on the Formica table. It smelled like my grandmother's kitchen, a mixture of sink-drain scum and cinnamon. I couldn't wait to get back home and tell Ryan what middle-aged Luanne was wearing: stretch pants and a moo-moo top!

"Do you want just the positive stuff or everything?" she asked.

Feeling momentarily brave, I said, "All of it. I can take it." I handed over my wedding ring as the personal item from which she would receive her psychic vibes.

Luanne entered into a trance-like state and began scribbling wildly on paper, recording her thoughts as she expressed them aloud. "You have a lot of doctors around you. A lot of books also. You are either a teacher or a nurse. Which one?" she asked.

"A teacher," I answered. Wow, I thought.

"You wanted to be a nurse, but doubted your abilities."

How true! I was sure that had I been a nurse, I would make a mistake sometime or the other and inject the wrong medication into someone with fatal consequences. But then I realized that I was hypersensitive to foul smells, especially, the kind that emanated from someone else's orifices. And sick bodies most definitely smelled.

"You are struggling with money issues, right now. It's related to your doctor visits, correct?"

"Yes." Now I was getting goose pimples on my skin.

"You have one son. His name begins with a J...Jack...No. Is it Jacob?

"Yes!"

"He adores you. He's very attached to you," Luanne went on without a hitch, as she described my son's personality. "He chose you to be his parents," she said.

Confused, I asked, "What do you mean?"

"Souls choose the experience they want to have. He chose you.

He doesn't like being an only child, but he needed to experience it."

Okay. I had told this woman nothing. There was no way she could even have known I had a child! I could feel the hair rising on the back of my neck.

Wow! He chose us? Why? Why us, of all the options he had? He could have been born to wealthy parents. He could have been born to a family with nine kids. Instead, he had chosen ordinary us. Why would anyone choose ordinary, when they could have fabulous and exciting? I was overwhelmed with a sense of privilege and honor to be Jake's mother.

She described my relationship with Ryan as running hot and cold.

Yes! So, so true. Unbelievable!

"Tell your husband to be careful on ladders. He loves you very much, but you don't always reciprocate," Luanne said, as she rapidly scribbled her reading on paper.

As this truth was laid bare, I felt utterly ashamed of myself. I had been exposed. I was not as demonstrative in my affection as Ryan was. It often made him feel insulted. It was not how I was raised. Sometimes, he simply chose the wrong time to say "I love you." I found it hard to reciprocate when I was still seething over a recent argument. My heart was guarded, while his was displayed openly on his sleeve. But I loved him. Strangely enough, when it came to loving Jake, I did not feel at all inhibited. I was completely open.

Finally, I couldn't stand the suspense any longer and asked, "Do you see other children for me?"

"I don't see a lot of souls around you. There is one more waiting, though. You know her."

"What? What do you mean?" It was just too abstract for me to grasp.

"A soul waits for you. You have to decide to receive her. I can't get any more clarity on that."

Well, I couldn't claim any clarity of thought either. Instead, I was more confused. Was I chasing a non-existent dream or not? This reading did not appease my inquiring mind. It simply left me hungry for more.

Luanne had made a reference to a "her." Was I going to have a girl? I should send in Ryan for a reading and see if he got a similar prediction. If we both had a female soul waiting for us, it would be a truth I could bank on.

Ally was quite impressed with her reading. She was amazed at the factual information that Luanne was able to read. The psychic told Ally that if she wanted a girl, she would have to have a fifth child. To this, Ally responded, "No thank you! I've already got enough stretch marks for five kids. Those boys have sucked the life out of me."

CHAPTER ELEVEN

J ake barely made the school bus, because I could not get out of bed. After eight bongs from that irritating priceless heirloom, I awoke to alarming stiffness and soreness. Most mornings were now beginning with severe muscle and joint pain. I was also sweating, as though I'd entered menopause. But this time, it felt as though someone had drugged me and beaten me with baseball bats. I could not pull my knees up to get out of bed. The last time I could remember feeling so bad was in college, after which I swore to never again touch Jack Daniel's or any other liquor. In my freshman year, I became the human guinea pig for testing genetic alcoholism. It was partly born out of the new yahoo freedom of being away from home and partly out of fear that my mother's disease would be my fate as well. I was relieved to discover that not only did I not care for most types of alcohol, but my body seemed to naturally repel the stuff as if it were poison. I couldn't understand why people willingly abused their bodies with alcohol.

But my current aches could not be explained away by an alcohol hangover. If it were not for Jake, I would not have attempted to get out of bed at all. Despite all my personal pain and grief, I tried very hard to be positive for my son and keep his life and routine normal. There had been many days since I started treatment, when I wanted to stay under the covers and hide from the world. I never forgot that although I was trying to have a child, I did, thankfully, already have one, one that needed my attention. I owed it to him to seem normal, even if it meant faking it. Occasionally, I found that in feigning happiness, I could actually make myself feel happy.

Five-year-old Jake had become my therapy, but only during the hours he was home. The fact that he was in kindergarten all day had its positive and negative aspects. It left me with too many hours alone and without enough to focus on, but it also freed up my schedule for doctor's visits. Jake was unaware of my innumerable doctor's appointments. A five-year-old child did not need to be burdened with worries about his mother's declining health. I missed him terribly. Some days, I wanted to keep him home from school just to keep me company. He was, however, in his glory spending his days with other kids. For the first time in his life, he did not seem as lonely. Ultimately, that was what I wanted, to ease his loneliness.

It had been my dirty little secret that after Jake left for school, I often snuggled back into bed to watch *Regis and Kelly* and *The View*. I was not a soap-opera junkie, but with cable television, there were plenty of good movies to watch. Lately, I had been watching all the old classics on AMC. For the past week, A & E had been running John Riley movies. I was a huge John Riley fan because he had graduated from my high school. He was also very easy on the eyes. "The Package," I called him.

While slumming and absorbing TV radiation, I had learned, moreover, to avoid the infomercials on how to be successful in life. When you were already down and depressed, nothing could make you feel more like a loser than an Infomercial touting, "Do something with your life. Get a degree at home. Start a new career. Get off that couch and call now, before this offer runs out." All they really wanted was your money. Ryan thought I was very busy with PTA projects and working on the house, but I was really, just...sleeping. I could not help it. I was just so tired all the time. I had become a hibernating bear. The more I slept, the more I needed to.

On one occasion, he came home from an especially arduous day at work and found me in my pajamas yet again.

"What did you do all day?" he asked accusingly.

"I...I...," I stammered, struggling to recall what I had actually done. "I loaded the dishwasher. I did the laundry, all day. I did... stuff." Actually, I had put a load of clothes in and it was still sitting there, as it had been "all day". Often, I lied and made up things just to pacify him. "Oh, the day I've had!" I would say. I couldn't admit that I was becoming a helpless, lifeless, defeated sack of itching and sweating flesh.

Finally, Ryan became thoroughly exasperated. "Julia," he said, "I think you're falling into a depression. I think you need help."

"Genius observation! What was your first clue?" I was well aware that the blues consumed me, but I was helpless to get out of it. Now I understood why people in depression slept so much. It was an escape; a place where tranquil dreams dulled the pain of your heart ripping apart.

Ryan sat on the bed next to me and counseled, "You can't lie around all day feeling sorry for yourself. I get sad sometimes too, but *I* have to go to work. I can't stay in bed all day."

In all fairness, there was a huge difference between what my body had been through and what his body had been through. "I don't stay in bed all day. I migrate to the couch or the recliner sometimes. And I don't feel sorry for myself. I feel sorry for you and Jake too." I started to leak tears, "And you lecturing me doesn't help."

True, he was in this thing too, but he simply could not feel the depths of sadness and despair that I did. For one, his body and mind were not being laced with chemicals that enhanced such dramatic moods. Imagine having super-maximum PMS on low dose LSD. That's what it was like being an infertile drug junkie. Surely, the next dose would be your last. One more hit would be the ultimate euphoric high and then you could abstain.

That particular day would not, however, be one of those glorious sleep days. I had to make it out to Eddington by 10 a.m. for blood tests to check my estrodiol levels. We were in our fourth IUI cycle and the problem of rash and hives would have to be addressed.

Last month, I had questioned Castlebloom again, informing him that I could not find anything I could possibly be allergic to.

"I'm sure it's just stress-related," he had replied. "You need to relax. Maybe, you should take a break from this for a while and put it out of your mind."

Did he just dismiss me? Again?

I turned red at the suggestion that I needed to relax. Everyone thought it was so easy to get pregnant! I lay in bed most of the time. How much more relaxed could I be? I'd like to relax him, the patronizing bastard!

During the times that I was not slumbering, I became hell-bent on proving him wrong. I did some research on the Internet and got lucky on the Mayo Clinic website. I loved the Internet! I found that the hormones could, in fact, cause skin irritation. One little footnote stood out like a red flag; it said that a drug allergy would more than likely show up as a skin problem, like itching or hives! Ah, ha! In your face, Dr. Castlebloom! Interesting, that such vital information was not listed in the brochures that came with the medication. I had the article to prove it and intended to make the doctor pay attention. But now, I was facing a whole new problem: severe joint pain. It was so bad, that these days, I crept down the steps of my home like an old woman, clutching onto the handrail for dear life. A long, hot shower and some anti-inflammatory tablets helped relieve the stiffness, but it was still distressing. I had been experiencing sore muscles and stiffness for a while, but that was nothing compared to this.

There were two different routes to Eddington Hospital. One was the twenty-eight-minute scenic route along Philmont Avenue. The other was the Pennsylvania turnpike which took eighteen minutes, if you could avoid a traffic calamity. Since I was late, I took the turnpike. It was a perfectly sunny day, but in the month of January, the temperature was down to a frigid twenty-two degrees. Traffic was not too bad, but Philly drivers were only second to New Yorkers for their notoriously poor driving etiquette. Staying alert was proving a challenge for me. And then I noticed that coming up on my left was the oddest looking orange vehicle I had ever seen. All around, cars began to brake. Finally, the orange bus-like vehicle moved alongside me and...oh wow!...It was a hot dog! It appeared to be the Oscar Mayer Weiner mobile. It was truly hilarious. I could not stop staring at it and trying to figure out where they had hidden the door. I could not see an opening to the hotdog anywhere.

Suddenly, I noticed that while gawking at the hotdog mobile, I had missed my exit at Willow Grove. Shit, shit, shit! You could not just turn around on the Pennsylvania turnpike. You had to drive all the way to the next exit, pay the fare and backtrack. Well, that was just dandy, because it so happened that I only had enough cash to pay for the exit that I was to take.

The next exit was Fort Washington. I pulled into the stall and pleaded my case, but then, could not even find the damned toll ticket. I searched everywhere in my car while impatient motorists honked at me. It seemed to have vanished. The gods of smooth sailing were obviously against me! Turnpike-Bertie was unyielding. She insisted that since I did not have a ticket or even enough money to pay two dollars twenty-five cents, I would have to pay the entire fare, which was around fifty dollars! Well, yes, that made sense. I did not have enough money, so charge me more! She acted as though it was a logic I should understand and graciously accept. As cars honked and beeped, I felt my hives bursting open. I should have followed my instincts and stayed in bed. I had planned on tapping the ATM when I got to Eddington. Now I would have to rob one! I really needed to invest in that EZ PASS thing.

When Dr. Castlebloom appeared after my blood test, I was ready to strangle him for every wrong committed in the world.

"Is something wrong, Julia?" he asked, sensing my edginess.

"Is something wrong? Look at me." Underneath my sweater, I wore a tank top to expose my arms. "I look like a leper! I can't go out in public because people stare at me like I'm afflicted with something contagious! I can't take this any more! And you were wrong." I shoved my Internet research at him. "According to the Mayo Clinic, these drugs can cause skin reactions. You did not take me seriously. I am not some uninformed moron you can play games with! You're the doctor. You should have known about this research."

Castlebloom recoiled a few inches from the heat of my fury.

"Well." He reflected for a moment, looking beyond me to some mysterious place on the wall. "Okay. Thank you for pointing that out. It's good that you are informed. Informed people make better patients."

Blah, blah, blah. "So now what? I can't tolerate this medicine anymore."

"Well, there is a new brand out that is more refined. It's taken subcutaneously with smaller needles. The size diabetics use." He thought for a second while I calmed down. "Why don't we suspend therapy for a while and see if your skin clears up? If it does, we'll try the new meds."

Suspend therapy? That was even worse than soldiering on. If I could not get pregnant with drugs, then surely, I would not be getting knocked up without them? As my posture drooped and I stared at my swollen hands, I knew that I did not have any other option.

Defeated, I went home and crawled back into bed. I did not come down to dinner. Ryan brought me Tylenol and herbal tea, that distasteful hormonal remedy that was supposed to provide a natural balance. He tried his best to pep talk me back to stability. The phone rang twice and he answered each time. First it was Ally, then Lauren, my realtor friend whom I had introduced to Alex. I could not talk to either of them. Finally, Alex called and I accepted.

"Hey. Ryan explained what happened. Are you all right?"

"I guess I'll live if I have to. It's just…I'm such a junkie now. I know the shit is killing me, but I desperately need it."

"I know," she soothed. And she did know. She was the only friend or family member who knew what it was like to crave Pergonal. This was why I found myself avoiding Ally and Lauren. I knew they were concerned, but explaining it all to them was just too much work. Although hives and joint pain were not Alex's experience, she at least understood that we were all unique. The understanding that I wanted from my doctor, I thankfully received from her.

"Enough about me. I'm sick of my life. Tell me something

interesting about yours. Has Dave done anything weird lately?" I inquired, because since he had asked for the divorce, oddball tendencies had surfaced.

"He claims that I'm not taking care of the house, which is bull. He flipped when he found out that I cancelled the cleaning lady."

"Why would he care? He doesn't live there anymore."

"He's decided that he wants it back. He thinks I'm letting it go to hell to sabotage his profit from the sale. But honestly, without him here, I find that I make very little mess. I don't need a cleaning lady."

"It sounds like he can't stand the idea that you're doing so well. When you didn't oppose the divorce, it probably hurt his ego," I suggested.

Alex gave a half-laugh, "Maybe. I think he sees the house as being more his than mine, since he had it before we were married. He sends these long, obnoxious e-mails, threatening me that I'm going to get nothing, because it was he who did all the renovations."

"What an idiot! His lawyer couldn't be all that great, if he believes that. Haven't you paid half the bills for the last twelve years?"

"Exactly. I think he's just trying to pester me into moving out sooner."

"Well, in that case, maybe you should booby-trap some things to fall apart soon after he takes over. You know, like loosen up some pipes. Remove a few essential screws. How about some Limburger cheese in the curtain rods? It will take years to find the source of that stench."

Alex laughed wickedly. "You're evil!"

"It's my drugs," I said almost proudly. At least, they were good for something. Maybe, I should become a crime-story novelist and put my malevolent Pergonal inspirations to good use.

"Seriously, though, I have considered removing the litter box and letting the cat piss all over the house. He hates Larry."

"Good one!" I cheered. "I guess he's finding it difficult to bring his girlfriend over to his mother's. He's getting restless."

"I'm just as itchy to move on. Lauren has found another house for me to look at tomorrow. It's just outside your neighborhood on Yardley Road. Want to come with me to see it?"

"If I'm feeling able by then. Oh, is it that cute Cape Cod with the funny mailbox?" If it was the house I recalled, the mailbox had been a sore spot with the community for several years. It bordered on obscene, but mostly, it was just hilarious. It was a handcrafted wood carving of a plumber bending over. The mail went—you guessed it—in the plumber's crack! The owner was obviously a plumber and part-time woodworker. When town officials wanted old Mr. Eshelman to remove it, he had argued that it also served as an advertisement for his business. The battle between the owner and the town supervisors made the local paper. Alex did not know about the mailbox, but assured me that if she bought the house, it would be the first thing she would replace. I was sure it was too much of a male touch for her. She would not be cajoled. A prominent view of a male coin slot was plainly unnecessary.

CHAPTER TWELVE

I met Alex and Lauren at the house on Yardley Road. From the road, you could tell the Cape Cod needed some work, but it was charming and sat on a half-acre lot which, for the area, was a nice size.

When I entered the driveway, Lauren and Alex were already standing in the front yard, shivering from the cold and looking at the house. I wrestled out of my van to greet them. Lauren's striking appearance grabbed my attention. She had been making herself over lately, becoming more stylish. Her hair was freshly cut in a new, bouncy do. Her name always surprised those who were expecting an Italian. She was Irish through and through, with red hair and blue eyes. Yet, she went by her married name, LaRosa. I met Lauren through Ally. Their older boys were buddies. Lauren and I had become fast friends. She had a comforting calm about her that immediately drew me in and made me feel more self-assured. Everyone needed a friend like that.

"Hi," I said, giving each a hug.

They both stared at me oddly without saying anything.

"What? Is there food residue on my face? Give me a compact."

Lauren was the first to speak. "Julia," she said, "Are you okay? You don't look well."

Scratching at my left arm, I said, "I'm fine, except for these damn hives."

Neither of them had seen me in person for a couple of weeks. In the past, I'd been able to hide the hives by wearing long sleeves, but now they had crept to my neck, threatening to take over my face.

"It's not that, Julia. It's your face," said Alex.

"You look different...bloated...distorted."

"It's not that bad," I protested. "You're looking at me like I'm Frankenstein."

We entered the house and were immediately engulfed by dank air. The place needed a good cleaning. I migrated to a wall mirror for a look at myself. Okay. I did look fat, bloated and flushed in the face. No. I looked a bit like Queen Adoree of Snow White. Mean and evil. Spiteful and vengeful. What had happened to me? I'd always had a pretty face, or so people told me. Where there had been a natural smile, there was now a frown. This was what life did to a woman's face, I surmised. Some of us became the evil, jealous queen, while some rare, lucky one got to remain Snow White, pure and unblemished. I'd noticed my first real wrinkle after Jake was born. The signs of age had started manifesting themselves after too many sleepless nights. This new angry look was not from lack of sleep. It was a sign of grief.

"Do either of you have any water pills?" I hollered as they moved through the hall toward the kitchen.

"You need more than a water pill, Julia!" Lauren shouted back from the hall. "How about a new doctor?"

The kitchen was antiquated, with brown and beige linoleum flooring and still more ancient appliances. A three-season room off the kitchen blocked the southern light that should have flooded this room. As Lauren was showing Alex around, I moved toward the bedrooms. There were three in all: the master bedroom and two smaller rooms. The bonus was the master bathroom—awesome for the house's modest size—in addition to the regular main bath in the hall. The master bath was, no doubt, the handiwork of Mr. Eshelman, the plumber. It featured a separate whirlpool tub and shower stall and a long, double-sink vanity—all tiled in varying shades of beige. For the bathroom alone, she should buy this house, I thought.

I thought Alex had agreed when she walked in and said, "Wow."

"You could fit a reading chair in here," offered Lauren.

"I thought the toilet was the reading chair," I joked.

We were all gathered in the kitchen again, when Alex asked for our opinions on the house.

"It needs a little love," I submitted. "Mostly just cosmetic, though. I'm sure you won't have any plumbing problems."

The typical realtor, Lauren interjected, "It's a great location. Decent neighborhood. Good school district. The taxes are reasonable. What do *you* think? How do you feel about it?"

"I like it," smiled Alex, looking at me.

"Would you like to make an offer, then?" I could feel the rush of excitement emanating from Lauren.

"How much is it again?" Alex asked.

"Only two twenty-six."

Only she says. Real estate in the North East was horrendously overpriced.

"I think it may need a new roof, though," I chimed in, "and the garage door looks as though it's hanging by a thread."

Alex let her eyes scan the kitchen a moment. "Well, this kitchen is completely disgusting. It would all have to go."

I could feel Lauren holding in her breath, waiting for an answer while Alex let her suffer. Finally, Alex said emphatically, "I like it. I want to make an offer. Can we get it down to two ten at least?"

Lauren smiled, "We can try."

Relief for Lauren. Joy for me. Amazingly fast for Alex. It was only the fourth house she had toured. "I'll help you paint. And did you notice the mailbox? Don't you love it?" I was excited at the prospect of having her in the neighborhood.

"It's going," Alex insisted. We all laughed.

Six weeks later, Alex and her cat, Larry, took possession of their new house. She did, in fact, remove the mailbox from the yard and replaced it with one of those baseball-proof plastic contraptions that do not complement the historic quality of the neighborhood. I arrived to help paint the main bedroom and living room. After changing into an old pair of painting shorts, I caught a glimpse of my legs in the full-length mirror in Alex's bedroom. Those couldn't be my legs, I thought. My legs were thinner, with fewer spider veins. And when had they become so ghostly white? This was the routine I went through every year, when I put on my first pair of shorts for the season. After not seeing my bottom half all winter, I hardly recognized it. Then I went through the five stages of grief, not as dramatically as I did with the deluge of every period, but still, a form of grief.

First, there was shock and denial at the sight of my legs, then anger and bargaining. It was not fair that my legs looked ten years older than I was. My mother was fifty-eight and had great legs. Even she didn't have spider veins. I did a few squats to tighten the muscles. Eventually, there was nothing left to do but accept the fact that I'd inherited my paternal grandmother's legs. Short, dimply and laced with spider veins. I should have stopped obsessing about my legs and been grateful that my overall health was restoring. Gradually, the hives and joint pain had subsided, validating my suspicions from the start. I was able to move without pain and had even lost six pounds. I had not even realized how ill I had felt, until I started feeling well again. It helped that I was focusing on other things, like getting Alex settled.

As she was finishing painting the trim in the living room, I rolled the last wall. "It's going to look great." I inhaled deeply. "I love the smell of fresh paint. It feels clean, doesn't it?"

"It does," she agreed. "It's time for a break. How about a glass of wine?"

"Let me finish this wall first." I was anxious to see the transformation from yellow to sage. It was going to be a beautiful room with the plum sofas and wide-planked wood flooring.

When Alex came back with our wine, we sat in the center on stools, admiring the fresh color.

"To your new life," I toasted.

"Thanks for all your help, Julia."

I waved my hand to say no big deal. "I haven't even finished the painting in my own house."

We both sipped the cool Chardonnay and scrutinized our paint job.

Alex broke the silence. "You're looking better."

"I'm feeling better. But you know, it feels like we're just wasting time, waiting for me to recover." Even though I did not, for one minute, miss the needles, the wasted months were torture.

"It won't do you any good to be pregnant if you're half-dead." She paused. "You don't seem very happy, though. It's like you have this dark aura around you."

"Really?" I was shocked. "I try hard to be positive. I haven't lost all hope yet."

"Maybe, you should consider a therapist."

"Why? Isn't that why I have you?"

"I can only understand what you're feeling. A good therapist can help *you* understand what you're feeling," she advised.

"Ryan said the same thing...that I should see someone." Actually, he had said he was worn out from counseling me. "Alex, did you ever have, you know, like...crazy self-destructive thoughts?" I could not bring myself to say the word: suicide.

She nodded, yes, sensing my true meaning. "And if you are, you really need to get some help. If you let it go, it only gets worse. I once swallowed a bunch of pills at my lowest point. After about ten minutes, I panicked and forced myself to throw up. That's when I started counseling. I also had serious fantasies of poisoning my husband. I thought if I could just get rid of him and be with someone else, I'd get pregnant. The thoughts you have when you're in Pergonal psychosis can be frightening."

To whom else but each other could we admit such deplorably dark secrets? "On the days when I had to drive out to Eddington for the blood work," I confessed, "I sometimes wanted to steer my car off the road. Just slam it into a tree or a guardrail. Especially, if it was raining. The rain always made it worse. But I'd think of Jake and soldier on."

"You keep thinking of Jake and Ryan and me—all the people who love you."

"Right. Well, I'm over that now. It was the drugs." I assured her that I was not in that place any more. Not today, anyway.

The doorbell rang and in walked a lovely and sophisticated Lauren with a basketful of goodies slung over her arm.

"How did you know we were having a party?" I asked, while rummaging through the wine, cheese and crackers in the basket.

"I wanted to bring a housewarming gift," explained Lauren.

Alex invited her to stay and visit with us. We cleaned up the paint mess and rolled out the new rug. We sat on the floor emptying bottles of wine and laughing over everything and nothing. It felt wonderful to laugh with such abandon.

Then Alex brought the fun to a halt by announcing that she was, indeed, going to follow through with her sperm-donor baby dream.

"Seriously?" I asked.

"Good for you," said Lauren. "So who's the dad?" Lauren was open to anything.

Alex sensed my concern. "I have a list to choose from, but I can't decide. It's too hard."

"Can we see it? We'll find one for you," said Lauren cheerfully.

Alex rushed off to find her list of potential candidates and Lauren said to me, "Don't be so old-fashioned. It's her choice."

"I know, I know," I agreed. "But these guys, you know they're all college kids looking for extra cash. They are not doing it for altruistic reasons. They just want the money."

"So what? Alex wants a baby," said Lauren.

"And what if the donor was overzealous and in the future, two of his sperm children fall in love and marry, only to have deformed babies."

"What if?" Lauren rolled her eyes at me, "I'm sure there are regulations for how many times they can donate."

I could not help but feel apprehensive and concerned. I had been defeated and the only thing I could do was jump on the bandwagon and be supportive.

Alex came back looking breathless and excited. Her face was glowing with happiness. I then truly understood that whatever the outcome, this was simply something her soul needed to experience. Sometimes, the desires of your soul overrode the physical world and you found yourself making decisions based on faith.

"Let me see that." I grabbed the list from her. "It's probably just like looking through the personals; you have to read between the lines."

Her list consisted of twenty-six candidates. Some even came with toddler photos. The donors were described racially, physically and intellectually. A health record detailed all pertinent test results, such as HIV and other sexually-transmitted diseases.

Lauren leaned over my shoulder and read, "'Dark, thin hair, blue eyes, average build, acute asthma.' Oh, come on. He's more likely fat and bald."

We crossed him off.

"What is your priority?" I asked Alex. "Intellect? Health? Or do you want the father of your child to look like a Greek god?"

She tossed her response around in her head and said, "All of those. Why not make the most of it?"

"Sure, make it easy on us," quipped Lauren.

"Maybe, you should narrow down the choice to those men who share your similar features, so the baby will have more of a chance of looking like you," I offered.

"One step ahead of you. I definitely want brown hair and eyes."

So, with that consideration in mind, we scrutinized Alex's candidates and narrowed them down to five, for her to make the final choice.

CHAPTER THIRTEEN

As a gift for my thirty-second birthday on the sixteenth of May, Ryan treated me to a play at the Walnut Street Theater in Philadelphia. This was a generous gesture on his part, one because I usually planned all our events and two, because he hated the theater. But he humored me and suffered through the clumsy rendition of *The Glass Menagerie*. Afterward, we walked two blocks down Eighth Street to Darby's Pub for dinner.

Having lost another six pounds, I was feeling very long-legged and sexy in my new Nine jeans, leather blazer and heels. It was a cool night, but lovely and romantic. While I'd been on the Pergonal hiatus, Ryan had confiscated my credit card, but with a little creative planning, I had figured out how to avoid further clothing arguments with him.

As I was writing out a check for groceries one day, I developed a money-laundering scheme: if I wrote the check for twenty-five dollars extra, each time, Ryan would never know the difference. Fed up with the daunting ATM transactions, he had begun regularly scrutinizing the checking-account statement online. But grocery receipts? He never checked those. To capitalize on my brilliant plan, I became a double-coupon shopper. And if something was on sale, I bought two. I had never really been motivated enough to bother with coupons in the past. But now it had become like a part-time job. I was saving left and right. And we had never eaten better!

I stashed my extra twenty-five bucks away, every time I shopped, and by the end of each month, an easy, untraceable nest egg of a hundred bucks or more was burning a hole in my pocket. With my birthday coming up, I treated myself to a new outfit. I was wandering the racks in Saks, looking for a cool pair of tan khakis or

Capri pants, when my eyes zeroed in on a rack of Nine jeans. Very hot and youthful. I thought I would just have fun and try them on, not really intending to spend a whopping $150 on one pair of jeans. Thirty or forty dollars had always been my usual limit. Well, let me say, they slid over my new slimmer self. I was back in tens, thanks, in part, to my new exercise routine which consisted of not lying around all day feeling sorry for myself. As I was admiring the cut in the three-sided mirror, a salesgirl walked by and said, "They look great."

"Do you think so?" I asked, as I twisted and turned, trying to view my rear end.

I had the devil on one shoulder saying, "Do it," and an angel on the other, saying, "Don't. It's a waste of money." Back and forth they argued. Guess who won?

Darby's Pub on Eighth Street was a most charming establishment, open and spacious, with a Pottery Barn feel to it. One section had leather couches in a grouping that reminded me of the TV show, *Friends*.

My hubby and I were sitting in a cozy booth enjoying each other's company for a change. We had ordered a bottle of white Merlot, and Ryan was not letting me see the bottom of the glass. This made me a little suspicious, but I was feeling so elated that I did not care. We feasted on steaks and listened to the music. We talked, not like an old married couple, but like young lovers.

"It's nice to be alone with you," he said lovingly.

I shoveled the last piece of steak into my mouth and said, "What do you mean? We see each other every day."

"Not like this."

"What's 'this'?" I asked, drinking more wine. He refilled my glass.

"We just go through the motions. And you've been spending a lot of time with your friends."

I set down my utensils. "Why does that bother you so much?"

He shrugged. "I think you don't like your life. I think their lives look more appealing to you." I knew he was referring to Lauren and Alex, those ghastly and immoral divorced friends of mine. "I'm afraid you'll find someone else."

He meant someone else with whom to have a baby.

"Are you kidding me? Don't you know it only makes you look more appealing?" I reassured him. "Even though they are happy to be free of their idiot husbands, they're lonely, especially Alex. They wish they had what I had.

"It would help if you told me that once in while," he said in a low voice.

I reached for his hand. "I'm telling you now. I mean it. I'm not going anywhere, Ryan."

With that affirmation, he said, "Let's get out of here."

In a very swift flow of events, he took care of the bill and guided me as I staggered toward the door. Outside, the cool air sobered me up a bit. We began strolling along, our arms hooked together. Then Ryan whisked me up against the brick wall of a building and began kissing me as though we were teenagers in a high-school hallway. It was nice, I had to admit. He rested his forehead against mine and said, "I have an idea. Let's get a room at that hotel over there."

I smiled. "Are you serious?" This was new. But honestly, I felt so warm and fuzzy that it sounded like a good idea. Unlike Ryan, however, I did not fancy sex in strange beds where thousands of other couples had left behind their body cells and other unmentionable fluids. "It'll cost too much," I said, appealing to his more practical side.

"It's only money," he replied, groping me—in public!

Once in a while, you just had to give in to the moment and throw your husband a bone. A sultry voice that seemed to come from deep within me said, "Okay, but only if I get a full body massage first."

His reply was to lead me by the hand in the direction of the hotel. In my head, I heard a chorus of Marvin Gaye and Barry White bedroom music. This was love sustained. After all these years, I still, occasionally, had the hots for my husband. We began walking again and he said, "That guy just checked you out."

"Where?" I said, a little too loudly. "No, he didn't. Maybe, he was looking at you."

Ryan always swore that other men were looking at me, but I was never quick enough to notice. The only ones I ever saw stealing a look were toothless road-crew workers. Yeah, that was a real compliment. So when he pointed one out to me, I had to verify what he looked like. As I turned around to spot my admirer, my right heel caught in a sewer grate and I fell, landing on my right knee.

"Are you okay?" he asked, kneeling next to me.

There was a two-inch rip in the knee area of my overpriced jeans and a scrape on my knee. "They're ruined," I whispered, more to myself.

"We'll get you a new pair," he consoled.

Not if you knew how much they cost, lovey.

Instantly, I knew that I should have listened to the angel on my shoulder, and not the devil, when I bought those ridiculously expensive jeans. A royal conflict raged in my head. I had two choices. I could let this little mishap ruin the moment or pretend that it did not matter. I wanted to wail over the waste of hard-earned money spent on these stupid jeans. I was beyond pissed. And I wasn't drunk enough not to know that if I revealed the truth about my frivolous purchase, my adoring husband would go ballistic. His it's-only-money speech usually only applied to his own purchases.

"Promise? Because I really liked them." Who was this person talking through my lips? It was a frigging pair of over-priced pants!

I chose the hotel. The sex was fantastic, almost epic for a married couple. For a change, it was not about making a baby. It was not mechanical married copulation. It was wild, bawdy sex, purely for the pleasure of it. But never once during our lovemaking could I completely lose the vision of those ruined jeans.

Two weeks later, I had still not gotten my period. I paced and paced for three more days. I had trained myself not to get excited over this. We had spent a small fortune on drugstore pregnancy tests by getting excited too soon. There were lots of reasons to be late, I told myself. Nothing had been regular since I started taking the medications. My body was still adjusting, still on its way to getting back to normal.

I could not stand it. I had to know.

When Ryan came home, I left him with Jake and made an excuse to go to the store. I made my purchase, buying two kits for extra measure. The need for immediate gratification consumed me and I didn't even wait until I got home. In the drugstore restroom, I peed on the first stick and waited.

No way! How was it possible? Two pink lines appeared on the test stick. I did it again, just to be sure. Again, two pink lines. Yes! I screamed inside. Maybe, those fertility statues had worked after all. I wondered what the gift they'd promised to send would be.

When I got home, I couldn't even get the words out. So I just showed Ryan the two sticks. I could see in his eyes a sense of pride over the fact that his seed had been successful at last. A slow, satisfied smile consumed his face.

I then proceeded toward further verification. Three days later, I had a blood test at my primary doctor's office. When they called the next day confirming the joyful news, I immediately called Dr. Castlebloom and asked to speak to him directly. I was not willing to leave a message with a secretary.

"Hello, Julia. How are you?"

"I'm great, actually. I'm pregnant and I won't be in need of your services any more." I felt so victorious to say that to him.

"That's great. But you need a blood test to confirm it."

Killjoy.

"I already did that with my primary-care doctor. It was positive."

"Okay, then. Can you have that faxed over to our office for your file? I would like you to come for an exam in four weeks, and then we'll release you."

"All right," I agreed.

"And congratulations," he said dryly. He was human, after all.

Even though I was elated and wanted to take out a full-page newspaper advertisement, I reserved my announcement for my closest friends, Ally, Lauren and Alex. Ryan and I were on a high better than any euphoria-inducing drug. Finally, we were able to look to the future and plan again. We had been living for so long playing the waiting game, afraid to plan ahead. It was part of the reason that I had not looked for a job. I could not make the commitment. The limbo life.

CHAPTER FOURTEEN

One week shy of the appointment with Dr. Castlebloom that promised to purge him from my life, I began spotting. Just lightly at first, then heavier. I was forced to eat crow and make an appointment with him. After the blood tests and ultrasounds were over, it was revealed that what I had imagined to be a pregnancy was actually something called a blighted ovum. It was a growing placenta producing pregnancy hormones, but without an embryo. Immediately, a D & C was ordered. The lack of an embryo did not make the experience any less traumatic or devastating. Only someone who had suffered a miscarriage could understand this. Our hopes had been raised, then denied. This state of existence was mental, physical, spiritual and emotional torture. Unable to sleep, I roamed the house at night and eventually ended up crawling in next to Jake. And when he was at school, I found myself weeping in his room, hugging his stuffed animals tightly. Even Taco sensed my pain as he tried snuggling against me to offer comfort. I had weathered the grief that followed each episode of failed insemination, but what I was enduring at that moment turned out to be the proverbial last straw that would send me into therapy.

Dr. Maureen Melmed was Ryan's choice for a therapist. Another counselor he worked with had referred her to us. But here was the point with therapists in general: it didn't matter how good he or she might be. It had to be a good match between patient and therapist. There had to be a certain empathy, a rapport, or the patient would not be able to open up.

I was sitting in a comfortable Queen Anne wing chair, swinging my crossed leg, nervously waiting to be called in. Dr. Melmed walked in and introduced herself. All my instincts told me to leave. This was not going to work. It was not exactly a sixth-sense kind of feeling that went through me. I just looked at her with her Shirley Temple blond curls, her mini-skirt, her heels and her clown make-up and I realized that I could never take her seriously. She was pushing sixty and dressed like a twenty-year-old. The way I saw it, the only sixty-year-old permitted to wear a mini-skirt was Tina Turner.

"So what brings you here, Julia?" she asked in a squeaky voice.

Really, there was no use beating around the proverbial bush here. "If you don't mind, I think I need someone else," I told her.

Perhaps that was the therapy—comic relief.

Dr. "Melonhead" seemed offended and shoved me off into the main waiting area for another available therapist. But I felt empowered somehow.

The next therapist was male: a Dr. Robert Snyder. He was an average Joe with no distracting attributes. Judging by the brown hair that was graying at his temples and the creases at the corners of his eyes, he looked to be in his mid-forties. He wore an unpretentious blue L. L. Bean polo shirt under his suit jacket. His style was carefree. His presence was calming. His office was not as nice as Melonhead's, though. It was very masculine with uncomfortable desk chairs. Esher prints adorned the walls.

"Tell me about yourself," he opened. He did not sit behind a desk, but sat approachably opposite me in a standard office chair.

"Starting where?" I asked, unable to make eye contact.

"Why are you here?"

"For answers, I guess," I shrugged, feeling a lot like an insolent teenager. I wanted help, but could not unabashedly reach out for it.

"What kind of answers?"

Woefully, I said, "Probably, only the kind God can offer. So, this is probably just a waste of time."

"Oh? You've lost faith in God?" He wrote something on his notepad.

"That and other things." I was fighting back tears. My throat ached. I refused to sit there and allow myself to break down. I will not cry, I told myself. I will not cry. An awkward silence pervaded the tiny room. I hated it when therapists did this. They tried to draw you out by forcing you to fill the dead air. But I did not cave in. I just kept examining my manicure or rather, the need for one.

"What's hurting you right now?"

Bingo! A knife ripped through my heart. My eyes swelled beyond capacity and overflowed.

He handed me a box of tissues.

I said something about hating my life, about my plans gone south, being infertile, my recent miscarriage...It all came out in one long, breathless sob. I was sure he couldn't possibly have understood what I had tried to say. I took a breath and said, "I don't want to be this resentful, grief-stricken, angry-at-the-world person any more. It's killing me. I don't know how to deal with it. I used to be a fairly nice person. Now I'm just bitter and sarcastic. And sad."

"So you are saddened by your inability to have another child?"

"Well, I used to be." I collected myself and said, "Mostly, I'm just really pissed off!" That felt good.

"What angers you?"

It took a moment for me to steel myself to admit what I really felt. In the name of restraint and good manners, I held myself in for a moment. I knew that if the floodgates were opened, this would become a bitch session. A sharp breath in, and out it all came. "What really infuriates me is the fact that it's so easy for some people. For instance, for those who don't even want to be parents. If I were sixteen, no problem—I'd be pregnant. I think if I were a crack addict, no problem. If I had a one-night stand, I know I'd be pregnant the very first time, although my life would be ruined. We are good parents to our son and it feels like we are being punished. Everywhere I go, I see awful people yelling at their kids or ignoring them. We try every month. And every month, I faithfully get my period. The bleeding is so heavy and painful; it feels like I'm dying from my center. I have all the right hormones to get a period, but not enough to make a baby. My womb is waiting to be filled up so that I can move on with my life and…" I had to shut up. "Is that enough for you?" I asked, while mopping up tears with a wad of tissues.

There was silence for a moment before he spoke. "What would you like to gain from therapy?"

"Some frigging peace. Could you do that?" I choked.

Calmly, he said, "We can try." He wrote something again. "Tell me, assuming that you haven't always been this way, how did you deal with your problems in the past?"

"Ben and Jerry have gotten me through a lot of tough times," I half-joked. They say you are what you eat. Well, I had become a "chunky-monkey". "I talked to friends."

"You don't talk to friends any more?"

"Not about this. It's old. Most just don't understand. I don't want to bring everyone down all the time. I need to have fun when I'm with friends. Then I get advice like, 'Be glad you have one healthy child.' Well I am grateful for that, but I want more. It's easy for people who have three kids to say that." I drew a breath. "Now, ever since I had this miscarriage, I get, 'At least, you know you can get pregnant.' As if that will make it all better."

After my session with Dr. Snyder, I was exhausted and passed out on the couch when I got home. Even the bonging of my husband's beloved clock did not wake me up. I was not convinced there was any benefit in spilling my soul to a total stranger, especially, when I ended up feeling abused afterward. It took a while to recover from the experience.

Then my anger became somewhat constructive. I became obsessive about cleaning the house. I projected my hurt and anger on the walls and floors. I cleaned out closets and filled bags with useless junk. I reorganized the kitchen cabinets and shelved all the canned and boxed food with the labels facing out. I was over and under furniture, vacuuming and scrubbing. I found my missing dolphin earring, a gift from Ryan. There was not a corner in my home that remained untouched, or that did not endure the onslaught of my wrath.

I finished painting our bedroom a plum color. Ryan hated it. It might not sound so great, but with the antique white trim and the floral bedding, it looked cozy and warm, a feeling I craved. The point was that I was finishing projects I had put off, and he should have given me due credit for it. When I ran out of domestic projects, I took my anger out on my hair. Going for a completely different look, I colored it auburn. Ally loved it. Ryan hated it. Jake hated it too. He wanted his mommy to be blonde again.

Just as my mood had been altered by the year's events, so had Ryan's. I allowed him his contrary opinions without confrontation. It was not long before intimacy issues developed.

One particular night, which I predicted would become a Dr. Snyder session, Ryan reached for me and I pulled away. I could not bring myself to engage in the act of sex. In my mind, there simply was no way of separating the act of sex for pleasure from trying to make a baby. Procreation had become the only reason for sex. I had gotten into a cycle of only having sex mid-month. For some reason, having forced sex eroded all desire and passion. So I had to save up my energy for the important time—mid-month. Ryan just did not seem to get it. He always kept trying for more.

He rolled away and sighed heavily. And sighed again. And again.

"What? Just say it, why don't you?" I challenged.

"Prisoners get more conjugal visits than I do," he mumbled pathetically.

"Oh, please. Ebbs and flows," I quoted him. "Isn't that what you always say? We're in an ebb right now."

He often liked to counsel me, but not follow his own advice.

"I have needs too, you know," he argued, now facing me.

"So do I. And I have a need not to have sex right now. So you'll just have to chill!"

He rolled away from me in a huff. "You don't need me any more. You have your friends. I'm just a paycheck to you."

That was his control card. He knew the reference to his being my financial supporter would inflame me.

Seeing red, feeling red, I said, "Well, I know how to give myself orgasms too. So I guess I won't need you for that either!"

It was a nasty thing to say. It seemed to come from my deepest darkest depths. I just didn't know when to quit sometimes. It was like I was my own worst enemy.

With that, Ryan threw back the covers, grabbed his pillow and stomped out of the room. I did not go to him. I did not deserve to be forgiven just yet. It took several days before we could speak to each other again, which meant I had to grovel in the worst way.

"Why do you think you have an aversion to sex?" asked Dr. Snyder a week later.

"You're the Ph.D. You tell me." I was feeling cross due to the ten-month pregnant woman I had just ridden with in the elevator. Why couldn't they all stay home?

"Okay. Maybe, you associate it with all your failed attempts to get pregnant."

I snorted a DUH!

"Being intimate makes you feel vulnerable."

I snorted again.

"Maybe, you blame Ryan for your not being able to get pregnant. Maybe, you think it's really his fault."

"No. I never thought that."

I really had always blamed myself. We had never fallen victim to that kind of blame game.

"Are you sure? Perhaps, deep down, you believe another partner would deliver results. You mentioned it yourself during your first visit."

"Did I?" I was shocked. "No, I don't blame him. It's just life. It's a couple thing. I know that."

"You know that intellectually, but do you acknowledge it emotionally?"

"Maybe, it's my mother's fault. Can I blame her? She smoked

the whole time she was pregnant. Maybe, all that tar has encrusted around my eggs cells."

"Why does it have to be anyone's fault?" He looked at me with earnest eyes, his head tilted at an angle.

"Because it does. That's the way the world works. It's always someone else's fault." *Duh!*

"Maybe, there doesn't have to be any fault at all. Maybe, things just *are*. Then the issue would be: how will you choose to deal with it? You can choose to let your hurt control you or you can control the hurt."

"That's deep, Doc. But I think I'd really feel better about this, if I could blame someone or something." In doing so, I thought I could deflect my hostility. But I hadn't been able to. I had ended up internalizing the blame instead. "You know...," I continued, "I think I was caught off-guard with this infertility thing. I never expected it to constitute my life's crisis. I thought I'd be in a psychiatrist's chamber some day, in the patient's chair, discussing my abandonment issues about my mother." Whoops, shouldn't have mentioned that. He was liable to take the Freudian approach and connect my mother to this. If anyone had issues with his mother, it was Freud himself.

"Tell me about your mother."

"No."

"Why?"

He shifted in his chair, apparently finding it as uncomfortable as I did mine.

"I prefer not to."

"Did you resolve your 'abandonment issues' with her?"

"I misspoke. I don't really have issues with her. Where she is concerned, I am surprisingly well-adjusted. I don't blame her. I don't hate her. I understand that she did what she had to do. End of story."

"Is she a part of your life now?"

"Minimally. We have an agreement."

"I see." He pondered this, and I could tell he was looking for another angle.

"Look, I can tell you that I have been dissecting it for years. The only connection to her is that I'm not achieving the kind of family I always dreamed of. I did not grow up in a two-parent family. Even when my mother was there physically, she was mentally absent. I promised myself that when I was ready for a family of my own, I would have many kids and ensure that there were two committed parents to raise them. I can't seem to break free of my physical and spiritual conditioning of desiring a family. As long as humans have been on this planet, we have been expected to be fruitful and multiply. No fruit is coming from this womb."

There was silence. He was waiting for more.

"Some women want to succeed in their careers," I went on. "I want to succeed as a parent. One child is just the practice round."

I was inadvertently referring to Jackie O.'s famous line that went something like, if you failed as a parent, you failed in the most important job. I had bought into the ideology.

"What is your definition of a family?"

Every time I tried to shut him down, he just kept throwing it back at me!

"It isn't one lonely child who craves a brother and bunk beds. It isn't three seats at the dinner table."

That one empty chair had been gnawing at my resolve for sometime now. I had considered removing the forlorned chair out of my sight rather than see it vacant. But then, I thought I would just look disturbed and the table would be lacking a necessary Feng Shui element.

Besides, my mother was not the problem here. I had a physical problem, not a repressed abandonment problem! I really was fine with my mother. It was not like I never saw her. We just were not intimate about our lives. Though it had taken a few solid years, I now understood why she'd had to leave. My mother was, sadly, an alcoholic. There was a self-destructive streak in her nature. Without alcohol, she was evil. With it, she was sloppy and neglectful. As a child, I had liked her better when she was drinking, but she was terribly unreliable. Her often irascible moods were embarrassing. My brother, Jeff, and I knew never to invite friends over for fear of Mother making a scene. By the grace of God, neither my brother nor I inherited the disease. When she left, Mother claimed that it would be better for all of us, that she knew she had a drinking problem and needed some time to go away and recover. But I always suspected that she never intended to return. She had already made her plans. She had someplace to go to. She did not flee in the dark of night like a protagonist from a Lifetime Channel movie drama.

Despite her alcoholic cravings, my mother, Carol Connelly, is an educated woman. She is one of those "functioning alcoholics." When other children asked me where my mother was, I would boast about her intelligence and the fact that she was a professor at California's University of the Pacific. I also lied that it was a job of a lifetime and that my father insisted that she should fulfill her dream. I made it sound as though my mother commuted monthly from Pennsylvania to California for her prestigious job.

Somehow, Mother managed to earn a Ph.D. at Columbia while still married to my father. According to him, the serious drinking did not really start until after Jeff was born. I followed two years later. Before she moved away, Mother was an adjunct professor at Bucks County Community College, teaching literature and writing courses. Through a Penn State classmate, she was offered a job at University of the Pacific and moved to California. To young children, California was a world away. I'm not sure what happened there. Perhaps, she was fired, for she was soon back in Pennsylvania and teaching at Penn State, but at their Fayette County branch campus in Uniontown, PA. Being a mere six hours away by car did not mean we saw her more often. She was forever inaccessible.

Though it was painful having her gone, it was peaceful when she left. And what hurt was not so much the fact of being without her, but simply being without a mother, any mother at all. We were a normal family of three, rather than a screwed up family of four.

Becoming a mother to Jake was somehow healing. He was my

life. He was my focus, my chance to make things right and be the mother I had wished for. I let go of the anger by concluding that, maybe, in some ways, my mother had done us a service rather than a disservice. After all, if she had been around, I would have learned little about parenting and nurturing from her. My notions of mothering came from two terrific grandmothers and my Aunt Sara. My aunt always said that my mother simply was not "mother material," that, maybe, she should never have had children. It was never said directly to me, however. I remember overhearing a conversation between my grandmother and her. It was one of those times when grown-ups thought you were so intent on playing that you were not really listening. But I heard. I internalized the information. I guarded it jealously for years, pretending no one else knew.

It was Aunt Sara who took me to buy my first bra and instructed me on how to use a tampon. She frequently took me shopping with her girls. I often slept over at her house and pretended that she was my real mother. I wanted her to be. She was everything I wished I had in a mother: stable, loving, affectionate and patient. As far as I was concerned, she was a shining example of what was normal. And she was instrumental in helping my brother and me come to terms with our troubled ideas about our mother. After her husband, Ed, had died a few years ago, she moved to Boston to be near her daughter, Emily, and her family. I missed being able to pop in at her house for a deliciously warm meal. Aunt Sara was now raising two more little girls, while daughter, Emily, climbed her way up the corporate ladder.

Dr. Snyder did have a valid point that I just did not want to consider or acknowledge. How did I choose to accept the problem with my mother? Could that same sense of acceptance be applied to my infertility? If I was ready to accept it, probably. In many ways, I just wanted my doctors to find a problem they could fix. Just fix me. Endometriosis as a sole cause for infertility was a dubious diagnosis. Many women suffered from far worse cases than I and still got pregnant.

CHAPTER FIFTEEN

September brought with it welcomed changes. Through a chance encounter in August with a former co-worker, I was offered a part-time position teaching high-school English, two classes a day. With Jake in the first grade and me slowly losing my mind without enough to do, it was the perfect opportunity to occupy myself gainfully and make an effort at restoring my sanity. A part-time job was ideal. I knew I did not have the stamina for full-time teaching just yet. Besides, I couldn't commit to a permanent full-time job, in case I conceived. It may have been irrational thinking on my part, but that was how I was living my life. I still needed to keep myself free, just in case. I did not need approval from Dr. Snyder to know that a job would be good for my fragile mental state. Work was always good for the soul. Perhaps, it was the experience of feeling useful that fed and nourished the soul.

I threw myself into preparations for general humanities classes, one each for the ninth and tenth grades. It was refreshing to be able to look forward to getting out of bed every day. I enjoyed the challenge. Pregnancy had almost become a distant thought, until one of my tenth-graders started getting ever larger in the middle. I forced myself to keep an emotional distance from the situation, but the reminder was there, every day, in the center of the second row.

"Tell me why it angers you?" asked Dr. Snyder one day when I brought up the matter of the pregnant tenth-grader.

"Apart from making me feel like I'm some kind of freak magnet for pregnant women, it just does," I said, trying to cop out. Was it my imagination or was Dr. Snyder getting better looking?

He shook his head. "Not good enough."

"You really need to get more comfortable chairs in here. Maybe, I would be more forthcoming if I could sink into a nice, soft chair," I said, still avoiding the subject. The concept of therapists having a couch in their offices was a myth in this case.

"I'll take that into consideration," he smiled. I could tell he liked me, even though I gave him a hard time. "But why does it anger you?"

My feelings didn't fit in with what I understood instinctively. "She's too young. The baby will have disadvantages. Teenagers very often don't bother to get married any more. She should have been more responsible. She probably got pregnant because she felt unloved by her own parents and she wanted someone to love her and thought a baby would do that. Now two people will be screwed up by the choice she has made. It's just not the ideal situation." I grabbed the tissue box. "Sorry, I'll bring my own next time."

Dr. Snyder smiled wanly. "If every child were born into an ideal situation, would that make the world right for you?"

He definitely was looking better.

"Yes...well, no...I don't know. It's not that I'm thinking of me. I'm thinking of the child. There are so many unwanted, unloved children in the world. Children don't ask to be born. So they deserve to be properly taken care of, don't they?"

Dr. Snyder shrugged. "Perhaps, there are reasons for those children to be born disadvantaged. Disadvantages often make us stronger. For some people, it's what creates their drive in life."

"Or they end up in the Russian mob because they have been neglected and suffer from attachment disorder. If you don't experience love as a child, how do you learn to love?" I challenged.

"I see." He scratched his ear. "But why do you feel animosity toward this particular teenager?"

Arrrrgh! He brought out the worst in me. "Because she has something I want. I'm jealous, okay?" Ugh! That was so hard to admit. "And let her be pregnant, fine. I just don't want it in my face every day!"

Every time, Dr. Snyder managed to needle me to the point where I shouted out such obscenities, I felt ashamed of myself. I admitted things to him that I would never confess to my closest friends, even Alex, who was the one person with whom I could be completely, unabashedly candid.

Sometime around my fifth meeting with Dr. Snyder, he lent me a book from his collection entitled, *Don't Be the Victim*. It was about positive thinking and learning to be proactive after a life crisis. It boasted chapter titles, like "Create Your Own Destiny", "Letting Go" and "Accepting Plan B"—each one a little summary of what my life seemed to be about. Unconsciously, I was already latching onto the idea that I needed to be more proactive in my life. I needed to make things happen, instead of just waiting for things to come. I could not allow the pregnant teenagers of the world to bring me down.

It took me a while to read the book and take it seriously, but I did. Slowly, I evolved and began to comprehend that being infertile was not all there was to my life. Infertility did not define me. It did not define who I was as an individual. Therefore, I should not allow it to take over my life. I completed all the lessons and worksheets in the book. I shared the book with Ryan. I wasn't sure if he processed it the way I did. I suspect he already had plans formulated in his head regarding the path he wanted to take.

After a few weeks, I resigned myself to making some positive changes. The revelation I needed to convince me that a change of perspective was called for, did not come to me in an instant, light-bulb moment. My self-awareness and the need for change grew in me steadily, brought about by a series of developments. So Ryan and I began an aggressive campaign to end the baby quest I had been fixated on for so long. We would look into the adoption process while continuing with the drug therapy for a while longer. Our decision was also prompted by the need to make better use of our time. So many months had been wasted in waiting. We had resolved to burn the candle at both ends. Whichever came first, I would live with it and not harbor regrets.

Dr. Snyder helped me to acknowledge my desire to save the children of the world. Yet, I was emotionally lazy. Even during leaps of consciousness, I procrastinated. While I had good intentions to do great things, like save a child, I had done nothing constructive to translate my desires into action. It was not possible to save all the abandoned children in the world, but I could save one or two.

Ryan and I sat up late that night and discussed our options. We both felt as though we were spinning around in a black hole. We were stuck and needed to break free of the thing that was weighing us down: infertility. The adoption journey involved an entirely new route for us to travel. It was going to be an educational and emotional adventure. I flipped through the phone book and started with the first agency I saw.

On my lunch break the next day, I made the appointment, thinking all the while, "But what if I get pregnant?"

The Giving Heart Adoption Agency was located in Cherry Hill, NJ. Ryan and I each took a day off from school and went on our first fact-finding mission. Ryan was excited and ready to say yes to anything. I knew he had to be restrained or we would end up having huge regrets. This was not like getting a puppy; this was a human life!

The agency assisted in domestic adoptions. But the social worker, Catherine, was keen on pushing the idea of our adopting older children or kids with special needs. She left us alone for a while to peruse a thick binder full of photographs of older children. Their bios were heart-wrenching. It was unconscionable to see so many orphaned children. I cried all the way home. It had not been the optimistic meeting I had imagined it would be.

The biggest obstacle to adopting a white baby, our natural preference, was the wait period. Bottom line: if we wanted a white infant, it would take three-to-five-years. In five years, Jake would be eleven. And part of the reason for this baby quest was to give him a sibling.

The cost for the adopted child was variable. It depended on many factors, mostly related to the birth mother. It was frightening to enter into a process without really knowing the financial obligation. We had limited resources. Did we want an open adoption, where the biological mother would have involvement? Or, did we want it closed, so that our anonymity was preserved? Would we consider an older child? What disabilities were we willing to accept in our adopted child? We were not sure we could handle any. Didn't everyone want the healthiest child possible? Didn't we deserve a healthy child? On and on it went. It was overwhelming. Instead of yielding a sense of relief, we found ourselves with even more on our plate. There were a few matters on which we stood firm. Neither of us could emotionally survive an adoption where the birth mother was allowed a retraction period during which she could change her mind about giving up her baby. It had to be an unbreakable contract. Jake's welfare needed to be considered. We would not have him emotionally scarred by bringing a child into our home, only to see it taken away. We could not alter his birth order by bringing home a child older than him. The decisions before us were like being on that game show, *Let's Make A Deal*. Instead of three curtains to choose from, there were one hundred and three.

Whenever I became weary of my own life, I called Alex. Hearing about someone else's problems should have made me more depressed, but it served as a necessary diversion. Sometimes, you need to look at another's situation to see your own more clearly.

After choosing Sperm Donor number twenty-three, Alexandria Martin had begun a course of Pergonal to induce her one remaining ovary to produce massive amounts of egg cells. She was near the end of the injection phase and ready for the next step which involved the retrieval of the eggs. I could not let her go through this alone without some emotional support. Granted, I wasn't the most stable candidate. But her seventy-year-old mother who could not grasp the concept of laboratory baby-making was hardly a better option.

The evening before the egg-retrieval procedure, I stopped by Alex's house to check on her.

"Are you ready for tomorrow?" I asked.

Very calmly, she answered, "Yes." She looked sure of herself.

"Well, it's not like you can back out now. How is the kitchen coming along?" I asked.

I could hear scuffling in the background, as workers busied themselves in her kitchen, financed by Dave Martin, aka her ex-husband.

"It's great, come look. They're putting the new floor down."

She pulled back the sheet of plastic covering the opening into the kitchen to reveal beautiful hardwood flooring in a cinnamon hue. That alone was a striking contrast to the brown linoleum. She had also solved the problem of poor lighting by adding skylights in the ceiling, thereby creating the impression of a well-lit open space. We settled in the living room so that she could put up her feet and take the weight off her blossoming ovary.

"So if this IVF works, how are you going to explain it to Dave?"

"How am I going to explain it to my mother?" she retorted.

"You are going to shatter everyone's comfy world." I meant that in the most endearing way. "Oh, hey...wait until Dave finds out you're giving this child the surname Martin! He'll flip."

Alex snorted with laughter. It was one of those embarrassing unintended snorts, and we laughed at her faux pas. It was a favorite pastime of ours, thinking up ways to torture Dave who had, I'd heard, quit smoking for his new girlfriend, because she did not approve of it. He had never made the effort when Alex wanted him to give up the habit.

"Well, it has been my legal name for fourteen years." On a more serious note, she said, "You talk like it's a certainty. It may not work this time."

"Alex, I know it will work for you. I just have a feeling. It's in the cards."

I could not explain how I knew, but some kind of deep female intuition told me that this was her time. In all the years she had been through infertility treatments with Dave, the IVF was the one procedure that had not been tried. At least, this procedure would be covered by insurance. I was sure she would not be going in for it otherwise.

I felt no envy toward my friend. I really wanted it to work for her. A part of me had always harbored some guilt over the fact that I already had a child, while she did not. Sometimes, I refrained from telling her cute stories about Jake for fear of hurting her sentiments. I was always cognizant not to brag about my adorable, funny and straight-A son.

"So, I met someone," she said shyly.

"Yeah? Someone you like?"

Frustrated, she groaned, "I can't even go there. Not yet. I have too much on my plate right now."

"No, you think?"

"Besides, the minute he finds out I'm doing this," she gestured to her stomach, "he'll be gone."

"Maybe, maybe not. That would surely be the ultimate character test," I reasoned. Noticing the time, I stood to go, "Okay, I have to get home and prepare a book test on *The Scarlet Letter*. Isn't that ironic?" I thought aloud, "that I am teaching that particular story at this point in my life? If you were living in that era, you would have a big, old red letter A on your chest, you hussy, you! No wait, come to think of it, what you're doing is so much more than adultery!"

With a smile on her face, Alex threw a pillow at me.

CHAPTER SIXTEEN

We all experience moments of intuition from time to time. Like knowing someone is going to call you, and they do. Or, thinking of an old song, and surprise! It comes on the radio. I have no true sixth sense to speak of, other than the usual female intuition, but one day, when I was shelving books at home, I had what can only be described as some sort of vision. At first, I did not know what to make of it.

On that particular afternoon, I was on my knees, rearranging our books on the shelves, when a sound caught my attention and caused me to look up. From across the room, I saw a dark-haired toddler calling to me, her arms outstretched. She ran to me and hugged me. But then, she ran through me. I could not hold on to her and I wanted to so badly. Like most of my vivid nocturnal dreams, the vision seemed to convey a message which came through, not so much in what I had actually seen, but in what I had felt. I was not scared, just unnerved. Yet, the experience was strangely comforting too. A curious blend of different feelings seemed to seize me. My heart raced. Sometime during the fleeting experience, I must have dropped a handful of books. They lay scattered around me. I was numb for a few moments before I could move again. I felt I knew the child. Somehow, I knew her. She was as familiar to me as my own son. It was almost a déjà vu moment. It was as though it had already happened. Or, perhaps, it was going to happen. All I knew was that I felt an intense love for the little girl I had seen.

When I sobered from that experience, I rationalized it by claiming that I was just losing my mind. It would be easy to do, I thought. Lately, it seemed easier to give up and be crazy, than to struggle and remain sane. Parenting was much the same. It was easy to be a bad parent and hard to be a good one. Jake had been testing our parenting skills recently. He had been having too much fun in first grade. He had received a detention for disrupting the class too often with his clowning. He had been accused of riling the other boys and making life difficult for his teacher. When the teacher's back was turned, he would make silly faces at his friends and start a giggling riot. He would occasionally shout out answers to questions in goofy voices. As long as his juvenile audience was laughing, he felt emboldened to carry on in the same vein. I was pretty sure that Jake's antics were not a cry for attention. He simply enjoyed making people laugh. It was a gift he possessed and it had brought even me out of the doldrums occasionally. How did you discipline a child for having fun and being silly? After all, to put things in perspective, it was not like he decked another kid or spit on the teacher! I thought this was it. This was when children lost their innocence and their ability to have fun. We adults pounded it out of them. Bound by societal norms, we issued the standard lecture about there being a proper time and place for fun.

And no Play Station for a week.

On a glorious fall morning, as I was driving Alex to her appointment, God sent me a sign. Or so I felt. I don't mean a celestial message, but a literal billboard sign. After years of praying for guidance and getting no response, I thought I might just be beginning to obtain an insight into what God had in mind for me. I had become aware of an uncanny sequence of events.

Since it was such a beautiful day, we had taken the scenic route. High-pressure weather conditions had pushed away all clouds, leaving the sky a brilliant blue. Cruising along Philmont Avenue, I noticed a billboard advertisement promoting overseas adoptions. I had traveled this route many times without noticing the sign. It had to be new. Could this be it? Was this the path along which I was supposed to travel? I argued with myself that we had gone to an adoption agency and it had not felt right. A three-to-five-year wait did not grab at our hearts. But something about this billboard sign did.

Alex and I sat quietly in the waiting room for her egg-retrieval. I had begun to scratch furiously at my skin again. It was my second month on the new Fertinex drug. The first IUI had, naturally, been a failure. My ovaries had not responded well enough to produce a quality ovule. For the second try, Dr. Castlebloom had increased the dosage and my old allergy friend seemed to be making a comeback.

Feeling miserably bloated from the over stimulation of her ovary, Alex was not very talkative that day. We were both flipping through magazines when another advertisement caught my attention. It was yet another agency promoting overseas adoptions with a photo of a white couple cuddling an Asian baby. She was the most adorable baby ever. In fact, she resembled the toddler in my vision. Honestly, Asian and black babies were so much cuter than Caucasian ones! White babies seemed to have all kinds of skin problems like discolorations and blemishes.

Goose bumps danced on my skin. I showed the photo to Alex. "Look at this. What do you think?"

Alex smiled and said, "What do *you* think? Could you adopt a child that belonged to a different race?"

"I don't know. Probably not. I just can't picture it. I've seen white couples strolling with either black or Asian babies, but it's never struck a chord within me. But a child is a child, right? And lately, I'll have to admit I've been thinking a lot about those poor Chinese baby girls that just get tossed aside because of China's one-child law. Someone has to raise them. Would it be depriving them of something vital to take them from their culture?"

"Everything in life is a trade-off. You know that. Look at me. I had to get divorced to try for a baby, because my husband refused to be a part of it anymore."

I thought for a moment, then admitted that I had been seeing ads like this one everywhere I turned. "It's weird, Alex."

"Maybe, you're just noticing them now because the idea appeals to you. You have to decide what it is that is most important to you.

Is it a baby you really want? Or is the idea of being pregnant more attractive?"

Hmm…That was a lot to chew on.

"You know, if anyone could do this," she said, pointing to the advertisement, "you could."

"What makes you say that?" Before she could answer, her name was called. It was time. I watched Alex struggle out of her chair, the way a woman in the tenth month of her pregnancy would have. We shared a small laugh over it and then I wished her luck. I removed the page with the adoption ad from the magazine and tucked it away in my purse.

An hour later, I was allowed into the recovery room to sit with Alex. "How did it go?"

Sleepily, she said, "They only got eleven eggs."

"Is that bad?"

"I guess it depends on how well they survive."

"You know, the nurses kept looking at me funnily. I bet they think we're lesbian lovers!"

Alex chuckled. "You can give them a good show, when we come back in three days for the implantation."

"Oh, and just to be safe. You know, in case there is a…mishap. God forbid." I pulled out a piece of paper and waved it at her. "I wrote down a complete physical description of all the other couples in the waiting area."

"You're a true friend," she said mockingly.

I was not paranoid, really. This was merely a reference to an episode of *20/20*, where two women ended up with babies fathered by the wrong husband's sperm supply. Apparently, the lab mixed up the catheters. How was it so obvious? The white woman had given birth to a black baby and the black woman had delivered a blonde-haired white child. It was pretty obvious that there was some sort of malfunction somewhere.

CHAPTER SEVENTEEN

Not only was the grandfather clock offensively reaching its climax of nine bongs, but the phone was ringing as well. Either the clock or I would have to go. We could not maintain a harmonious co-existence anymore. I had been plotting to dismantle it for years. It was an heirloom from Ryan's grandparents and being a sentimental guy, he loved it, because it brought back fond memories of them. I had always harbored a certain contempt for unnecessary noise. In my teenage years, when I could sleep like the dead, I might not have noticed all that chiming and bonging in the middle of the night. But motherhood seemed to have robbed me of the ability to sleep soundly. On many a night, I found myself being awakened by that damn bong.

And now the phone had to be answered. I was in our home office, grading papers for the next day.

"It's Alex," she sniffled. "Are you busy? Can you come over?"

"Bad news, huh?"

Oh, God. This was going to be bad.

I promised to be right over. But first, I needed to stop at the 7-Eleven to get some supplies: chocolate ice cream, Pop-Tarts and Alex's weakness—crunchy cheese curls. I arrived armed with comfort food, knowing it was the day of her pregnancy test. It had been two and half weeks since her IVF, and we had both been on pins and needles, waiting for the results. I often caught myself pacing during the wait like an expectant father.

She answered the door with a wad of tissues in her hand and a face puffy from crying. In her blue sweats, with her hair disheveled, she looked a wreck. She led me into the newly-renovated kitchen, all cherry cabinets and granite counters. I felt a fleeting pinprick of envy over her kitchen. Since I had known her, this was her second kitchen remodel, whereas, I had still not begun my first.

"Want some tea?" she offered, already working over the new stainless-steel appliances.

"Sure," I hesitated. "I'm sorry, Alex."

"It's not what you think."

"What, then?"

"I'm pregnant," she said glumly.

Clearly, I was confused by her lack of enthusiasm. "What is it, tell me?"

"I'm pregnant, but, I think I made a huge mistake!" she sobbed over the teacups. "This was all wrong. I shouldn't have done this. I can't be a single mother. How can I raise a child on my own? And...oh, God! What if I have triplets!"

I took the cups from her before she dropped them and turned her around by the shoulders to face me. "Look at me. This is wonderful! It's really good news! It is what you wanted. If you have multiples, you will hire help. I will help." I smiled brightly, my heart bursting for her. "Alex, it's good. It's all good."

She crumbled again. "It didn't seem real until now. I couldn't go to work today. I've been absorbing it all. It's unreal. I never thought it was going to really happen."

Alex sat at the island, while I continued to make the tea. I toasted two Pop-Tarts. This was no longer comfort food; it was now celebration food. "Look, you're probably suffering a hormonal imbalance," I told her. "Get used to it. There's more to come. There's someone else in your head that's going to be there for the next nine months!"

We sat there for two hours, eating and sipping tea to calm her nerves. I deduced that her greatest fear was having multiples. Although six fertilized embryos had been implanted, the odds of more than one or two were not so threatening. Owing to recent sensationalized stories of fertility multiples, there had been a misconception that anyone who used fertility drugs would have twins or more. Not true. Besides, unlike me, she had a lot of sisters who would be more than willing to help out. Not to mention friends and a mother. I assured her that she was not alone, just minus one useless husband and the better for it. Alex was the kind of woman who would thrive in her independence. She would not become a withering flower. I was sure that I would not be as productive, if I were in her situation.

I needed my husband in my life, and for more than "a paycheck," as he claimed when he was angry. Sometimes, my greatest feelings of love for him were aroused when I watched him playing racing cars with Jake. Or doing something for me, like cleaning the snow off my car. I appreciated the little things, the small gestures of chivalry. No, I wouldn't have functioned well living alone, which was evident to me during our two weeks of silence and non-interaction. I was forced to put an end to the isolation by admitting that sex was a necessary, if not burdensome part of marriage.

The problem, however, lay in the way each one of us needed it. He needed it to feel better, to feel loved. I needed it as an end to a means, to make a baby. I also needed to feel healthy and loved before I could do it. After much head-butting, we had arrived at something of a compromise. Well, he hadn't. I had. I just had to sacrifice my body twice a week to keep him happy! Pathetic, but true.

Dr. Snyder did not approve of my mindset, but being bound by testosterone himself, I concluded that it was a concept even he, the doctor, couldn't comprehend. We evidently needed a change, and it came marching and shouting into our lives like a wild summer thunderstorm with the culmination of two events.

Our third IUI with the Fertinex was apparently going to be my last, at least for a while. With a case of full-blown hives to suffer through, it was obvious that I needed to suspend my drug therapy. In addition, my poor ovaries seemed to be plain old tired. They did not respond as well as they had with the Pergonal. Injecting the Fertinex was less painful than introducing the Pergonal. It was administered with a diabetic-size needle subcutaneously, in other words, in the fat layer as opposed to the muscle. I had plenty of fat. However, because of my needle-associated hysteria, I still needed

Ryan to administer the injections. Except for the time when he went out with work friends for poker night and forgot me.

He had promised to be home by 11 p.m. to give me the injection. It needed to be taken around the same time every night during the cycle. Midnight came and went. No Ryan. I was forced to attempt it myself. It couldn't be that bad, I reasoned. After all, I barely even felt these smaller needles go in. After talking myself up, I prepared the syringe and carefully tapped out the air bubbles. I took a deep breath, grabbed a handful of belly fat with one hand and angled the syringe with the other. Okay, one, two, three…I couldn't do it. Try again. One, two, three…No. Deep breath, relax. Again. One, two, three…Arrrggghhh! Now my palms were sweaty. Okay, maybe, if I closed my eyes, I could do it. It was just the anticipation of seeing it go in that was stopping me. Okay, here goes. Eyes closed. One, two, three…Ooowww! Somehow, I had missed that enormous roll of belly fat and jammed the needle into my hand, hitting bone! I prayed that I never became a diabetic.

One last time, with eyes open, I finally got it in. Just as I had cleaned up, Ryan strolled in, reeking of cigars and beer. "Sorry, I forgot. Are you ready?"

"You're late. I had to do it myself. Don't do that to me again. It was hell."

"Really? You did it yourself? That's progress."

"No thanks to you."

CHAPTER EIGHTEEN

Ryan stood behind me on this third Fertinex/ insemination cycle, holding up the wall, as Dr. Castlebloom inserted the catheter to deliver my husband's sperm. My egg cells were no longer languishing; they were downright rejecting admittance to the throne. The ultrasound image revealed that only one out of five stimulated eggs had ripened enough to be fertilized. Yes, it only took one. But after being on a stimulating drug, there should have been many ripe eggs to increase the chances.

With my feet in stirrups, I broke the doctor's concentration. "Dr. Castlebloom, this is not working for us. If I don't get pregnant this time, it's over…for a while," I said, sounding like I was breaking up a love affair that was going nowhere.

He looked at Ryan and asked. "What are your plans?"

"I'm not sure. I just know that this stuff is like poison to me," I retorted. I had a plan; I just did not feel like sharing it with him, especially, if he couldn't show me the courtesy of eye contact. He did not deserve to know my plan.

"We could put you on Lupron or birth-control pills for six months, shut your system down," he suggested.

"No, no more drugs. I'm done. There is only so much abuse I can take. Your 'six to nine months' are up." After all we had been through, Lupron was just what I needed. It was a caustic drug that shut down your endocrine system, so that cysts and other inflammations caused by over stimulation could dissolve. However, it also deepened your voice and caused facial hair to grow. The thought of going on birth-control pills to give my tired body a break was like a cruel joke. Sure, the pill had many benefits besides contraception, but I could not wrap my brain around that hideous plan.

The other turning-point event occurred at a birthday party for one of Jake's classmates. We had taken our son to the skating party and I had initiated a conversation with Kim Hartly, the mother of his classmate, Annie. Standing close by her side was two-year-old Katie, a shy Korean girl the Hartlys had adopted sixteen months earlier. Katie was incredibly cute. Like me, Kim had a biological first child, but no others. She had been through the same emotional trauma I was experiencing at the thought of not being able to have a second child. Lately, I had been frequenting adoption websites and storing up stories and photos of families who had adopted offspring. I had begun to secretly contemplate the idea of Asian adoption for sometime, because sad though it seemed, going overseas for a baby appeared to be less risky and to have more potential than a United States adoption. Meeting Kim was an affirmation.

I squirreled away the pertinent information she offered about the agency they used, but one simple statement made emphatically by Kim sealed the deal. "I loved being pregnant, even the delivery part," she said. "It was all joyous and wonderful. But the day Katie came to us was just as joyful and exciting, maybe, even more so, because I was healthy and not exhausted from giving birth."

All said and done, perhaps, that's what I was craving, the pure and simple joy a new baby brought to a family; just the way a home came alive with a new little person in it. I observed the Hartlys' interactions with Katie and saw nothing but love between them. Even the sibling interaction was amazingly affectionate. Why was I placing so much importance on giving birth, anyway? It wasn't as if I enjoyed having the most intimate part of me ripped open. I had not tolerated the pain so well either. And I had a difficult time getting my hormones back to normal afterward. The daily sweating for three months had been disgusting. Feeling like I constantly needed a shower made breast-feeding even more difficult. Yet, it seems that I had somehow glorified the whole process.

"How long did it take to get her?" Ryan asked, still mortified at how women could share intimate birthing details at their very first meeting.

"The whole process, from start to finish, took about nine months," Kim replied.

Nine months! That was nothing! I would have to wait just as long if I got pregnant right this minute. Sign me up! I stole a look at Ryan and read his mind.

It was as if the pieces of a puzzle had all come together, fitting perfectly into place. God *was* speaking to me. He had been speaking to me all along. I simply had not been listening. Maybe, I was not ready to hear what His plan was for me. But I did not doubt it now. It all swirled around in my head: the psychic's odd words about a waiting soul, the adoption advertisements, the vision of the Asian toddler, meeting the Hartlys and my body's rejection of fertility medication.

The hives suddenly stood out like the loudest voice from God. He hadn't forsaken me. It was as though He were screaming at me that fertility drugs were not the path I was meant to traverse. Finally, I got it! It was a lesson in spirituality like no other. What had I expected to happen? That God would actually speak to me in a thundering voice from the clouds? No, He spoke to you through your heart, your pain, your experiences, your relationships and through brief encounters with people like the Hartlys. The messages were absolutely everywhere!

I glided into Dr. Snyder's office on a life high. I was anxious to tell him the good news that we would be adopting a Chinese girl and saving her from a life of shame and neglect in the orphanage. I was also looking forward to it being my last session. Therapy was getting costly. And that life-transforming book he had given me had been the real cure. I figured that the darn book had cost me $500 or so. Had he offered it to me in the beginning, I could have saved so much money. No matter, I felt I had resolved certain things and it was time to move on.

As I crossed the threshold to his office, I noticed the change. The difference was striking. New chairs. He bought new chairs! I ran my hand along the smooth leather and lowered myself gently into one at first. Then I let my whole body sink and relax. They were exactly like the club-style reading chairs found at Barnes and Noble, the kind you could curl up in for hours without feeling your rump go numb.

From behind me, I heard, "Ah, so do you approve?" Dr. Snyder took the chair opposite mine, presumably holding my chart in his hand.

I smiled appreciatively. "They're great. You did this for me?"

Damn, he looked especially good today. Funny, how at first I'd thought of him as just an average Joe. He simply had the perfect look of distinction. I loved the way his jaw tensed when he was thinking.

"I wish I could give you full credit, but you weren't the only client to complain."

Darn, I'd thought I was special. "It's too bad that I won't get to enjoy them," I announced.

"What do you mean?"

I enthusiastically recounted my path to spiritual enlightenment and our decision to pursue a Chinese adoption.

"Good for you. I'm happy for you. I think it will be a positive step." As he was saying that, I imagined I heard, "However..." I waited, but the words did not come.

"Is that it? You aren't going to say that I need more enlightenment?" I asked.

"If you need me, you'll come back. My door is always open. I will have to warn you that the adoption process will not be as easy as you might think. They can put you through the wringer emotionally. It will force you to examine your readiness."

"Oh, I'm ready. No doubt about that," I assured him.

"But have you fully worked through your grief over not being able to become pregnant?"

Okay. I started to choke when forced to think about that. Alone, the word, "grief", evoked tears like a hypnotic suggestion. True, choosing to adopt did not take away my grief and feelings of loss. But it was early days yet. I needed time for the pain of all our failures to dissipate. I did not believe that grief ever went away, anyway. It just became more bearable over time. A tear escaped, which did not say much. For some reason, with him, I always seemed to *feel* more than usual. Most days I walked through life and pushed my feelings deep down. Maybe it was the new chairs, but now sadness overwhelmed me and the tears flowed softly.

"Now why did you have to do that? I was feeling jubilant when I walked in here, and now look at me!" I reached for his box of tissues.

"Julia, have you accepted, truly accepted the fact that you have not gotten pregnant naturally?"

I looked at the ceiling. Hmm, it needed some paint. I looked at the gray carpet, finding a stain. I examined my scuffed loafers. I looked out the window and watched the first flakes of snow starting to fall. "No," I said softly.

"Then it looks like you'll be enjoying that comfortable chair, after all."

WELCOME HOUSE SOCIAL SERVICES OF
PEARL S. BUCK INTERNATIONAL, INC.

REQUIRED DOCUMENTS FOR WELCOME HOUSE:

____ Fact Sheet of Application: Return with non-refundable fee of $300.

_____ Service Agreement: Sign and return entire agreement.

_____ Social Services Fee Policy: Sign and return entire agreement.

_____ Financial Statement: Notarization is required for international adoption. Include W-2 for both spouses and copy of most recent 1040 Income Tax Form. Affidavit must be signed and notarized.

_____ Medical Exam Report: One for each applicant

_____ Photographs: Three photos may be sent to the overseas agency with your home-study report. Do not include pets. Include 1 photo of applicants and any children living at home, 1 photo outside of home, without family members, 1 photo of inside of home, without family members.

_____ Letter From Employer: Include current position, salary, duration of employment and a statement addressing job security, on letterhead with original signatures.

_____ Personal References: No relatives. 1 must be a neighbor, 1 must be from licensed therapist/ psychologist, etc. One referral per couple.

IF ACCEPTED INTO THE ADOPTION PROGRAM, A COMPLETED HOME-STUDY REPORT WILL BE REQUIRED AT THE COST OF $1400. Includes completion of parenting seminar.

CHAPTER NINETEEN

Large areas of open land were a rare sight in Bucks County, Pennsylvania. The lower part of the county, especially, had been infested with cookie-cutter houses and mass overdevelopment. Midway up the county, where we found ourselves on our way to the Pearl S. Buck Foundation, we passed the occasional tree or turf farm. I had always thought either of the two the perfect commodity to farm. It would be good for the environment. My sensitive nose had never been able to handle the stench of farm animals.

Devoid of vegetation, the winter landscape was stark and unbearably dismal. It was cold and drizzling. Icy droplets of rain threatened to make our trip home treacherous. The deer which usually swarmed over this area were hunkered down in anticipation of the impending storm.

We crossed over a wooden bridge and turned into the sixty-five acre estate, which was now a museum of sorts. The Pearl S. Buck home was off to the right, available for daily tours. A gift shop stood a few yards from the main house. There was always a gift shop, wasn't there? But this one specialized in international treasures. Further along to the left sat the Welcome House offices, a subsidiary of the foundation begun by Buck. An American author most widely known for her Nobel-prize-winning novel, *The Good Earth*, Buck had a deep interest in Asian culture. Raised in China by missionary parents, she was a pioneer in stimulating Western interest in Asian culture and furthering our understanding of it. After she returned to the United States and settled back here in Pennsylvania, the author set up an adoption agency that was the first of its kind in promoting bi-racial adoptions. Buck herself adopted seven children from various countries and fostered many others.

Welcome House had existed now for over fifty years and had maintained strong government ties in Asia. That the agency was a long-established one was a factor that attracted us. Although using their services would cost us more money, we were not about to risk losing money by dealing with a fly-by-night operator.

I could not help but regard the long, winding road leading to the offices as symbolic. Indeed, we had traveled a long road to get to this point. On Kim Hartly's recommendation, we had scheduled our first meeting with the adoption agency. The rain was incongruent with my ecstatic mood. The sky should have been radiant with sunshine. We were going to be parents again in only nine months! If it all went well, maybe, we'd even take siblings or twins. How common were twins in Chinese families? And how did the one-child-per-couple law introduced by the Chinese government to curb the serious risk of overpopulation accommodate twins or triplets? What did a couple do then? This deplorable law was the reason for thousands of baby girls being rejected by their families on the pretext of wanting to ensure that their one child would be a son. For a son in Chinese society not only carried on the family name, but was expected to take full responsibility for his elderly parents. It was a tradition that had been passed down from one generation to the next.

Ryan pulled into a parking space that was as far as he could possibly find from the entrance to the office.

"Why are you parking here?" I inquired. "There's a spot in the front row by the door."

"It's for employees," he barked.

"No, it isn't. I don't see a sign saying so."

"It is, trust me!" he snarled.

"Why do you have to do that?" I responded, hurt by his tone.

"Do *what?*" Again, that tone!

"This is supposed to be a happy occasion," I reminded him, "and now you've ruined it for us!"

I was afraid we would look back on this day and remember our disagreement, not our jubilation.

He drew in a deep, exhausted breath. "No, *you* ruined it," he accused me.

"I just asked about a stupid parking spot, and you have to get all, 'I'm not wrong, you are,' on me!"

"I'm going inside." He yanked open the car door, stepped out and slammed it shut violently. He proceeded to walk toward the front door, leaving me to steam up the windows with the exhaust of my raging anger. Inside my head, I was screaming. I wanted to just drive away and ditch him. Owing to his inability to locate a better parking spot, we wanted to strangle each other! He had me, and he knew it. I could not just sit there, unwilling to leave the car, because if I didn't follow him, the social workers might just see how dysfunctional we really were as a couple. Were we the kind of couple they entrusted babies to?

I knew that this was simply going to be a meeting where information would be provided on the various options available to us and the requirements that would have to be met, but there seemed to be no end to the reams of paper that kept flowing in our direction. Six couples were seated around a huge round table in a conference room. Before me were twenty-eight pages of information about dossier requirements from China, South Korea, Thailand, India, Russia and Guatemala. The lead social worker, Diane, fielded questions from a group of prospective parents like us, but all I could hear was a garbled version of some foreign language.

I flipped ahead to the fact sheet on China and was disheartened to see that neither our wallet nor the time-frame we had in mind would suit their requirements. Both China and Russia required from adoptive parents a two or three-week visitation period in their country. The officials of each country claimed, of course, that it was to help adoptive parents learn about the child's culture. I could not help feeling, however, that the only purpose of such a requirement was to extract more revenue from overeager and anxious parents who might already be in a financial bind. The greatest disappointment over the way the Chinese and Russian authorities handled the adoption of children from their respective countries lay in the time that would elapse between the selection of a child by prospective parents and the moment they would finally be allowed to take it home. Neither government was swift in processing the paperwork involved in finalizing adoptions. This meant that the baby you agreed to accept when it was five months old, could be eighteen months old before you actually brought it home. It was distressing that a baby chosen for adoption would have to languish for so long in an orphanage, when it had loving people waiting to welcome it.

The biggest kicker of it all was the price tag. Agencies claimed that you were not buying a child; the money you paid simply went toward the payment of facilitators' salaries, lawyers' fees, orphanage subsidies, transportation costs and overseas government fees. No matter how it was packaged, you still ended up feeling that you were, indeed, buying a child. But you had no choice. It was not unlike the experience of paying the outrageous price charged for fertility drugs. Adoption was like any other market. Supply and demand ruled the day.

We arrived home in time to play a few rounds of Old Maid with Jake before bed. He loved the card game, because our rules specified that whoever got stuck with the Old Maid got monstrously tickled. He had not yet mastered the artful poker face and was, therefore, a frequent target of the tickle torture.

After Jake was in bed, we sat in ours pouring over the adoption information and the details relevant to each country's requirements. I glanced over at Ryan as he leaned back on the headboard with his glasses on. For a fleeting second, I saw him as an old man reading in bed. We weren't so young anymore. The road we had been down and the path up ahead of us felt like we had just bought a ticket into true adulthood. I had felt like a child when we got married. I still felt as though I were eighteen and carefree when we had Jake. But our infertility experience and, now, this adoption issue represented a true and defining grown-up moment, one that needed to be carefully considered.

"What do you think?" I asked Ryan.

He looked up from his reading. "Well, I know you wanted

China, but honestly, South Korea seems like a better country to work with. They don't require travel. Nor do they need as much in the dossier."

"Yeah, I was thinking that too. The cost is the same, except for the travel." I pointed to the paper. "And look. It says here that Korean babies arrive at an average age of four to eight months. That's certainly better. I want a baby as young as possible." I was concerned about the bonding problems that might surface with an older child. "And, South Korea has a foster-care program."

The idea of foster care over an orphanage was a significant selling point for me. South Korea's program placed babies in foster homes when they were only three days old. Only one baby at a time was placed with the host family, which meant more individual care and, hopefully, more comfort and love. Korean families apparently approached the care of these babies with much pride. Koreans were a proud and affectionate people and did not want negative blemishes ruining their reputation.

"It says here, though, that you don't get to choose the sex of your baby," observed Ryan.

"No, it has to be a girl," I insisted. It just had to be.

"Don't you think a boy would be easier to raise? It would be better for Jake. And we already have so much boy stuff."

He wanted to go with the comfort factor.

"It has to be a girl." I repeated.

I told him about my vision of the Asian girl. I hadn't mentioned it to him before, because I doubted whether what I had experienced was real. Now I was sure.

"Wow."

"I felt it, Ryan. It's supposed to be a girl. Besides, don't you want to get the most out of this experience? We've done the boy thing. A girl would be new and special."

He contemplated the idea for a moment and said, "I suppose so. But how are we going to pay for this?"

"The Hartlys refinanced their home and took out a second mortgage. Do we have any equity in the house?"

I knew there wasn't much, because our fixer-upper home had been the proverbial money pit. We had refinanced it two years ago to pay off our reconstruction debt and our credit-card liabilities. Since we already lived paycheck to paycheck, the idea of racking up another credit card was out of the question. We could not afford to make the monthly payment on a new credit card or a home-equity loan. Wherever the money came from, it could not be in the form of a payback loan. If we'd only had the foresight, years ago, that we would be adopting, we could have planned it better. What we had, instead, was a new roof, new windows, new wiring, plumbing, siding and the addition of a family room with a second bathroom.

"I can sell the stock, but that's only three thousand. We're short by $22,000."

I hated money. There was never enough. People with tons of money just did not understand the good they could do with it. But lack of money was not going to stop me. Kim Hartly had said that if they could do it, anyone could. We just had to find a way.

"Maybe, we should call Oprah. She's always making people's dreams come true."

Ryan rolled his eyes. "Yeah," he said, "I think that website is Oprah@show/me/the/money.com."

Wishful thinking. Middle-class people like us did not get freebies in life. We paid the way for everyone and everything. You would think that for something as wonderful as adoption, there would at least be a decent tax credit. As the law stood, we were only entitled to one amounting to no more than $5,000. I knew it was better than nothing, but it seemed to me that more people would adopt if the financial pressure on them were eased.

Ryan ran his hand through his hair in a symbolic gesture that suggested he was about to pull it out. We were breaking the golden rule of a happy marriage by entertaining a discussion about money in bed.

"What about your fertility treatments?" he asked. "Don't you want to try for an IVF?"

I shrugged, inwardly cringing at the thought of more chemicals invading my body cells. "Maybe, somewhere down the road. But I think it would be a better gamble to spend $25,000 on adoption and be guaranteed a baby, than to spend twelve thousand on an IVF and get nothing."

It was like playing high stakes at Harrah's.

"Okay, that sounds smart," he said, but I could feel that there was something troubling him more than money, because he kept staring at the ceiling. He was in his deep-thinking mode, his brows furrowed.

"What? What's wrong? You're not sure, are you?" I asked, worried.

"It's just...well...I need to be sure of you," he said cautiously.

"Me? I'm fine. I want this."

"That's not what I meant. All of a sudden, you seem obsessed with adopting. It's like you have tunnel vision now and can't see anything else."

That was absolutely untrue. And I was absolutely not in the mood for 'Let's point out Julia's faults tonight'. "I'm not obsessed; I'm focused for a change," I shot back. "Somehow, I think adopting has always been in my destiny."

"I'm talking about me."

"Why is this about you?" I asked defensively.

"If you'd let me finish, I could tell you." He shook his head in exasperation. "I don't want to bring another child into our home without a guarantee that you are going to be here for the long haul. Because that would be awful—to adopt a child and then get divorced. It's not fair to the child."

"What? Where is this coming from? Is this the sex thing or the lack of it? Is that what's bothering you?"

"No. I just need to be sure that you are committed to me, is all, because lately, I feel like you aren't."

"Oh, Ryan." I tossed the papers aside and gave him an earnest look. "I love you. I love Jake. And I am committed to my family. I'm not like my mother. I'm not going to run when it gets tough.

Besides, I can't leave you. No one else would put up with me the way you do."

"That's true," he agreed. I wasn't sure whether it was my mother's history that generated his doubts about my intentions. It was interesting that I, on the other hand, never doubted him. I knew he would always be there. He was just that kind of person, a reliable one. He would not run off in pursuit of an affair during a mid-life crisis, like Dave Martin. He'd purchase a Harley instead.

I snuggled up to him, knowing that if I touched him, it would be perceived as foreplay. "This past year has been hard on us. We need to move on, to have something exciting to look forward to. That's why I'm passionate about this. It's exciting and positive for a change. It feels right." I snuggled closer still. He smelled deliciously of Irish Spring soap. "And...well...I don't think that I could do this with anyone but you. You're so...so...confident about it all. It makes me more confident."

With that affirmation came the tender peace offering of a love session. It started with soft kissing and ended on the floor. I was not merely pretending to be interested either, because once I got started, I realized how much I missed the closeness.

What I had confessed was true. I could not envision myself adopting a child with another man. Ryan had seen the bigger picture right away. Being a parent meant raising a child, not merely sowing the seed for one. As the days passed, it seemed more and more likely that this was our destiny.

CHAPTER TWENTY

Once it was decided that we would go with the South Korean adoption program, the floodgates opened. We had a sea of forms to complete, starting with the first $300 application fee. Ryan sold his Smithkline stock for $3,265. It was a start for the initial payment of $2,500. The rest paid off extra bills.

There were miles and miles of lists to be completed and documents to be filed and notarized. We decided on a plan of attack for the overwhelming process. He would handle the financial end, which meant finding the money. I would deal with the paperwork, which began with the problem of obtaining five personal references. Three of them could be friends or family. One reference had to be from a neighbor and one from a psychologist. This was to be the first insult of many that we would encounter along the way. Not only did we have to divulge a piece of private information to one of our neighbors, we also had to ask for a reference testifying to our suitability as parents. We were not exactly close to any of our neighbors who were all elderly. We were merely cordial.

The personal references were easy. I had good friends I could count on. I was sitting in Alex's kitchen sipping tea, while she sipped ginger ale. She was nibbling on a cracker to ease the all-day morning sickness. She had been having a rough time adjusting to the pregnancy. I was sure it had something to do with flushing out the extra chemicals from the fertility medication. I wanted her to be happier, to be able to enjoy it more, but she was too ill all the time. Together, we completed a referral form. Ally was easy. Her life was hectic and she had said, "Write whatever you want and I'll sign it."

"It says here," Alex pointed out, "that your references have to be from someone you've known at least five years. I've only known you...like two years."

I looked at her dumbfounded. "And so, you will fudge it a little," I mocked. "You think they're really gonna check? You've known me since Jake was born and I am a patient, even-tempered mother who never ever raises her voice."

"Ha!" Moving on. "What is the condition of your home?" She read from the prompt questions.

"Immaculate," I answered.

"Oh, come on. Are you trying to appear obsessive-compulsive or functionally normal?" She smiled. "I'll just say it's very clean, but lived-in."

"Lived-in implies it's a mess," I argued.

"How about very clean, organized—ha!—and appropriately lived-in."

"What does that mean? 'Appropriately lived-in'? That makes me sound uptight. Just say, 'Clean and fairly well-organized'," I suggested. "At least, it will be before the home-study visit."

"Why don't you just write this yourself?" Alex chided. In reality, she had felt honored when I asked her for a reference.

"I can't, I feel too weird describing myself." As though I hadn't just done precisely that. "Just finish it. I can't stand this. I hate feeling like I have to have everyone's permission to be able to care for a baby. Not only do I have to pester my friends, I have to notify both of our employers for financial affidavits and job security. Why do our employers need to know we want to adopt? It's none of their business. Then we have to provide photos of ourselves, I guess, to verify that we don't have third eyeballs or something." There was also the slight fear at the back of my mind that when we brought social workers in to scrutinize our lives, they would, perhaps, detect some horrible dysfunction in us and take Jake away.

It was crazy, I know. But would you want a social worker examining your private life? We'd all done and said things we regretted. And with our houses in such close proximity, I was sure our neighbors had been entertained on occasion by my arguments with Ryan. I tried to recall if I had ever slipped and used the F-word a little too loudly. I'd better be sure to get my neighbor reference from eighty-year-old Mrs. Fuller who was nearly deaf. I knew it was selfish of me to feel insulted. It's just that we were not yet ready to announce our plans. We had not even told Ryan's parents and here we were, getting distant neighbors involved in our lives. Other prospective adoptive parents might have found the criminal and child-abuse background checks invasive, but being educators, we were used to that. That was one item on the extensive list that we were comfortable with.

"You want them to be thorough, you know that," Alex consoled, making choking sounds. "They don't want to miss anything and be up for a lawsuit," said my wonderfully supportive friend, just before she vomited into the sink.

"Alex, my God! Are you like this all the time?"

I moved around the island and searched in the drawer for a clean washcloth. I soaked it in cold water and put it on her forehead. No wonder she was not enjoying being pregnant. I had not even suffered from morning sickness with Jake. In fact, I remember having a hard time being convinced that I was pregnant until I felt movement somewhere in the fourth month.

"Have you spoken to your doctor about this? There must be something you can take to ease your nausea."

"It should be over soon," she said stoically.

Why did women glorify pregnancy? Why did I? In reality, it sucked. It was the worst possible thing a woman could do to her body, yet the experience was something we all coveted. Some of us wanted it so badly, we became drug addicts for the cause.

CHAPTER TWENTY-ONE

Panic and fear settled in, as I prepared for our home-study visit. Between my job and completing endless amounts of adoption paperwork, I had become crazed over my own personal checklist—the one where I superficially organized my house in preparation for impressing Jeanie Carlisle, our social worker. In order to create the illusion of a well-managed home, I had to take a day off from work on the pretext that I was indisposed. The thing was, my house used to be what Alex and I described as clean, but lived-in. However, with my job and the endless papers I graded every night, my home and its condition had slipped down my list of priorities. I needed a wife, failing which a laundry maid would do, since laundry seemed to be the most challenging of the chores at hand.

Much as I might tell myself not to worry, I worried, anyway. Logic told me that Jeanie was not going to enter my home wearing a white glove to check on the level of dust, but I cleaned as if she would. Better to be safe than sorry. I cleaned out all the old food from the refrigerator. I dusted the ceiling fans. I washed the glass on the French door, smudged with Taco's muddy footprints, and made sure that Jeanie would not be finding popcorn and crushed cereal under my sofa cushions. Every surface shone.

Though appearance was important, smell was paramount. I knew how revolted I became when I entered someone's home, only to find it smelling of bacon, sweaty shoes or wet dog. I was in a quandary. Should I make my home smell like fresh-baked cookies or orange/ lemon clean? I conquered the problem by giving Taco a bath and putting orange blossom outlet scents in every room.

Then there was the matter of Jake. He had to be given a haircut against his will. He was beginning to resemble a wanna-be rock star. Then he had to be prepped for the occasion. I couldn't risk having him blurt out something awful like, "My mom walks around the house in her underwear," or "My mom can burp louder than my dad." No, Jake could not be trusted, especially, not after his funnyman stints at school. Children could be notoriously loose-lipped.

I stood Jake squarely in front of me and angled his chin to make serious eye contact. "Now Jake," I told him, "this meeting tonight is serious. If we want the social worker to think we are good people, worthy of adopting a child, then no funny stuff from you. You need to be careful about what you say. You're not to repeat everything you hear. I want you to use good manners and be on your best behavior. Understand?"

He looked up at me with those blue puppy eyes and said, "Do you want me to lie?"

"No! Just be careful about how you answer questions. Don't divulge too much information."

"Okay," he said with a tone resembling his father's. "Can I go play now?"

By the time Ryan walked in the door after work, I was consumed with fatigue. I was not used to the full day of hard labor that cleaning obviously involved. I would have liked to say that I was the kind of wife who greeted my man at the door and offered pouty lips to kiss. He would have liked me to be that kind of wife. What usually happened, though, was that Taco became the official greeter at the door and Ryan had to search me out. By four o'clock in the afternoon, I was more often than not, lying prone somewhere in the house.

He found me stretched across our bed on my stomach. "Where is my real wife?" he asked, leaning over me. "What have you done with her?"

Sleepily, I asked, "What? What's wrong?"

"Nothing's wrong. It's just that everything is right." Then he gasped, noticing the carpet. "You got the carpet fixed! All right, what have you done with my real wife, the one who never finishes anything?"

I rolled over and said in my own defense, "I *do* finish things, though not in your time-frame. Did you notice the curtains? I hung them today."

"I did. Looks great. Everything looks great. We should have home-study meetings more often." He snuggled up next to me on the bed. "What's for dinner?"

Can I tell you how much I despise that question? A bowl of Frosted Flakes would be fine with me, but the husband expects "dinner"—a hot meal. There was only so much Happy Housewife in me. "You must have me confused with Betty Crocker. You don't expect me to cook as well, do you?"

"Take-out again," he groaned. "You know, I don't think it's been worthwhile having you working. We spend even more money than we used to. Where has all your salary gone?"

It just seemed to evaporate. "Bills, work clothes, Pergonal and take-out," I answered promptly. "How's the search going for our hidden treasure?"

"It looks like we can pull $19,000 in equity. But we have debts to pay off.

We're still short.

He received two checks a month. One was earmarked for the mortgage; the other paid all of our bills and maybe some savings. Yeah, when I was young, I couldn't wait to be married and live happily ever after!

By the time Jeanie arrived at 6:30 p.m., I was pleased with the house. But I had forgotten to take care of something: *myself.* I caught a quick glimpse of myself in the mirror just before I answered the door. I looked ragged and worn-out, with disheveled hair and mascara smudges under my eyes. I still wore my "maid" uniform, covered in dust and damp from splashes of water from the toilet. Just before I was to open the door to Jeanie, I turned to Ryan and hissed, "What's wrong with you? Why didn't you tell me I looked like hell?"

I raced upstairs for a quick change, leaving him to greet the social worker.

Jeanie made me feel uncomfortable in my own home. She was quiet and reserved. A slow, calm talker, her speech pattern left too much dead air between her articulated thoughts. She was younger than either of us. It should have created in me a feeling of security, if not superiority, but it didn't. I fought the urge to chew my nails, as she examined our home and chatted with us. Then she asked to spend some time alone with Jake and I was overcome by a rush of panic. So far, my son had been very well-mannered. He took her upstairs to show her his room, leaving Ryan and me to sweat it out in the kitchen. When she was out of sight, I made a gesture of collapse and fell into a chair.

Ryan whispered, "Be cool."

I buried my face in my hands, wishing that I could go to sleep and wake up when it was all over. Being scrutinized like this was enormously stressful. My heart rate was elevated. My armpits were sweaty. My mouth tasted of dust, but I couldn't take a drink to get rid of the feeling.

Jeanie and Jake finally rejoined us and I served her some tea and cookies in the kitchen. She spread a file folder in front of her and began to ask us some form questions. She described her conversation with Jake. "He's looking forward to being a big brother," she said.

Our posture straightened as Ryan and I beamed with pride.

"He was so cute," she went on. "He showed me his soccer trophies, his artwork and his closet. He said, 'These are my school clothes, because my mom says I have to dress for success. But I don't like them.'"

Jeanie paused and looked at her notes. "So, it says here that you are signing up for the Korea program."

"That's right," I confirmed, as Ryan nodded.

"Discrimination against Asians is more subtle than it is against black people," Jeanie observed. "It is, therefore, less obvious to white people. Adopting an Asian child will call for more sensitivity on your part. After you adopt, your family will be forever interracial. How do you feel about that?"

"We don't have a problem with it," I said, answering for both Ryan and myself. "At first, I wasn't sure. I was too worried about how those around me would react. But I realized that I wasn't usually bothered by what others thought. So, I decided not to let a racial difference worry me."

"A child is a child," said Ryan.

"A strong support group is vital, though, don't you think? Do you think friends and family will be supportive and comfortable with your decision?"

I knew this one. It was like playing Millionaire. Ally had given me this answer one warm day, when we were attempting to walk off our winter flab. Ally may have been the first to articulate the words, but I had long felt them in my heart.

"First of all, we have terrific friends," I said to Jeanie. "As far as others are concerned, I think people will follow our lead. Our love and acceptance will hopefully make people feel secure enough to open their hearts as well. Those closest to us have already been very encouraging."

"What will you do, if someone makes a racial slur?"

"I don't know," I shrugged.

"Set them straight," Ryan said. "I suppose life will forever be a teaching moment for us."

"How can we predict that?" I interjected. "Race doesn't have to be such an issue, you know. We do live in quite a multicultural area. It somewhat factored into our decision." As we were talking, I looked over Jeanie's shoulder and spotted Jake leaving the hallway bathroom without switching off the light.

Jeanie tossed her long brown hair over her shoulders and adjusted her glasses. "Would the child have his or her own room?"

Would the child have a room at all in Korea? She would be living in an overcrowded orphanage.

"Yes, we have to move the office," Ryan answered.

"What are your plans for maintaining some of the child's ethnic culture?" asked Jeanie. "Would you contribute to developing his or her own identity?"

Are you kidding me?

"All children have their own identity," I replied. Jeanie clarified that she had meant cultural identity.

On that issue, we had no clue. My brain had not yet processed the fact that this child would be racially or culturally different and I thought Jeanie's emphasis on the issue a little over the top concerning a baby. The child's interest in life would be my guide. That's all I knew. How much cultural interest could a baby have, anyway? That was years down the road. American culture represented every culture of the world. I thought we were supposed to be integrating, not separating. As I was about to fudge my way through some intelligent response after Ryan, I noticed water flowing into the hallway. Fecal water!

I jumped up. "Ryan!" I yelled as I shoved at my husband because he was closer to the mess.

Instinctively, he bolted. "Holy fuck!" shouted Ryan, quickly assessing the damage and leaping into action.

Brilliant Ryan, I thought. Please say you did not use the F-word in front of the social worker. We're doomed! I can just picture a huge red stamp on our file saying, "DENIED". The ominous feeling that something would go wrong involving Jake had come true in the most grotesque fashion. He had overstuffed the toilet with paper and the old pipes had coughed it all back out onto my clean floors. We might laugh about it some day, but at that particular moment, the situation was beyond horrifying. And oh God, that smell! Not what you wanted to go wrong when a social worker was observing your every move. The little perpetrator was upstairs playing his Play Station, oblivious to the mess and destruction he had left behind.

Sometime during the pandemonium, Jeanie said her good-byes. I was confident that our home-study report would be less than glowing, particularly, after Ryan's slip of the tongue over the mess Jake had made.

WELCOME HOUSE OF PEARL S. BUCK INTERNATIONAL

520 Dublin Road
Perkasie, PA 18944 215 555-1445

May 2004

Ryan and Julia Leary
1400 Hampton Ave.
Attleboro, PA 19040

Dear Mr. and Mrs. Leary,

Congratulations on your approved home-study report. Your adoption coordinator has submitted your completed home study. We are pleased to accept you both for the placement of a Korean child.

We have forwarded your home study to INS to complete your immigration application. Please let us know when you receive your INS approval (I-I71H)- Notice of Favorable Determination Concerning Application for Advance Processing of Orphan Petition.

You will be receiving a bill for the processing fee of $5,000. After receipt of payment, Welcome House will forward your home-study report to Hill Children's Services, Inc. in Seoul, S. Korea.

Sincerely,
Karen Roberts
Karen Roberts
Adoption Services Manager
Welcome House Adoption Program
KGR/hjl

CHAPTER TWENTY-TWO

On a sunny Saturday morning in May, I invited Alex over for a late breakfast out on my back porch. I had fed Ryan and Jake earlier, so they could head off to baseball practice. It was one of my favorite spring and summer treats, to have a leisurely breakfast outdoors, with the birds singing and the smell of flowers floating on the breeze. I had created a Martha Stewart ambience with table linens and fresh flowers. The moment would have been picture-perfect, had it not been for my compulsively subversive neighbor deciding to seize the moment to mow his lawn. Hadn't he just mowed it three days ago?

Alex was just under six months pregnant, but barely showing under her jogging suit. I felt like a proud parent, as she shoveled down pancakes, sausages and fruit. She was over the nausea and had started eating normally again. But Dave was back in her life. He had started coming around the previous month, paying "friendly" visits and offering to do work like replacing her gutters and repairing the broken fence. Like a smart woman, she let him. Those things needed to get done. But then he'd started wanting dinner and heart-to-heart conversations. He wanted to be friends again, he said. He missed her, he said. He did not confess to being a jackass for leaving her, though. He had either broken it off with his girlfriend or she'd dumped him. But he was alone again and re-evaluating his life. They always came back after they realized they'd made a mistake. But for Alex, it was too late.

At first, he would kiss her hello and good-bye on the cheek. Then he attempted the intimate kiss, hoping, no doubt, that it would put her under some kind of spell. Even that was okay with her. Then he moved on to touching and fondling and Alex shoved him away. When she announced that she was pregnant, Nice Dave disappeared and Nasty Dave resurfaced. Anger and indignation consumed him as he shouted obscenities at her. Naturally, he assumed her pregnancy was the result of a passionate love affair, and she did not correct him.

"Did he think you were going to wait for him to have his fling and come back?" I asked.

The noise of the lawnmower died down and my peaceful breakfast was back on track.

Alex shook her head in bewilderment. "I tried to be nice, friendly. I started thinking, we *did* spend fourteen years together. We should be friends."

"I think most men take friendliness for foreplay. You can't be nice," I said.

"What can you be? If you're nice, it's foreplay. If you're mean, you're a bitch." She took a bite of pineapple smothered in maple syrup. "And you know what else? I'm really angry with his mother. After fourteen years and all I did for her, she has never once called me since Dave and I separated. Wouldn't you at least give your daughter-in-law a call and say something comforting? He's the one who wanted the divorce, not me. At least, I got my gutters replaced." She shook her head in disgust. "I hear from a few people that he has been asking around about who I'm dating. He's trying to find his rival."

"What about that guy you had lunch with? What was his name? Burt?"

"Bart, Bartholomew Christopoulos," she corrected, rolling his name off her tongue as if she had practiced it to perfection. She shook her head. "We're just friends."

"Does he know that?"

Dismissively, she replied, "Of course."

"Does he know you're pregnant?"

She shook her head. "That's why we're just friends." Alex studied my hair. "You're definitely a blonde."

I was back to boring blonde again. The lush auburn color I

loved kept fading and was too hard to maintain. So I had recently gone back to being the California blonde that Ryan loved.

"So this Bart...you're like what, lunch buddies?" I asked. I was sure there was more than she was letting on. He was a lawyer for the health insurance company where she worked.

"Something like that," she said evasively.

"Does he have kids? What's the dish?"

"Divorced, no kids. His wife wanted a career, not a family. And what's the point? Like I said, we're just friends. He won't be interested anymore when he finds out I'm pregnant."

"I'm not convinced that men and women can be just friends. If he's having lunch with you every day, he probably likes you."

"It's not every day," she said, looking embarrassed. "So how's the adoption coming along?" she asked, segueing from a subject of angst for her to one of angst for me.

The truth was, I had been having a difficult time keeping up with the paper trail of documents I needed to file. Working and making myself available to Jake had left me with little time to make the necessary phone calls and appointments. I did have one item to complete that I could soon take off my list. We needed a referral from Dr. Snyder. If I had not been seeing him, we would have had to consult someone else to vouch for our psychological health and pronounce us suitable adoptive parents. Again, the fears crept in. We already *were* parents. So if they found me unstable, would they take Jake away? Lately, due to lack of time, I had been seeing Dr. Snyder only once a month. Like my students, I was counting down the days to the end of the school year. Maybe, with some blessed time off, I would be able to refocus my energy on the adoption.

Then there was the money dilemma. Ryan had completed the refinancing of our home and received $19,000. But after paying off the Visa card charges and other smaller bills like major car repairs, we were down to $10,000. Going against everything he believed about savings and retirement planning, Ryan had cashed-in an IRA for another $10,000 dollars with a hefty penalty attached to it.

"So, we're still five thousand short," I explained to Alex, feeling somewhat crushed. "It just never ends. We also got hit with income taxes this year for the first time ever. The two thousand I had saved from my job went to pay Uncle Sam. From the financial point of view, my job really was not worth it."

"Can't you make payments for the adoption?"

"No, it all has to be paid in full before they send the paperwork overseas to be matched with a child."

"Then how long do you need to wait after there's a match?" Finally, she was full and pushed her plate aside.

"Four to eight months. I guess I'll have to go back to pilfering grocery money again, when my job ends this summer."

"Why do you have to swindle money like that? Doesn't Ryan provide you with spending money?"

"Sure, but he lowballs me. Things are a lot tighter on one income. It's easier for me to work around him than to have arguments over it. I hate the confrontation."

Especially, since money was the number one cause of marital strife.

Alex shook her head in disbelief. "I am so thankful that I don't have to live like that anymore. Whatever I make is all mine. No one questions me about how I spend money."

"It works for us," I told her. "Why rock the boat if you don't have to? And I have a new twist to add to my old laundering plan. The grocery stores now sell all kinds of gift cards to other stores. They have everything. So I figure I'll just buy myself a gift card each time I shop. Then, when I need new towels or something, I'll whip out my cards!"

She snickered at me. "So what's your story, when he asks where the new sheets came from?"

"I'll just say they were a gift from a friend. Favors repaid."

Two long weeks later, the completed home-study report I had been anxiously awaiting arrived from Jeanie. Other than an unfavorable FBI background check, this was the only document that could deny us the privilege of adopting. But Jeanie, God bless her, saw past the nervous tension, the toilet overflow and the verbal outburst by Ryan. In her report, she wrote:

"I found the Learys to be a close, affectionate and devoted couple who share a mature and fulfilling relationship. They are very supportive of one another and treat each other with respect. They enjoy parenting their son, Jake, and look forward to the opportunity of raising another child. I am confident that they will provide an adopted child with a loving home. I recommend the Learys for the placement of a healthy Korean child, zero to three months at the time of referral."

It was funny how other people perceived you differently from the way you did yourself. Yes, we were some of those things that she mentioned. But we were so much more—both good and bad. I was terrified that Jeanie would see through the polished surface and report on our dark side. Thank you, Jeanie! We had been accepted! To be approved was the greatest compliment we could have received. I should have been jumping for joy. But the placement process would not begin until we coughed up $5,000 more.

Okay, God. It took me a while, but I got your message that we should adopt. But what now? We couldn't do it if we could not afford it. We couldn't rack up more credit and not be able to pay it back. What was I missing? What else could we sell? What stone had I left unturned? I needed a long walk to think things out. Walking was the only exercise I could tolerate. I was not an indoor machine junkie. I needed fresh air and scenery. As I walked through the streets of my neighborhood, past homes that were centuries old, I thought of what life must have been like say, 300 years ago. The Brody house which had once served as an emergency hospital during the Revolutionary War was in the midst of repairs. The Deveraux house on Bellevue Avenue was being turned into a bed-and-breakfast. The Middleton house further down Bellevue was rumored to be haunted, although several families had owned it in succession and hadn't fled screaming into the night. And then there was the travel agency that was haunted by James Watson, one of the original owners of the town. The travel building had been a bank a hundred years ago. The current residents claimed that Mr. Watson's ghost had set off the alarm system by pacing back and forth to the vault or, at least, to the spot where the vault used to be. It was impossible not to feel a rich presence of past souls in this town and wonder what trials they had suffered. Certainly, the lack of money had been a cross to bear for all people at one time or another in life.

As I was strolling down Green Street on the final leg of my route, I was mentally planning Monday's class lesson for *Of Mice and Men* which, ironically, was partly about the struggle for money to fulfill a dream. All the characters had deferred dreams like me. It was probably not the best piece of literature for me to be reading right now, but I had to follow the curriculum. Poor Lenny. I became mournful each time I read the novel and had to deal with his euthanasia. My students laughed at me when I had trouble holding back the tears while reading the scene of Lenny's demise. Society had come a long way in the understanding and treatment of mentally-challenged people.

Something was floating on the breeze, bringing me out of my trance. The further I walked, the more it seemed to angle directly toward me. It was a piece of paper. Then suddenly, it fell right at my feet. It was money—a five-dollar bill! How cool was that! That didn't happen every day! I had found dollars and coins before, but never as much as a five-dollar bill! I stuffed it in my pocket and continued on my way home.

When I got back, I showed it to Jake. "Look what I found on my walk."

"Cool. Can I have it?" he asked, wide-eyed.

I gave him the money grudgingly, because I knew it would only be spent on dollar store junk. I had promised him earlier that I would give him some cash for helping me spread the mulch on the flowerbeds. That was exactly how easily money flowed through my hands. It was not mine for five minutes. I just got to decide who would receive it next.

CHAPTER TWENTY-THREE

As we were scrambling to fulfill the requirements from the home-study checklist, we were also scheduled for our certifying visit with Dr. Snyder. Ryan did not immediately feel comfortable. Despite my assurances, my husband was convinced that I roasted him every time I went to therapy. I insisted that I had plenty of unresolved problems in my life besides him. He was not my only pain in the ass.

"So, as you know, this meeting is to clarify some concerns that you may have regarding your desire to adopt. And well, Julia, we do need to assess where you are emotionally with your grief over your infertility."

Ugh. No. I really did not need to talk about that today, as I sat there bleeding to death. Ever since I had gone off the drugs, my periods had been excruciatingly painful. The cramps were not normal; they were frigging labor pains! I swore I was about to give birth, any minute, to a tumor. All I wanted to do was lie down with a heating pad pressed against me. Over-the-counter painkillers barely touched the pain. And not to be so gross, but chunks of tissue were falling out of me and plopping into the toilet like dead fish. I could not get through the night without at least two "diaper" changes. I was seriously considering buying myself some Depends, because that would be the only sure way to save our mattress from period desolation.

Despite my looking forward to the joys of adoption, I became dismally weepy when I found myself in this disgusting physical condition. And I still grieved, though not quite so intensely, over not being able to bear a child. Every month, I was reminded of what my body refused to do for me. It wouldn't allow me to become pregnant. Yet, the curse of my period visited me faithfully. Alex said I had crossed a threshold, partly due to age, and my period might never be the same again. This was not mentioned in any of the middle-school literature. There were no references that some women might have difficulties in conceiving or that their period would go through changes in consistency. If anything, I had naively thought the flow would diminish with age.

In Dr. Snyder's office, I started bawling. "Look, today is not the best day to talk about grief." I explained how wretched I became with my period. Every emotion was raw and magnified. "If you try to take me down that road, you won't get an accurate response. This isn't how I am every day."

Thankfully, he understood, or seemed to, as he rocked back in his chair, considering my plea. Due to limited space in his office, Dr. Snyder was seated behind his desk, leaving us the comfortable chairs. "Let's move on, then," he suggested. "So when you have conflicts in your marriage, how do you deal with them? Do you verbalize your feelings to each other?"

"I can assure you that communication has never been a problem," answered Ryan proudly, as if he'd just correctly answered a trivia question.

"In what way?"

"Well, we are both very verbal people. We have always talked things over."

"Or, yelled," I added. I could not let Ryan make a fool of himself by painting too rosy a picture. "We get things out, one way or another, but it comes out."

I was not about to shatter the good doctor's image of me by recounting the food fights Ryan and I used to have in the early days of our marriage. Once I had spent all day preparing a potato and beef casserole, a twist on Shepherd's Pie, but forgot to pre-cook the potatoes. Ryan had started to needle me with his facetious comments. "Kinda crunchy, don't you think, Jule?" he had said. "I almost broke a tooth...Is this some kind of family recipe, handed down from one generation to the next?"

I had grabbed a handful of casserole off my plate and thrown it, smacking him square in the face. I'd been the butt of his jokes over that past week and could no longer control my temper. And I might have been on my period. As I was storming off, a loaf of bread collided with the back of my head. Then it was open war. We had thrown other less messy food items before, but the casserole was to be the last. Later, Ryan had refused to help clean up the food stains from the walls and I had decided that fighting wasn't worth it, if *I* was the one who had to do the cleaning up.

Dr. Snyder wrote something on his notepad. I wished he would go to the restroom so I could sneak a peek at my chart. But he guarded it like it held the formula for Cold Fusion. "Ryan," he said, "describe your marriage for me in one word."

"Solid."

This, coming from the man who felt threatened by my spending time with my friends!

"Explain, please."

"It's just that we have been through a lot of heavy crap and we're still here. We're both committed to the marriage and divorce is not an option for either of us." Ryan looked at me and took my hand. "She'll always be my...girl."

How was I to follow that comment? I did not deserve him. I felt like a turd when he said things like that and I did not respond in kind with something equally loving like those cheesy quotes pinched from greeting cards.

"Julia, describe your marriage in one word and explain why."

"One word is too hard. I guess I'd say...accepting." I was grasping for straws. "We know we both have faults, but we accept each other's shortcomings." What bullshit! Other more appropriate adjectives came to mind like, enduring, trying, imbalanced and under-funded! But maybe, I was just feeling negative right then because of my decaying uterus. Or because Ryan had polished off the last of my Mt. Dew that morning, when I desperately needed a kick and had saved it for myself. I'd even taken care to hide it behind the apple juice. "Let's be realistic," I went on. "We have a marriage.

It's no better and no worse than other people have. There are ups and downs. But we are still together and I do not doubt that we will remain together, no matter what comes along. This interrogation from you and from the agency...it's like both of you are looking for some neatly-packaged description of us."

He reflected on that for a moment and jotted something on his notepad. "Let's talk about finances, since most of the troubles in a marriage involve money."

"You mean the lack of money. That's the problem," I said.

"Well, you're right. So how do the two of you approach each other, when it comes to money struggles?"

Ryan took the lead. "Well, we used to have some pretty heated arguments over Julia's frivolous spending. She always overshot our budget. But she has been doing a great job lately." He bestowed upon me a look of pride which I felt I did not deserve. "I mean, she did work last year and so we had some extra cash. But before that, she was on her way to a twelve-step program for spend-a-holics. Even now that we're reduced to making do with one income again, she spends within limits."

If the way my feelings of guilt surfaced and spread across my features was any indicator, I could have been hanged! I could not even look at Ryan for fear that my whole money scheme would be revealed by the expression on my face! Hiding deep in my purse were two gift cards, one good for purchases at Gap, the other at the Linen Store. Both acquired from the grocery budget. Hadn't my husband noticed that we were eating more potatoes and pasta lately?

"Julia, do you agree?"

"Huh?" Now would be a good time to confess, *girlfriend*. "Oh, yeah...I had some issues with unnecessary spending, but I'm cured now," I lied outright. Oh, I had to stop this! It was getting out of control.

Dr. Snyder scribbled more notes. He probably saw through the thinly-veiled lie I had spouted and had written that we completely worked around each other instead of with each other.

"Okay, moving on. Adoption. Give me one word that describes it for you and why. Julia?"

"Exciting. Because I'm really looking forward to having a baby around again. I always felt that my parenting skills would be wasted, if I couldn't raise another child. I feel I have so much more love to give, and this will be my chance. I'm looking forward to the whole experience, especially with Jake. He too, is really excited."

Ryan nodded his blonde head in agreement. He needed a haircut, but always let his hair grow unruly in the summer. "Hopeful," he said. "I hope it takes away some of the pain we have felt in the past several years. I think it will be good for all of us. It's exciting."

"Do you have any anxiety over the racial difference?"

Ryan shook his head.

"I don't care if she's green," I said. "It's about loving and nurturing another child. It's like people keep expecting us to have racial anxieties. But I don't. I have to live my life and deal with the issues as they come."

I could not worry about racial problems that might never arise. And I was secure enough to put people in their place, should an insensitive comment be made.

"I agree with Julia. Our adopted dog is ugly as hell and we love him like he's our child."

Dr. Snyder smiled at Ryan's analogy.

Then Ryan added, "The only anxiety I feel is in telling my parents."

This had been an issue for us. We had initially decided not to tell his family until a match was made. That way, we could give them more definite information instead of being plagued for months by their questions to which we would have no specific answers. By this time, however, it seemed that everyone, except Ryan's family, knew about the intended adoption. There was also the apprehension that the people who mattered most to us might not accept our decision.

By the end of our session with Dr. Snyder, we agreed that our anxiety could be put to rest, if we conveyed the news to Ryan's parents now, rather than keep it for later. I already knew how my father would react. He would be happy for us and graciously supportive. My brother, an Air Force lieutenant stationed in Florida, would be completely unaffected. He had always been something of an absent brother and not much of an uncle to Jake. He was immersed in his own life and flying jets was his personal heaven. But we did owe it to Ryan's parents to inform them about the impending adoption, especially, since they lived locally and could accidentally come to know of it from one of our many friends in the area.

We were on our way to their house for a quick visit when my cell phone rang.

"It's Alex. Where are you?" She was calling from work on a Tuesday in late June.

"Just leaving my shrink's office. What's up?"

"Something's odd about Bart."

"Bart? You mean your lunch buddy, Bart?" I asked, a trifle sardonically, because I was so sure that Greek Bart was more than just a friend.

"He's been distant for the past month. When he's around the office, he just isn't himself. When I asked him what was wrong, he said he was just busy. Julia, it felt very odd. I think Dave got to him."

"How do you mean? Could it be the fact that you're pregnant? Maybe, it makes him uncomfortable."

"He's okay with that, I've told you already. We still talk from time to time. It's something else. I've heard from a few sources that Dave has been asking around here. He's threatened my lawn-care guy, my dentist and my contractor. They all happen to be single. He's gone crazy."

Bart might have said he had no problems with his "friend" being pregnant, but I was sure the situation could still make a man feel awkward. He probably needed some time to absorb it all. What's more, she was still closely guarding the truth about how she'd gotten pregnant, and I could understand that. Somewhere in her sixth month now, she could no longer hide her pregnancy from Bart or her co-workers. Her belly seemed to have exploded overnight. She was huge now.

"Why don't you just tell him the truth?" I suggested.

"Who? Dave or Bart?"

"Well, both. Come clean. You're letting them both think there is someone else."

I was not able to speak freely, because Ryan was sitting next to me, overhearing my side of the conversation. I did not want it to appear that I was withholding information from my husband, but this was Alex's business. Ryan's rapport with Dave was not as much of a threat anymore as it might have been once, for their friendship had slowed. I suspected Dave felt awkward keeping up, knowing that I spent so much time with Alex. I did, however, learn from Ryan that whenever Dave spoke of Alex, he always referred to her as "my wife", not "my ex-wife". It seemed a bit possessive, given that they were legally divorced.

We pulled into my in-laws' driveway and took a deep breath in anticipation of the announcement that was about to be made.

"Look," I said to Alex over the phone, "you're going to have to force a talk with your lunch buddy and see what's going on. I'm at my in-laws' now. I'll call you later."

Since my in-laws did not approve of unannounced visits, we made sure to call ahead. I could not speak. I left this one to Ryan. It was his territory, after all. We sat in Lois's nauseatingly pink living room. I mean *everything* but the lamps and wooden tables were pink. I sat there like a coward, waiting for Ryan to start.

He cleared his throat and said, "Well, we...uh...we felt that we...uh, needed to tell you both that we are planning to...uh... adopt a child."

Even though I was not the one speaking, I expelled a long sigh of relief.

"That's wonderful, honey," said Lois graciously. "But we already knew this was coming."

I cocked my head curiously. "How?" I asked.

"Well, Jake spilled the beans months ago. He's very excited about getting a brother."

Jake. I had forgotten about our little spy. Of course, Jake! There were no secrets with a child in the house. "Did he tell you that it would be an overseas adoption? Maybe, Korean?"

"No, he didn't. Why overseas?" There was a pause and a look on Lois's face that was hard to read. George just nodded his head.

"Because at this point, a domestic adoption for a baby could take three to five years. Going overseas will enable us to do it in less than a year and, in a way, more securely," answered Ryan.

"Do you have an agency in mind?" asked George, very businesslike.

"Yes, Dad, we're way beyond that," explained Ryan.

"Have you checked their credentials, their records...?"

"Yes, Dad. It's all taken care of."

"How about a lawyer? You'll need a good lawyer. I know someone..."

"Dad, it's done. The agency provides the lawyer."

Each time I sat in that pink shrine, I could not help redecorating it in my head. It was a little mental pastime of mine. Not that I had interior-design credentials, but at least, I understood the rule of three colors, and I would never place family photos on a wall, like Lois. In my head, I had redone Lois's pink paradise in almost every shade on the palette. I started by mentally gutting the entire room. I imagined all of her precious belongings piled high in a huge dumpster on the front lawn. Next, I let the original hardwood floor see daylight again. Then I went to work, mentally selecting the best pieces from Thomasville or Lane, keeping it simple.

"We know several people with Asian kids, don't we, Lois?" said George.

Of course, you do.

Here it came, the unsolicited information. "Just last year, the Sussmans's daughter and son-in-law adopted a Chinese baby." We had no idea who the Sussmans were. George always referred to people as if we should know them.

"I should call them and have you two meet. I hear that Asian adoptions are becoming quite popular among Americans," continued the local gazette. "Maybe..."

"Uh, Dad. So that's that. We just wanted you to know. We really need to get going." Ryan stood up first. I followed, thankful that he had put a halt to his father's stream of comments on adoption. "Got to pick up Jake from his friend's house."

It had not been as bad as I had envisioned it, but then, most things paled in comparison to what my hyperbolic imagination conjured up. I knew that my in-laws meant well, but for our own sanity, we had to maintain an emotional distance. Not having them overly involved in our lives was, so far, the only way we had figured out to accomplish it. Sometime back, I had almost buckled and suggested that Ryan should ask them for a loan, or better yet, a gift. So many times, I had wanted to ask my own father. He would have willingly lent us the money, except that I was sure he did not have much to live on himself. My mother took half of his retirement pension as part of the divorce settlement. It was easier to sell off our retirement funds than to ask either of our parents for money. There was an intrinsic drive to succeed on our own, to be self-sufficient. They had had their hard times. This was ours. We could make up our financial losses when I returned to work some day.

CHAPTER TWENTY-FOUR

Hello?" I answered weakly, fighting back tears. I was still in bed at 10 a.m., watching the continuous CNN news. "It's Alex. What's wrong?"

"Haven't you heard?"

"Heard what? Are you okay?"

"He's dead!" I sobbed.

Alex drew in a deep breath. "Oh my God! What happened?"

I started to speak, and then choked. It was all so unbearable. "A plane crash off Cape Hatteras. He's gone!" I wailed. "I was going to marry him!"

"Wait. Who are we talking about?"

"John Riley, the actor. Who did you think?"

Alex made a noise indicating relief. "Jesus, Julia! You almost induced labor! I thought you were talking about Ryan."

"It's awful. Horrific. I can't stand it. His mother did not want him to fly. She knew it wasn't safe. But did he listen? No. Turn on CNN."

"Did you know him?"

"We went to high school together. I had been in love with him since ninth grade."

In a high school of 2,000 students, John Riley hadn't known that I existed. He had been two years older than me and one of the few people voted most likely to be famous who had actually fulfilled that promise. As the macho action hero, he had steadily risen to stardom in the last five years. By all accounts, he had apparently remained an ordinary guy. Or, at least, as much of one as a man could be with extraordinary fame, ungodly wealth and a perfect physique.

"And you were going to marry him?" asked Alex.

"It was my fantasy, yes." Mine and thousands of other American girls who had witnessed his evolution through the eyes of the media. He had lived mainly in New York City. Each time I was in the city, I would carefully scrutinize every hunky male on the streets, hoping to spot him and finally get up the nerve to announce that I existed. The older he got, the better-looking he became. As much as I despised the way the paparazzi stalked him, I relished the occasional updates on his life. Now it was all over. No more news flashes, no more private photos for the world to drool over. Now he was just another promising life cut short.

"Well, I think I have something to cheer you up. Can you come over?"

"Now?"

I did not think that I could tear myself away from CNN.

"Turn off that damn TV and come over here," she ordered.

"But...but..." It somehow felt disloyal not to remain in front of the television to absorb every grim detail.

"Julia, get a grip. It will be on the news for the next month. You won't miss a thing."

Jeez, she sounded like a drill sergeant.

It took some effort to drag my butt out of bed and tear myself away from the news coverage. Alex was right. The story would swamp the news channels for the next month, at least. Jake did not need me right now. He and Ryan were challenging each other on the Play Station. The only other goal I set for myself that day was to finally plant some impatiens and marigolds in the flowerbeds. Then we would be off to the pool. Such was the beauty of summer for those in the teaching profession, although we were technically unemployed in the summer.

"So what's so urgent?" I asked Alex when I got there.

She gave me a calculating look. "Sit down. I have a surprise for you." I sat at her kitchen counter island and she handed me a cup of tea. Her belly was full and round. She was one of those pregnant women who carried it all in front. She handed me an envelope, beaming in delight over her big surprise. "Open it. Go on."

I tore open the plain white envelope to reveal a check for $3,000 made out to me from her. "What's this?"

"Well, do you remember the plumber mailbox? You won't believe this. But I sold it on eBay!" she squealed. "It was just a silly idea I had. I saw it sitting in my garage and I thought I'd give it a try. Of course, I only expected to get, maybe, two hundred at the most. I couldn't believe it. People actually collect junk like that."

I was overwhelmed and started to choke. "Alex, I can't accept this. You'll need it for the baby. You could put this in a college fund."

She waved me off. "I'll be fine. Insurance will cover everything. This wasn't money I worked for. It was just some object that I was lucky to sell. I want you to have it for your adoption, so you can start the matching process."

By her effervescent smile, I saw she was serious. We had $2,000 saved from my last few paychecks. This was it. This was what had been holding us back. With this money, come Monday morning, we would be officially in the program. Tears spilled over and streamed down my face. Between accepting this gesture of love and digesting John Riley's death, I was one blubbering mess. I swallowed enough air to squeak, "You're the best friend I ever had."

We decided a girl's-night-out celebration was in order and long overdue. Ryan could not exactly argue about it after receiving such a generous gift from Alex. But I had to promise to be home by at least midnight. He claimed that he worried too much about all the drunken fools on the road. I responded with, "How much trouble can we get into? Alex is pregnant, so she'll be the designated driver. Lauren is too worried about water retention to drink too much. And my body won't tolerate anything more than a few glasses of wine. That leaves Ally to be the drunken lush of the night."

"Okay, it's not you girls I'm worried about. It's those slobbering divorced old men who prey on good-looking women like you." He sauntered in close and grabbed me by the waist to pull me toward him. "Besides, if you come home any later than 12:00 a.m., I'll be too tired to take advantage of you," he said softly, kissing my neck.

"Okay, twelve. I promise."

At nine o'clock on a Saturday night, the four of us gathered in a corner booth at Bongos. It had been ages since I had frequented a meat market hangout that was designed to hook up single twenty-somethings. We were quite a group of mixed hair colors. No one could have mistaken us for sisters, with Lauren, the bouncy redhead, Alex, the coifed brunette, Ally, the Calico cat, and me, the California blonde.

"Who chose this place?" asked Ally, scanning the crowd.

"I did," volunteered Lauren proudly. "This band is becoming pretty popular in the area." The band, Sugarloaf, was playing "Mustang Sally". I found myself swaying to the rhythm.

The very sexy young waiter came back with our drinks, two rum and cokes, a Chardonnay for me and a club soda with lime for Alex. With absolutely no sense of shame, Lauren gave him the most obvious eye-contact flirtation.

"Watch out for her tonight," I whispered to Alex.

We ordered two combo platters of chicken fingers, bacon-wrapped scallops, fried shrimp, crab-stuffed mushrooms and stuffed potato skins.

Alex raised her glass of club soda and said, "To Julia, and your pending adoption. I hope it all goes well."

I responded with, "To you and your pending labor. I hope it goes well."

"I'm planning on a C-section," interjected Alex.

To Lauren, I said, "To you and your next sale."

Lauren said, "To Ally and her next hair color. May it, hopefully, be something monochromatic."

Ally made a face and, in her own defense, said, "I'm not afraid to try new things."

We clinked glasses and Ally said to me, "So are you requesting a boy or a girl?"

"I was hoping for a girl. I had this weird vision thing about a girl." I recounted the experience I'd had while shelving books. "Ryan sort of has his heart wrapped around having a little girl now."

"It's so great that you're doing this, Julia," said Ally. "Adoption is a wonderful thing to do. Even if you gave birth to a biological child, it wouldn't look like you, anyway."

Sometimes, Ally did not clearly articulate her meaning. Sometimes, she drank too much. I was thinking that, maybe, she had started throwing down drinks before we began.

There was an uncomfortable silence, while the three of us threw a please-explain-yourself look toward Ally. I was concerned that Alex and Lauren would find Ally's comment disturbing, since Lauren had two adopted kids and Alex's baby was coming from a sperm donor.

"It's just that on the Discovery Channel, there was this episode about natural paternity," Ally said. "It said that before blood and DNA testing, nature has always had a way of assuring the man of his paternity."

"How's that?" asked Alex.

"It's in the physical likeness that is apparent in the nose, the forehead and the shape of the eyes. Scientists think it plays more of a role than trait dominance. Look at my three boys. Who do they mostly look like?"

"Your husband, for sure," I said. It was true, they did not resemble Ally in the least, but they definitely had her personality and mannerisms. "Jake looks mostly like Ryan, but he has my eye color. You're right, though. His eyes and eyebrows are the same shape as Ryan's."

Ally continued, "It's meant to instill confidence and acceptance in the caveman mentality so that he sticks around and provides for the child."

Lauren chimed in with her observation, "But I've seen plenty of children who look like their mothers. I look almost exactly like my mother."

"That happens later on in life. In the beginning, the baby bears a strong resemblance to the father. Check out your baby photos sometime. How often have you heard grandparents say, 'He looks just like you when you were little?'"

"Well, that's just great, Ally," said Lauren sarcastically. "Thank you for the enlightening information. You do realize that with the exception of Jake, the three of us are never going to know the biological father in order to make that comparison?"

Ally turned red. "It was just some interesting show about natural human connections, that's all. My point is that for women, children don't have to look like us to be ours. The cavewoman in us allows us to be able to love and nurture any child. So you see, we are superior, yet again."

Except that some men like my husband who had evolved, could easily love a child he hadn't fathered. In a roundabout way, this was Ally's way of asserting how the female of the species was superior to the male. We'd had many conversations during which she had educated me on the Druid matriarchal societies that supposedly once existed. I had even attended a slide-show presentation at the Franklin Institute with Ally, where we learned that in these societies, men used to be slaves to women, but eventually rebelled and took over the reins of power. The centuries of misogyny that followed were meant to ensure that women never rose to supremacy again. Since the suffragette movement, women were slowly, but surely regaining power, which, ostensibly, intimidated men.

We were on our second round of drinks and tearing through our food, when Lauren asked, "Does he look the type that would go for an older woman?"

She was staring at our waiter. From across the room, they made eye contact and Lauren smiled. She made flirting look so easy. Or, perhaps, I had just forgotten how to do it after my years with Ryan.

"Does any man ever turn down sex?" asked Alex.

I put on a thoughtful face and said, "I don't think so."

"Very rarely," said Ally. "Only under extreme circumstances."

I chuckled. "Yeah, it's probably another one of those female superiority things, right, Ally? We can easily choose sleep over sex, but men struggle with it."

Alex offered her very clinical viewpoint. "It's because all the blood drains from their brain to the other head, and they can't think rationally until the deed is done."

This was precisely the reason why Ryan was intimidated by my time out with girlfriends. He was sure that we had male-bashing conversations like this one. And, invariably, we did. Of course, I always lied and said, "Nah, we have so much more to talk about than you lazy, good-for-nothing men."

But did we really? I turned to Alex and said, "Help! Change the subject. How's Burt?"

"Bart," she corrected.

"Bart, right. So is lunch back on?"

"Yes, but now I can't sleep at night."

"Heartburn bothering you again?"

"No, I can't stop thinking about sex—with Bart. And when I do sleep, I dream about sex—with him."

My eyes widened and I pointed an accusatory finger at her. "I thought you were just friends?"

"Well, officially, we are. But I'm still hot for him. Not that it will ever happen with us, with me all fat and pregnant. It's probably just pregnancy hormones, right?"

"Right. But is the sex you're having in your dreams, at least, good?"

Alex smiled mischievously. She was so clearly in love with this guy. Meanwhile, Dave was still lurking around in the shadows.

"Have you told Bart about, you know, No. Twenty-three?" I whispered, so that Ally and Lauren could not hear over the music.

"No, I can't. I just said it was a relationship that did not work out and it was definitely not my ex-husband." Alex gave me a stern look. "That's the story I'm sticking to, all right? It's what my mother also believes. It's for my privacy and the baby's in the future. I don't need people making hurtful comments."

"I understand completely. I wish I could raise my child without the whole world knowing that she or he was adopted. But since the child will be Asian, it's going to be pretty obvious, isn't it? Why would anyone need to know the private details?"

The general public did not look at Lauren's children and see the adoption tag on them. Only family and intimate friends knew the story. It's not that she was not proud of her children. They were *her* children. But she did not have to go through life, explaining to people why she had adopted or deal with the term's negative connotations. She did not want others to refer to them as "your adopted son and daughter".

"People have a voyeuristic nature. Take Dave, for example. He's just going crazy trying to figure out what's going on in my life. He should be paying attention to his own."

Dave, the ex-husband who wouldn't go away. One evening, he'd staked out the parking lot outside Alex's workplace. Having watched her leave with Bart on several occasions, he'd decided to mark his territory. Whatever Bart said to Dave that evening must have deflated him somewhat, but he still popped up every now and then.

"What do you think he could have said to Dave?"

"I don't know. Bart is pretty smooth with angry people. He knows how to get them to back down. It's a gift."

"Have you ever seen each other besides lunch?"

"Once, we had dinner. It was nice. No big deal."

"Why are you in denial?" I accused.

"What? What do you mean?"

"You obviously like him a lot. It's all over your face. You even have love dust in your eyes. You need to have that talk."

Alex drew in a deep breath. "I just can't. If I weren't pregnant, it might be different. I don't feel sexy. I don't feel like I could attract a man, you know."

I did know. It was hard to believe yourself to be sexy when you felt like a gestating cow.

"Well, okay. Maybe, if you keep the friendship going, you'll have something later on. I guess you can't force it. But you would be surprised. Some men find pregnant women very alluring."

Ally caught the tail end of this conversation and interjected, "Only because they feel so primitively proud of seeing their own seed blossom."

"That and the swollen boobs!" said Lauren.

The band kicked up again, this time, with a sultry female vocalist singing blues-rock classics like "Slip Away" and "The Dark End of the Street". I couldn't sit in my chair any longer, wiggling to the music. I needed to dance. Lauren and I weaved our way through the crowd and found a small spot for ourselves to shake and shimmy. Our waiter passed by and Lauren jiggled her assets in front of him, embarrassing both him and me. Ally had ordered a pitcher of Long Island iced tea and, against my better judgment about mixing alcohol, I had one. I was free of my dancing-in-public inhibitions. I was lost in comforting feelings of a positive future. I couldn't wait until Monday, to call Jeanie, our social worker and fork over the remaining $5,000.

With my eyes closed, I was sashaying my hips to "I Can't Stand the Rain", lost in lovely thoughts, when I felt someone touch me. Slowly, I opened my eyes, expecting it to be either Ally or Lauren brushing against me. Oh God! It was Greg Magatz, aka Maggots, aka the Eddington pharmacist! He looked a little less hefty, but it was unmistakably him, dancing next to me with a smug smile on his face.

I stopped. "Greg. Wh-what are you doing here?"

When I observed him more clearly, I noticed that he had definitely lost some weight, maybe, thirty pounds or so.

"Dancing with you, babe," he replied, shaking his still sizeable girth in front of me.

Gross. It was just gross. "Excuse me," I said, starting to walk away.

He grabbed my hands. "Come on, Julia! Dance with me like you used to."

I swiftly jerked my hands out of his grasp. "I'm here with friends," I told him, "and we," I pointed from me to him, "...are in the past." Something about him touching me made me cringe with disgust. I could not believe I had once wasted time dating this person. "I don't know you anymore."

Greg put a hand over his heart, as if my words had stung. "You're killing me," he said. "Just one dance, come on."

"I'm here with my girlfriends."

"So I see. Where's your husband tonight?" he asked cockily, as if he had something over me.

I put my hands on my hips. "He's home."

"So, what happened?" Greg reached around my waist with one arm and pulled me toward him again in a threatening hold. My heart skipped a beat, *not* in a surge of lust, but of panic. "Did the fertility thing not work out and now you're out looking for a replacement? Is Ryan shooting blanks?"

In my code of ethics, he had broken a cardinal rule of trust and confidentiality by making such a statement, based on his awareness as my pharmacist of the type of medication I was taking. Wasn't there some law prohibiting this? If not, there should have been.

I had to defend my husband's honor. The self-defense training I had taken when I was younger seemed appropriate right now. Purely on reflex, my knee collided with his crotch forcing him to release the tight grip he had on my waist and drop to the floor.

"Just so you know, you never had a chance with me," I snarled at him. "And my husband's sperm could get you pregnant, you wimp!" I stormed off, leaving him cupping his package in a crowd of gawkers.

"Oh my lord, Julia!" shouted Ally back at our table. "I'm taking you out more often! You were awesome!"

I drained another Long Island iced tea to calm my tingling nerves. "What's in this stuff, anyway?" I muttered. It went down smoothly. There couldn't be very much alcohol in the tea drinks, if I could chug one so effortlessly.

"Are you okay?" asked Alex. "What was that about?"

"You're not the only one with a guy from the past lurking around. Some jerk I used to date," I explained, as I watched Greg stagger out of Bongos. At least, he'd had enough sense to leave. "He insulted my husband's sperm quality. But it's not going to ruin my night with my best girls. We're here to celebrate. Let's do it!" Dancing and kicking a guy in the crotch had worked up quite a thirst. The idea, however, that I had actually hurt Greg physically made me feel a bit guilty. "Maybe, I overreacted," I conceded.

"Aggressive men require aggressive action," chimed Ally.

"I did not get to witness the whole thing, actually, but it kicked up the evening a notch," said Alex.

"I might have to move away from you," teased Lauren. "After that scene, you're like, man-repellent."

I realized that although Lauren had come out with us, she might not be leaving with us.

CHAPTER TWENTY-FIVE

It was dreadfully bright in my bedroom the next morning. My arm was slung over my forehead shielding my eyes from the piercing light. My bladder was sure to burst, if I did not get up soon. I seriously considered peeing in bed and dealing with the consequences later. Oh, it was no use! I wrestled out of bed and felt my way to the bathroom, reluctant to open my eyes. The need to vomit tickled my esophagus. Even at my age, I had been dumb enough to succumb to peer pressure and drink as much as my friends.

After a long, hot shower to awaken and stimulate my senses, I went downstairs in my robe, following the scent of bacon frying in the kitchen.

"Good morning, sunshine!" shouted Ryan, a spatula in his hand. He was showered and dressed, advertising the fact that he was the superior morning person.

"Gundmorgnging," I mumbled.

"Rough night, sweetie?" he asked with a broad smile on his face.

"A little. Why are you shouting?"

I poured a cup of tea, not caring if it had cream in it or not. Neither of us was a coffee drinker. We used our coffee pot to have tea brewed and waiting each morning.

"What time did you get in?" he asked casually, flipping a pancake.

"Twelve o'clock, like I said," I responded quickly. Then I had a flashback of entering the house the previous night, a little tipsy, with that damn grandfather clock bonging away. But it had only bonged twice. Fearing that Ryan would wake up and discover how late I was in coming home, I'd mimicked the bonging sound ten times to make it seem like twelve. I hadn't done too bad a job of it, actually. I must have been convincing, because my husband did not seem irritated at all this morning. Usually, he was very strict about me keeping my word. As I have repeatedly said, what he didn't know, wouldn't hurt him. The tea was soothing as it warmed my throat and cleared my head. Ahh...

"I think the grandfather clock is broken," Ryan announced.

I pondered over this before sticking my foot in my mouth. Had I done that? Had I actually sabotaged the clock the night before, as I had always threatened to do?

"Why?" I asked, puzzled.

"Because last night, it bonged rather strangely ten times and said, 'Oh, shit!' Then it giggled. Then it tripped over Jake's Tonka truck and farted."

Having said this, Ryan sloped backward, clutching his stomach with laughter, the spatula still in his hand. His face was beet red with delight.

"I'm glad you find it so amusing," I said, hanging my head in my hands.

"Thank you, Julia. Thank you so much!" he said, coming over to me.

"For what?"

"For reminding me why I love you so much. Life will never be boring with you, that's for sure!"

Then he hugged me tight and his chuckling made me laugh too. But it hurt too much to laugh. "So that's why you married me? I always thought it was my voluptuous bosoms."

"Well, that too," he said, cupping them. "You better rest up before tomorrow. We can't show up at the agency with your face all puffy and alcohol emanating from your pores." He was referring to our journey to Welcome House to make our final payment.

The memory of that five-dollar bill I had found came back to me. "Oh, wow, Ryan. The money...remember the five bucks I found on my walk? Only a few days later, Alex gave us this huge chunk of cash, and we were up to the five thousand we needed. It was a sign from God, don't you think? I bet God was sending me a message with that five-dollar bill. I mean, it just came from nowhere and floated right up to me."

How blind of me not to see it as such at the time! I now wished I had not given Jake the money. I should have framed it and hung it on the wall as a memento.

"Maybe. Could be. Maybe, we shouldn't worry so much about money anymore. It always seems to work out. We need to do something really nice for Alex."

The view from atop Bowman's Hill Tower was a spectacular canvas of color. We stopped on the way home from the agency to bestow upon Jake some Bucks County history. Ryan, Jake and I climbed the gazillion steps to the top of the stone lookout tower that was built in 1776 during the Revolutionary War. On a clear day, you could see all the way to Trenton, New Jersey, which was why the Patriot soldiers had erected it. They used the tower to keep watch over the Hessians on the other side of the Delaware River. We were 110 feet above ground level, and the breezy air over the treetops was clean and crisp.

"Look at that view, Jake," Ryan urged. "You're not so big and important when you stand up here. Makes you feel kinda small, eh?"

"I guess. Are we done, now?" asked Jake, clearly unimpressed by the awesome view. We lived in such a congested area, with houses packed in like sardines, that the sight of farmland and open space was soothing to the eye.

"Jake, this is important," Ryan admonished. "This is history. Your ancestors stood up here, keeping watch and fighting for this land. This tower was preserved and reconstructed to honor them. The least you can do is *look* at it."

To Jake it must have sounded like blah, blah, blah and more blah.

"Okay, can we go now? Aren't we going to the pool today?" Jake asked.

Ryan gave me a hopeless look. I shrugged in response. My only hope was that someday in the future, Jake would think back with fond memories of all the cool places his parents had taken him. More than likely, he would turn out like the preacher's son who hated church. Jake would, probably, never be interested in history, simply because his father was a history buff.

At the age of seven, Jake was about as impressed with Bowman's Tower as he was with the Liberty Bell. On that trip, his thoughts were clearly visible on his puzzled face. Big deal. What was so important about a dumb crack, anyway? In keeping with the mindset of a throwaway society, our son asked, "Why didn't they just get a new one, if the old one was cracked so bad?" The significance of history was evidently lost on a seven-year-old boy who only wanted to be hanging out with his friends.

At least, I found the view from the tower calming. I drew in deep, cleansing breaths, trying to erase the tensions from the morning we'd just spent at Welcome House. We had been feeling elated and relieved upon arrival, as this was the day our adoption matching would begin. After making the final payment, our paperwork would be sent overseas to the Korean government for screening. Every meeting we had attended at the agency had been arranged in a serene private room. Unlike the so-called private-consultation areas at the drugstores, where everyone could overhear your intimate conversations, the agency was concerned about providing privacy. It was one small gesture that I appreciated. We signed several disclosing legal papers. Then Jeanie ran through a checklist of all the completed documents we had submitted, only to find that we had overlooked something very crucial. We had provided the agency with an approved home-study survey and affidavits verifying our income, job security and home ownership. We'd supplied original birth certificates, W2 copies, a marriage license and our health records. We'd submitted five references, a recommendation from Dr.

Snyder, and child abuse, along with FBI background checks. But it seemed that we had overlooked one tiny detail: fingerprints!

"It's a requirement for prospective adoptive parents," explained Jeanie.

I could see that the look on Ryan's face mirrored what I felt. To be fingerprinted would make me feel like a criminal. As though we were some kind of risk or threat to society. We were about to do something positive and wonderful, and the idea of having our fingerprints recorded in some government file somewhere was more invasive than having a catheter jammed up my urethra while fully conscious.

"What if we refuse? Isn't it against our constitutional rights or something?" I asked.

"I'm sorry. I know it's not very pleasant, but it is a necessary step if you want to adopt. Because of a few sensationalized adoption malpractices in the past, every office involved now aims for an airtight adoption. No one wants a dubious case to slip through the cracks with embarrassing repercussions later."

"But we aren't criminals. We just want to be parents," Ryan protested.

"I know. And you will be," Jeanie reassured him. "The sooner you get this behind you, the better you'll feel."

"Where do we go to get this done?" I asked resentfully.

"The US Department of Immigration, in Philadelphia. You'll want to call and check their hours. I think they only fingerprint two days a week."

"But we're not immigrants," Ryan expostulated.

"You will be sponsoring one, and that is what they require."

Great. So like common criminals, we would be tagged. And knowing our luck, somewhere down the line, someone could quite possibly mistake our photo and fingerprints for someone else's and we would have to spend thousands of dollars in retaining a very skilled lawyer to clear us. Then we would have to move from our quaint neighborhood, because it was in a small town and small-town people thrived on gossip. By the time the original story got whispered down the lane, people would be claiming that we had illegally wired into cable and that Ryan was smuggling in drugs from Colombia. Drugs and teachers did not mix. He would lose his job. Then I would have to go to work full-time, shattering my covert dream of slumming off my husband for the whole of my married life.

It wasn't so much of a paranoid fantasy as I made it out to be. Just a month earlier, there had been a story in the newspaper of a twenty-six year old man wrongly accused of being involved in a robbery. He was a mature, successful, law-abiding family man who had been hauled off to jail and was forced to go through a costly legal battle to get his name cleared, all because some young girl falsely identified him from a photograph in the directory.

We took a suffering Jake to the local swimming club and ordered pizza to be delivered for dinner. The neighborhood pool was the summer social scene, as much for him as for us. Ryan and I had once indulged in a brief flirtation with the idea of having an in-ground pool put in our own yard. For both of us, it was probably a fantasy carried over from childhood. It always seemed the cool thing to do. As a kid, I had envied others in the neighborhood that had pools. After thinking it over for a while and studying the situation through adult eyes, we had realized that if we had one installed, we would never leave our yard. We would either be isolated from friends or be constantly forced to host poolside parties. Then there were the children to worry about. Did we really want the responsibility of being perpetually vigilant when Jake's friends were over? It was so much better to let someone else go through the hassles of having a pool.

While Jake ran around with his buddies, Ryan and I sat under the shade of an umbrella and stewed over the idea of being fingerprinted.

"Why do you suppose it makes me so angry?" I asked Ryan who was busy reading his *This Old House* magazine.

"Huh? What? The fingerprints?"

I nodded.

"Because you don't like being told what to do," he said freshly, then added on a more serious note, "I guess it's that whole criminal connotation. Look, it will be fine. We'll just get it over with as soon as possible. It's not like we have a choice."

"Exactly. We don't have a choice. That's what bothers me. We have to jump through rings of fire to adopt a baby and everyone else can just snap their fingers and get pregnant. Criminals make babies all the time. No one questions them. People with AIDS bring babies into the world and no one makes them provide a health record, verifying their ability to care for the newborn." I was getting hot and could continue to gripe for hours.

"But eventually, social workers get involved, hun. Maybe you should dip your head in the pool to cool off. Julia, that's just the way it is. Are you going to change the laws?"

"I wish I could." I wished I could straighten out all of the idiotic laws. Like the drinking-age-versus-the-driving-age laws. Why not raise the driving age to twenty-one and lower the drinking age? Wouldn't it make more sense to purge the irresponsible drinking first before those kids got behind a wheel? How could you tell an eighteen-year-old that he could not have a beer, yet he was welcomed to go fight some political war and die for his country? He was even allowed to get married and start a family. Supposedly, a person was an adult at eighteen. I wondered if they would let an eighteen-year-old adopt a child. I'll have to check on that.

As I was drafting a mental list of all the witless laws that existed, a couple walked into the pool area with an Asian girl who looked to be five or six years old. I glanced at Ryan to see if he had noticed them as well. We exchanged knowing looks. That's going to be us, I thought. I observed the mixed family and their interactions. I watched the other pool members and their reactions. I had been doing this quite a lot lately. Before, I had never even noticed mixed-race families. But now, I saw them everywhere. Like an interloper in their private lives, I hid behind my sunglasses and examined their glances, their caresses, their joy and their laughter. I had never scrutinized people quite so thoroughly before. It was research, I convinced myself. Then it occurred to me that one day, the tables would be turned and people would be looking at me in the same way.

People were fascinating. I could sit for hours at the pool or in a mall and watch them. I had noticed that most people presented a posture that reeked of insecurity and lack of confidence. Most people seemed self-conscious about their bodies. Women who were thin seemed to think they were too fat. Men sporting bloated beer bellies strutted around proudly without a care and didn't have enough sense to put on a shirt. Budding teenage girls struggled with the changes taking place in their bodies. They folded their arms across themselves a lot and tended not to walk the pool deck without a towel wrapped around their whole body. My favorites were the uninhibited toddler girls. They always seemed to have one butt cheek hanging out of their swimsuits and they were completely unashamed.

Ally entered the pool gates carrying a hefty bag of towels, followed by her three sons. Something was wrong with that picture. She dropped her bag on the table next to us. "Hello," she sang out to us. "Are you recovered from the other night?"

Ryan and I exchanged fleeting glances. With a smirk on his face, he buried his head in his magazine.

"I'm fine now." It took all of Sunday to recover from the poor judgment of drinking liquor. Never, and I truly meant *never*, would I drink liquor again. The stuff was poison for me. Two days later, and I still did not feel normal. When would I ever learn? My limit was a couple of beers or two glasses of wine. Tops!

"Oh Julia! You were hilarious," she said, as I felt a panic attack coming on. Telepathically, I unsuccessfully willed her *not* to expound on the evening's misadventures, for fear that she would divulge even more that I could not remember. "Poor Lauren," she continued sarcastically, "she thought you were bad for her image after you took care of that guy."

I exhaled the anxious breath I had been holding. She'd done it. She'd exposed me.

Ryan came back to life. "What guy?" he asked.

"Um...uh," I stalled, hoping that a meteor would land on us spontaneously and spare me from having to offer explanations.

At that moment, David came running up to Ally crying, "Mom, Michael took my Game Boy!"

Ally turned her attention to her son so that she could extract the whole story and immediately marched off to find the brutish older brother.

"What guy?" Ryan repeated, giving me an inquisitorial glare.

"Okay, look. Before you get all full of testosterone, just calm down." It was awkward explaining my interactions with men to him, for fear that he would become unnecessarily jealous. It wasn't that I was guilty of misconduct or anything; it was just easier not to go through the third degree. "Well, okay," I began nervously, "I didn't tell you this, because there was nothing to worry about. It's nothing, really."

"It's certainly something, if you feel you can't tell me."

"The pharmacist at Eddington Hospital is Greg Magatz." Recognition dawned on his face. He would never forget his so-called rival.

"I ran into him when I had my first order of Pergonal filled. He was almost unrecognizable. Must have gained eighty pounds or so. He looked awful."

This made Ryan relax a bit. "He asked me to lunch, you know, to talk," I carried on, "but I said no and I never went back there again for prescriptions. Then he happened to be at Bongos Saturday night. He made a distasteful comment and I...well...I kind of, might have kicked him really hard in the balls."

His eyebrows rose in inquiry and he snickered slightly with satisfaction. "You *what*? What did he say to provoke that response?"

"He insulted your sperm quality." Now Ryan had turned red. "Look," I went on hurriedly, "he was drunk. It was a little harsh of me, but I took care of him. I'm sure he will never be a problem again."

"I'm sure he won't."

"Don't bother with it, Ryan," I warned, sensing that he was planning a man-to-man talk with Greg, if only to assuage his own insecurities. "Look, you're the one I married." I stood up and touched Ryan's face. I kissed him passionately on the mouth. "It's not like you were my second choice or anything. And, he's huge now." I spread my arms the way children did when they pledged how much they loved you.

I excused myself by saying that I was going to go and meet the couple with the Asian girl. The boost-Ryan's-self-esteem lesson was not over yet. I would surely have to perform that night. He was so obsessed with the idea that I might find someone better and leave him. No matter how much I reassured him, I constantly had to prove my loyalty. It was as if he could not believe that I had married him. Leaving was not an option for me. Anyway, I didn't believe divorce resolved people's problems, except in cases of abuse or neglect. In a more normal situation, with children involved, the ex-spouse would always be in your life, anyway. And then the relationship would be worse, because you would only end up hating each other. With children involved, you could never really get rid of an undesirable spouse.

Still, I did fantasize, once in a while, about living on my own. Mostly, what I wanted was my own room. Jake thought it was completely unfair that his mom and dad got to share a room. He would have loved a brother to bunk with. I comforted him by saying that I would love to have my own room. Here's the fantasy: I would decorate it like an ultra-feminine French boudoir, complete with an abundance of flowers, a vanity table, a changing screen and lots of fabric textures in romantic reds. I would sleep in the middle my king-sized bed with pillows tucked front and back. There would be no episodes of snoring. There would be no roaming hands in the middle of the night to disrupt my tranquil slumber. If I wanted to,

I could sleep with the radio on low. I could read in bed until two in the morning.

Just a fantasy because, the truth was, people always think the grass will be greener on the other side. But it never usually was much greener. Unless you did not want grass. Then that would be a different story altogether. It seemed to me that most people who moved on to second marriages ended up marrying the same person in different skin. Good Lord, one spouse was enough!

CHAPTER TWENTY-SIX

Three days of drenching rain had made the weeds grow ferociously. Crabgrass was taking over my lawn. Dastardly weeds were encroaching upon the brick walkway alongside the house. I had been attacking them with a vengeance. Rather than spray herbicide, I pulled them out by the root. Later, I would sprinkle Borax and brush it into the cracks to keep them under control until the first frost. I hated weeds. But what I hated more was succumbing to the obsession of the immaculate lawn spiked with harmful fertilizers that seeped into the water table.

"Julia?" said a familiar voice, breaking my concentration.

I looked up into the glare of the sun to see the form of Dave Martin. "Dave. What are you doing here?"

"I was supposed to meet Ryan," he said carefully, sensing that he should explain the reason for his unexpected visit. "He's lending me his nail gun." Dave most uncouthly discarded a cigarette stub on my lawn and stepped on it. I kept staring at it pointedly, hoping he would pick it up.

It did not seem plausible that Ryan would agree to lend out a power tool. He was very protective of his more expensive tools, having learned in the past that people who borrowed things didn't always treat them with the same respect that he would.

I tried to remain neutral, but it was difficult to look at Dave and not think about Alex. I kept thinking, *stalker*. "Um, Ryan is not here right now. He's cutting a neighbor's lawn on the next street over."

This was awkward.

I stood up, feeling the tightness in my back, right at the spot where my spine had been punctured by the epidural needle when I had Jake. "Would you like something to drink? I have some iced tea." Not the Long Island kind! Never again! I picked up the discarded cigarette and started to walk toward the back deck.

"Uh, Julia? Actually, I'd like to talk to you."

No, please, I thought. I didn't want to be in the middle. It was so much easier to choose a side and stick to it.

"What about?"

He looked embarrassed, but not enough to retract his intended questioning of me. He also looked much thinner than I remembered. "How is Alexandria? I understand you see her often?"

"She's fine. She's good, Dave."

"I really screwed up, huh?"

"Are you looking for absolution or answers?" I poured us some iced tea.

He took the glass and shook his head in response to my question. "I guess she hates me?"

After a long refreshing swallow, I sighed heavily and replied, "No, Dave. She does not hate you. But she wants to move forward. She does not want to get back with you. Things have changed. She has changed."

"Yes, she has. She has what we planned to have together."

"Are you referring to the baby?"

He looked down at his shoes and nodded solemnly. "But now there is someone else."

"Dave, I know it must hurt. Changes are hard to accept. But you have to know that there is no new lover. It was a brief encounter. There is no other man." At least, not officially.

"It's that Greek guy, isn't it?" he asked, as though he had not heard me. I felt terrible for him, despite all the awful, selfish things he had done to Alex. He was clearly a broken man, cut adrift from his emotional moorings.

I heard the telephone ringing as the side gate swung open. "Hey," said Ryan to Dave, shaking hands with him and sparing me from further questioning.

I excused myself to answer the telephone, leaving Ryan to

counsel his friend. Despite the empathy I felt for Dave, it was too difficult to be objective about the situation. As a woman, I sat firmly in Alex's corner of the ring. She had made her choices based on the punches he'd thrown at her. She had chosen to take a positive route instead of letting her life fall apart over being scorned. This was precisely why I could never have been a social worker or a psychologist. I jumped on the bandwagon too quickly and took sides. I became emotionally involved.

"How do you do it? How do you listen to other people's problems all day and not want to jump off a bridge?" I asked Dr. Snyder the next day.

He shrugged. "Professional detachment, I guess."

"That's a copout. Honestly, please. Do you not really listen? Do you just concentrate on certain things? I bet you draw pictures the whole time, don't you? That separates your emotions, right?"

"No," he smiled. "It's problem-solving. I help people find solutions."

I smoothed out the wrinkles on my linen trousers. "What's mine, then?"

"You're a tough nut to crack. Excuse the pun."

"Funny," I said dryly. "Why am I so difficult? Why can't you fix me?"

"You aren't being honest with yourself. I can't get below the surface with you."

In my own defense, I argued, "How can you say that? I've divulged my deepest, darkest thoughts to you."

He cleared his throat and shifted in his chair. "There's more there than your infertility issues."

"Oh, yeah? Such as?"

"Your mother. You always avoid that subject."

"She is not the reason I came here. If you remember, I started here because I had a miscarriage. I was depressed and somewhat suicidal. My mother is not responsible for those feelings."

"Very often, when there is pain in the past, we push it down deep, not realizing that it is the root cause of other roadblocks. I think that your feelings toward your mother define how you feel about motherhood in general. At the very least, on some level, perhaps, you feel that you don't deserve to have more children. Or, maybe, you're afraid that you will screw up eventually, just like her. I'd say that turning out to be like her is one of your greatest fears."

Yes.

"So, you want to take the Freudian approach and have me believe that my mother is the reason for all of my negative feelings about my infertile self?"

"Not exactly like that. I think that you deny yourself your true feelings about her; therefore, you have never dealt with your resentment in a constructive way. I think you do not feel positive about motherhood."

Sparring with him was becoming too much work, so I relented. "Okay, let's do it."

"Will you be honest with me?"

Impatiently, I answered, "Yes, yes, of course."

"When was the last time you spoke to her?"

"I don't know. Six month's ago, maybe?" I called sporadically to check in and be dutiful. She was usually the one to call me. I had to work myself up to call, because it was always so exhausting. I usually bit off several fingernails before I could dial her. I could never predict how the conversation would go. Sometimes, it was normal and calm. At other times, she was so abrasive and full of complaints that I signed off as quickly as possible.

"Would you like to speak with her more?"

"Not really. It's too hard."

"Why?"

"There is so much lost between us. It doesn't feel like she is my mother."

"What is a mother?"

"Someone who takes care of you, loves you, stands by you and cheers you on from the sidelines. A mother does not abandon her child."

"You are about to accept a child that will be abandoned by its mother. You have stated that putting a child up for adoption is the right thing to do, if you can't take care of it properly. How do you think you will feel toward the birth mother of your new child? Do you think you might harbor negative feelings toward her? Because if you did, I think it would not be healthy for the child. Children sense things."

"Absolutely not. I will feel grateful that she realized she could not take care of the child and gave it to someone who could."

"Isn't that, in a way, what your mother did?" he asked.

"Oh. Okay." I needed a moment to digest this twist on semantics. "I guess so. Maybe, yes. But I get so angry when I think of all she has missed in my life and my son's life."

"But you do understand that she was ill, right?"

"I do. It's just that, sometimes, it felt like she was being selfish, like she did not try hard enough to get well."

He nodded in understanding. "It's perfectly normal to feel resentful." He paused and shifted in his chair. "Have you ever forgiven your mother, verbally that is?"

"Now you sound like the preacher man. No, I haven't."

"Would you be open to dialogue with her?"

"Please tell me you do not have her hiding in the closet."

He uncrossed his legs and leaned forward. "Julia," he said, "the only reason I push you on this is because you are classically headed for a crisis in your life, maybe, bigger than your infertility crisis. Imagine the scenario when she dies. She will someday, you know. What will it be like for you?"

"How would I know? It's hypothetical."

"If she leaves you with unanswered questions, your feelings for her will be unresolved and you will never be at peace. It will always gnaw at you. I'm not suggesting that she be suddenly over-involved in your life. I'm suggesting that you need to tell her how you really feel about the things that bother you."

He sat back in his chair and crossed his legs.

My throat ached, because I refused to show him that it hurt

to think of my mother. I wanted to believe that I was completely functional despite her. Yet, every decision I had made in life seemed to be based on what my fantasy mother would do. Yes, my aunt was a role model, but she was not my mother.

Furthermore, why was I even here today? What I originally came for seemed to have been put to rest. With his help, I had acknowledged that my grief over my infertility might always be there, but would lessen over time. There was good grieving and bad grieving. I had to feel it and let it out. Now, with the adoption looming, I was in a good place mentally. I did not even have to make this appointment. I just wanted to talk to him. His seductive speech pattern was soothing. He understood me, no matter how much I tried to derail his efforts to do so. I enjoyed being in his presence. He dressed very nicely. Yet, he was relaxed, casual. I'd begun to make a little game out of what color the polo shirt would be under his suit coat.

Suddenly, an embarrassing thought overwhelmed me. Oh, no! I had a crush on Dr. Snyder! I did not come to talk mental problems with him. I liked jousting with him. I liked his attention. I liked his warm smile. I liked that he cared, that he seemed to know my soul. I looked forward to our visits. I carefully planned what I would wear. The night before my sessions with him, I rummaged through my closet to select something that would make the right statement. Nothing too seductive. Just comfortable. And smart. I always dressed smart and wore tailored outfits, like some kind of country-club wife in a twin set, something that might attract a man of his caliber and education. Dressing either for success or to make the right statement was something my Aunt Sara had taught me. If you wanted respect from people, you should dress respectfully, she believed. Oh, God, I'd become a freak!

Had he noticed that I was doing that? If he was so good at seeing through to my soul, did he know that I had the most awful junior-high-school crush on him? I would never be able to sit across from him again without cracking up over my own ridiculous behavior. I had become just another cliché, the patient who falls for the healing doctor.

"Do you agree?" he asked. "Julia?"

"What? Oh," I managed, while the wheels were still spinning in my head. What had I missed? Had he said something important, while I was off on a cerebral tangent?

"So, does that sound like an option to you?" he asked.

"Yes, of course." What?

"So when do you think you would like to schedule that meeting with your mother?"

"What? No! No. I'm sorry." I peeked at my watch and said, "Oops! I forgot I had another appointment." I stood to go and secured my purse strap around my shoulder. "I'll have to cut this short today. I double-booked. I uh...I'll think about what you said." What had he said? I needed to get out of there fast, before my blushing face betrayed the nature of my sordid thoughts.

CHAPTER TWENTY-SEVEN

Alex was in splits over my infatuation with Dr. Snyder and my eternal obsession over dressing like a country-club wife. Her immense belly, now heavy with child, danced up and down with her laughter. She was eight days from her due date and we were at the Baby Superstore, shopping for a crib, a front-pack carrier and newborn diapers.

"It's not funny!" I protested. "What's wrong with presenting yourself in a positive manner?"

"Julia. It is so funny! You're in a pickle. How are you going to face him again?"

"I don't know. That's the hard part."

Alex shook her head and squinted at me. "I bet you shave your legs for your ob/ gyn visits, don't you?"

"Don't you?" Doesn't everyone?

"If I feel like it that day." She stopped at a white no-frills crib.

"Oh, come on! What about brushing your teeth for the dentist?" I asked.

Alex moved on, running her hand over various cribs. "Yes, that I always do. I don't want to have bad breath or promote cavities."

"One time, during those awful IUI sessions with Dr. Castlebloom, I had a huge mortifying pimple on my left butt cheek. I almost cancelled the whole session, because I didn't want him see it," I confessed. "I cleverly covered it with a Spider-Man bandage, as if that wasn't a red flag." At least, the bandage was more attractive than an inflamed boil on my ass.

Again, Alex cackled most unattractively at my intimate confession. "Trust me, you can't imagine the grotesque things nurses and doctors see. They might notice a bulbous, erupting pimple, but not your unshaven legs."

"Tell yourself that. I don't want to be that one memorable patient they have a good laugh over at the water cooler."

Crib styles, I noticed, had changed somewhat in the seven years since I last shopped for one. The more upscale styles were now standard fare in most modest-priced stores. It was like shopping for a car, as we inspected springs and fasteners. Given my own experiences with Jake, I advised Alex to go for a crib with a nice, quiet gliding rail. The glide on my son's crib rail would often squeak when I needed to lower it in the middle of the night to reposition him. As a baby, he was such a light sleeper that even the popping of my knees and ankles would wake him, forcing me to duck and hide until he settled again. I recalled tiptoeing into his room and literally holding my breath. It was like he was waiting for me.

"What do you think of this one?" she asked, standing near a cherry-stained crib. It was the infant-to-teenage model that could be dismantled later to make a twin bed and dresser.

"These are great. I mean, they're expensive, but well worth it in the end. You won't need to buy a headboard or a frame when the baby is ready for a regular bed." I did not like referring to her baby as an "it", but Alex did not wish to know the sex of the child before it was born. She claimed that knowing that would be like knowing what your Christmas gift was, before you had opened it. I was anxious to buy baby clothes for her, but it would have to wait.

Alex's baby shower was the first I had attended in years, where I did not spend a considerable amount of time sobbing in the bathroom. I'm sure she would have understood had I not been able to attend, but I did not feel it would be appropriate to decline the invitation. In fact, I had not even been in a baby store for years because the sight of baby paraphernalia always struck a nerve and triggered a crisis. If a gift were needed, I'd always leave it to Ryan to choose one. Usually, I took the cowardly way out and bought gift cards and mailed my congratulations to the ecstatic parents-to-be.

Alex decided on the cherry crib and had it delivered. I was impressed with the decisive manner in which she went about her shopping. I'd been sure we were going to be there all day, looking for the best value we could get. We moved on to the backpack aisle. Here was something I knew I would need. I was studying them, as much for her as for myself. Front packs or slings were favored in Korean families. We had been advised that this could be our best purchase, because babies felt reassured by the familiarity of being held that way. I was not, however, mentally prepared to make purchases for "my" baby. At least, not until we had been matched by the agency. Purchasing anything too soon would surely be tempting fate, I thought superstitiously.

"Did you read in the paper about that woman across town who was arrested for soliciting?" Alex asked, as she examined backpacks. Our quaint little town had a new scandal to boast about. A local soccer mom had allegedly set up a home business in prostitution. I did not know her, but the community was in an uproar over it. Puritan notions about sex were surfacing everywhere.

"Who doesn't know about it?" I replied. "It's all anyone is talking about."

"Can you imagine? She has a husband and kids. Whore by day, Mrs. June Cleaver by night."

"Easy money, I guess," I said. "I suspect it's more popular than people think."

"There can't be anything easy about having sex all day long. And what if your husband wants it at night? What do you do then? She must be one of those sex-a-holics or something."

"What's wrong with prostitution, anyway? Other than the adultery factor, I mean. Why is it a crime to get paid for having sex? I wouldn't mind if Ryan gave me a hundred bucks each time. I might have the incentive to do it more often."

I was joking, of course, but Alex gave me a sharp, shame-on-you-Julia look. Ryan would never give me money in exchange for sex. First of all, he didn't have any money to give. Secondly, he strongly believed in his conjugal rights. But we did barter and trade for things we wanted, like a back-rub for a session or a new deck.

"Seriously, Alex. Think about the hypocrisy. Anyone anywhere can have sex with whomever they want—for free. Why is it so shameful to get paid for it? If he wants to pay and she wants to give it, then where's the conflict? Other than the adultery factor, mind you, or being hired out as a sex slave by pimps. Why should it be anyone's concern?"

"I guess you're right in a way," she conceded. "If you think about it, marriage is just a form of legal prostitution, anyway. Right?"

"Exactly." Now we were on the same page. "How do you think I get Ryan to do all that home remodeling?" I said facetiously.

She laughed and shook her head at me, then suddenly made a strange gasping sound.

"What is it?" I asked.

"I think my water broke," she announced uncertainly.

"Oh, shit...uh...okay..." I dropped a front pack while trying to replace it on its hook. "...uh...I guess we should leave then." I was starting to panic, even though it was only a little fluid leakage and just the beginning of labor. Everyone knew first babies took like two days to actually arrive after labor had started. "Can you walk to the car? Or should you wait here, while I go get the car?"

She waved me off as we headed for the door and started dialing her doctor on her cell phone. St. Mary's hospital was only five minutes away. Unfortunately, Ben Franklin, the hospital designated by her insurance company, was twenty-five minutes away in North-East Philadelphia. And it was lunchtime rush hour.

I opened the car door and guided Alex into it, the way they did on those cop shows, making sure her head cleared the frame. Then I noticed something unmistakably wrong on her white Capri's. The fabric covering her lap revealed a red-tinged wetness.

"Oh, Alex!" I exclaimed.

She was busy calling her sister's work number. "What?"

I pointed to the stain. "That isn't normal, is it? It can't be normal."

She looked down to see what I saw. "Oh, jeez," she said, strangely calm.

"Does it hurt? What happened?" I hurried over to the driver's side and scrambled in with shaking hands.

"It could just be heavy spotting. Or it could be a placental abruption."

"Is that bad?" I asked. As if I were not nervous enough, the sight of her blood sent me into a panic. I started the car and instead of going in reverse, I jerked forward, bumping a shopping cart before I could slam on the brakes. "Shit! I'm sorry. Are you okay?"

"I'm fine. Calm down."

"I'm trying. I'm trying." The shopping cart started rolling down an incline of pavement and gaining speed. Why did these stupid things always seem to happen to me? Okay, moral dilemma: should I focus on my friend or stop the car and chase down the cart, so that it didn't slam into the car it seemed to be heading for?

Alex won my loyalty, as my rear-view mirror revealed a sailing cart colliding with a parked Mazda. I winced at the damage I had caused and scanned the parking lot for witnesses. There appeared to be none, but you never knew when a hidden camera might pop up. Or an adulterous couple could be secretly parked nearby, their identities concealed behind blackened windows, both vowing to leave their spouses but never really intending to. Not as long as the milk was free, anyway.

"Remind me to call the store when you get settled at the hospital." I urged Alex. I had to address the damage I had done and make amends or I would never be able to shop there again.

We were making good time down Route 1 toward Ben Franklin Hospital when a Septa commuter train slowed our progress. I tapped my fingers impatiently on the steering wheel as we waited and waited. I yearned to get out and pace around the car.

"Come on, come on," I urged. "Is that the longest train you ever saw?"

Alex moaned in pain, holding her belly, as she remained all the while on her cell phone. She was calling the hospital ER to report her condition. As soon as the train had passed, I took off, not even waiting for the safety arms to rise.

Alex reached out and touched my arm. "Julia, calm down. It will be all right."

"I'm sorry. I guess I should be consoling you. It's just...I love you like a sister, Alex, really. But there is no way in hell I can reach between your legs and be responsible for delivering this baby!"

She winced at a sharp pain and said, "Don't worry. I don't think it's coming out that way, anyhow."

"I'm serious. I can't do it," I said, not hearing her words. Then I stole a glance at her. The bloodstain was growing larger and brighter.

Backed up again in traffic on Roosevelt Boulevard, I noticed Alex squirming and moaning in pain. That was it! I only had a few miles left to go, so I hit the flashers and pulled out onto the right shoulder, sailing past dozens of cars while honking to get their attention. Two rights and a left and we were at the hospital.

As I pulled up to the emergency-room door, a nurse was waiting outside with a wheelchair, thanks to Alex's phone call warning them of her condition. With the nurse's help, she struggled out of the car, leaving a huge bloodstain on the cloth car seat. Now, between Jake and his messy eating and Alex practically giving birth, my car had really had it. I couldn't wait until Ryan, who was forever giving me flak about the way I kept my car, saw this one.

Pre-registration was a truly brilliant idea, especially in hairy situations like this one. Without it, we would be mired in paperwork at this critical juncture. Alex was whisked off behind the double steel doors and immediately strapped to a fetal monitor. Within seconds, they had an IV line secured to her arm. Even more blood was now soaking the bed linens.

"There's fetal distress," someone announced.

"Okay, prep for OR," announced another. "Is her doctor here?"

"Not yet."

"Who's the Attending?"

"Martini," someone answered.

"Yes, thanks. I could use one right now," someone joked. I got the feeling that this was an old, played-out joke, every time someone mentioned Dr. Martini.

"Okay, *vamonos*, people!"

The emergency crew started off with Alex and I remained where I was, unsure of what to do.

"Julia? Aren't you coming?" she asked.

Me? "But...your sister...What about her?"

I was not so sure that I could witness a real, live C-section, although it would be a privilege to be Alex's support. The sterile, antiseptic hospital smell was already making me queasy. To think I had once wanted to be a nurse! I would have spent all that money on my education, only to find out that I could not stomach it after all.

"I'm here! I'm here!" said a breathless Maryanne, Alex's sister.

Saved!

In the flash of a second, Alex and I exchanged brief looks. Hers was one of last-minute disappointment, as though she had decided that she would rather have me with her than her sister. My look was one of apology. It said, "Your sister is here and I can't step on her toes."

I stepped outside the ER doors to a hint of autumn in the crisp, late-August air. I collapsed on the curb and breathed for the first time since we had left the Baby Superstore. As I waited, I prayed for Alex and the baby. I threatened God that if anything went wrong, I would...would do something...Well, I would just be very disappointed with Him or Her and all of my progress with Dr. Snyder would go down the drain!

Thirty-five minutes later, Maryanne came out through the ER doors and said, "It's a girl! Seven pounds, nine ounces."

"And Alex? How is she?"

"Oh, she's going to be fine. She's pretty knocked-out right now. You might want to go home for a while. It will be a few hours before you can see her."

I stood up and stretched. "What did she name her?"

Maryanne shook her head and said, "She hasn't decided yet."

I did not see Alex that day. Suddenly, I felt out of place. Soon, her large family would swarm the hospital and take over. There would be no room for me. I decided to let the excitement run its course and go home.

When I pulled into my driveway, I could not bring myself to get out of the car. I was in the grip of ugly thoughts. The green-eyed monster had taken over my brain and those old feelings of inadequacy had resurfaced with a vengeance. I glanced over at the blood-soaked passenger seat. An untimely birth had nearly taken place in my minivan. This car was really shot to hell. I hated this stupid family van and all it represented. We had bought the van when Jake was one, because it was too difficult to maneuver him in the backseat of our two-door SUV, the "cool" car. At the time, we were going to have four children to fill this van. Now it seemed like a curse. I kept hoping someone would steal it and I could get a new, sportier, less-family-oriented mobile. But every day, I came out to the driveway, and there sat the reminder of what I did not have.

Ryan tapped on the driver's window, arousing me from my self-pitying trance. He was clad in his slovenly summer attire: cutoffs and a Grateful Dead T-shirt that would be more useful as a cleaning rag.

I rolled down the window.

"What's wrong? Are you crying?" Then he noticed the soiled passenger seat. His eyes widened and he asked, "Did you murder someone?"

It did look like a crime scene. "Alex went into labor," I answered absently. "Her placenta erupted...or disrupted...something like that."

He gave me a horrified look, replete with a thousand unasked questions.

I shook my head reassuringly. "She's fine," I said. "Emergency C-section. She had a healthy girl."

"Then why are you crying?"

Why, indeed? I was happy for her. Really, I was. But I was

desperately sad for myself at the same time. I was not supposed to feel that way about Alex. I had rooted and cheered for her. I no longer had to wallow in guilt anymore that I had a child and she did not.

"Mommy! Mommy!" shouted Jake, running out of the house toward us.

I did not want him to see the bloody mess in my car, so I quickly scrambled out and met him halfway.

We hugged and he said, "Guess what? I lost another tooth!" He smiled from ear to ear to show me the double gap in his top front row.

I held his face in my hands to examine the new development, "This calls for a photograph. Where is my camera?" I said, leading him into the house. I couldn't wait for him to lose his two front teeth and have that goofy smile. Only in children did missing teeth look so adorable.

CHAPTER TWENTY-EIGHT

Courage. If I only had courage, like the cowardly lion. I avoided Alex all of the next day, until finally, I felt so much of a heel, that I had to force myself to go and see her. It was nearly the end of visiting hours, before I nervously tapped on the door. Her room was overflowing with flowers and balloons, a testimony to the fact that she had an army of people who loved her.

She looked over and smiled. "What took you so long?"

"I didn't want to be in the way of your family."

"Bull." I knew she would say that.

I breathed deeply, "Okay. I was apprehensive. I was not ready to see a newborn baby." I sat lightly on the edge of her bed. "I brought you some food. I know they don't feed you enough in here, especially, when you're breastfeeding." I handed her a box of Graham crackers. "And these." A bouquet of flowers.

"Thank you. Are you okay?" she asked, sensing my nervousness.

"I should be asking you that."

"It's all right, Julia. Whatever you're feeling, it's all right. You're allowed to have mixed feelings."

I nodded, trying to be strong. "So where is she?"

"Getting a bath. I'm sorry about your car."

I stood to arrange the flowers in the vase I had brought from home. "It's nothing. Ryan took it to have it detailed. It needed a good cleaning, anyway. He thought I had finally gone off the deep end and murdered someone."

"Okay, here we are! Back to Mommy!" sang the maternity nurse as she wheeled Alex's baby back into the room. "All clean and fresh for you." She deposited the cart there and left.

"Thank you," said Alex.

I could not breathe. "You need more water. I'll get you some." I started to reach out for the pitcher when Alex stopped me.

"Julia. Could you hand me the baby, please? I need to try and feed her."

"Um. Okay." I stumbled. What the heck was wrong with me? I was tripping all over myself. Awkwardly, I reached in and lifted the baby. She wore a pink cap on her tiny head and was swaddled tightly in that clever way only hospital nurses could manage. At first, I held her away from me, giving us both some time to adjust to each other's presence. But slowly, I drew her closer to me and cradled her in my arms. I barely remembered babies being so small and seemingly weightless. She was simply beautiful. Her skin was milky white and free of any signs of newborn acne. "What's her name?"

"Jessica."

"That's nice. Hello, Jessica. Welcome to the world. I'm Julia and I'm going to be your babysitter, when Mommy needs a sanity break."

Jessica looked up at me through one brown eye and smiled as if she knew a secret. My heart turned over and I fell in love with her in that instant. What was this magic that babies possessed? Once I had her in my arms, I did not want to put her down. I wanted to soak up the newness of life, as if through some form of osmosis, I might absorb the ability to start anew from this fresh new person in my arms. I wanted to breathe in her clean, soapy scent and watch her sleep. Then I understood the reason for my initial apprehension and nervousness in handling Jessica. Because of my barrenness, I did not feel as though I deserved to hold a baby, especially, a newborn so fragile.

When she finally became restless, I relinquished her to Alex for a feed. A tap at the door interrupted us. "Oh, is now a bad time?" said a brawny male voice, preceded by yet another bouquet of flowers. The physical presence behind the voice was just as brawny. He wore summer khakis with a long-sleeved white oxford, rolled up to three-quarter length. He had that sexy five o'clock shadow.

He was lean and naturally tan, not the product of tanning beds and creams like me. His white shirt hinted at taut pectorals, biceps, triceps and whatever other "ceps" there were. No introduction was necessary. This was Alex's Greek "lunch buddy".

"Bart? How did you know I was here?" asked a flustered Alex.

"Office gossip." He confidently walked around to the other side of the bed and kissed her on the cheek. "How are you feeling?"

In response to his affection, Alex blushed. A surge of energy swept the room all of a sudden. He positioned his bouquet of flowers on the windowsill and turned to look at her with the same affection I used to see in Ryan before we became an old married couple darting through life's obstacles.

We're just friends. Right. He was totally smitten with her. How could she not see it? Was she so angry with men that her judgment was impaired?

"Uh, Bart. This is my friend, Julia. Julia, meet Bart."

We acknowledged each other. "It's nice to finally have a face to match all I've heard about you," I said, letting him know that Alex spoke of him often. My peripheral vision took in Alex, glowering at me.

"Same here," he said. "I understand that you were the surrogate ambulance driver." Bart smiled, revealing a gentle dimple on his left cheek. Wow. Was he hot!

"Yes, that's me," I managed. "Well, listen. It's almost past visiting hours. I should go. I'll check on you tomorrow." I leaned in to give her a goodbye kiss on the cheek, but whispered in her ear, instead, "You better call me later and tell me everything, you hold-out artist you."

HILL CHILDREN'S SERVICES, INC.
INITIAL PHYSICAL EXAMINATION

This report is intended to give the adoptive parents' pediatrician a picture of the child's initial physical and developmental appearance.

Number K 2004-955____ Date 10-3-2004

Name Sun he Jung Sex/ Race KF DOB 9-27-2004

Age 6 days

Hair Color dark brown Eye Color dark brown Ht 48.4 cm Wt. 2.4 Kg <25% <3%

Head Circumference 32.4 cm Chest Circ. 28 cm >10% <3%

Immunization Hepatitis-B 10-3-1999 Medical History Normal full term C-section. Birth Weight 3.1 Kg. Good condition on admission.

Laboratory Results:

Urine_____   Sugar_____Albumin_____

Microscopic_____

Blood 9-3-2004 VDRL non-reactive Hb/Ht._____ PPD____

Stool _____ Parasites _____ Total Bilirubin 12.1 mg/d l

Chest X-ray_____

Physical Examination:

General Appearance cute and alert

Nutrition Moderate

Skin and Prominent Marks Mongolian spot on back, jaundice

Head normal Fontanel 1FB AF opened

Scalp normal

Hair clean, normal

Eyes normal Ears normal Hearing Rt. Startled at sound Lt. Same

Otoscope Rt. Ear normal Lt. Ear normal

Page 1 of 2

Number K 2004-955 Name: **Sun he Jung**
Nose normal Mouth normal Tongue normal
Lips normal Palate normal
Tonsils normal Throat normal
Neck normal
Chest symmetric Lungs clear breathing sound
Heart regular heartbeat without murmur
Abdomen soft, umbilical stump Hernia none
Liver not palpable Spleen not palpable Spine normal
Upper Extremities normal
Lower Extremities normal
Neurological Data: DTR normal, moro, sucking, rooting, placing reflex: good
Mental and Social Development n/a
Motor Development symmetric
Speech n/a
Assessment of Developmental Age: normal full-term baby
Recommendation: This child is **Adoptable**
Summary and recommendation: Phototherapy and follow-up bil total

Doctor's signature
Me Kyung Kim
Me Kyung Kim, MD

CHAPTER TWENTY-NINE

She stood across from me, all of two years old, but with the posture of a fifteen-year-old terror in training. Her hands were anchored firmly on her hips, waiting impatiently for me to notice her untied sneakers. Purple was her favorite color and she wore it nearly every day. The choice for that day was a purple taffeta dress, worn backward and a pair of high-top sneakers. "Mommy, tie shoe!" she commanded with brows furrowed in an attempt to look serious. How could I not laugh? She willfully chose her own clothes and was defiant in her opinions about what matched and what did not.

For the past month, I had been repeatedly having fleeting dreams of a little Asian girl. I knew it was her, this soul that awaited me. I knew it as positively as I knew Jake would be a boy when I carried him inside me.

When the phone call came that afternoon on October 7th, my intuition had been confirmed. She had already been born in a bustling city hospital on the other side of the world. Cautiously, I answered the phone.

"Julia?" said Jeanie, confirming that it was I who had answered.

"Yes."

"It's Jeanie. Are you sitting down?"

"Yes." I wasn't, but the reply escaped my lips unconsciously. I was folding laundry in my bedroom and still held my husband's socks in one hand.

"We have a match for you. It's a girl. She was born six days ago in Seoul."

I felt as though my mouth had been injected with Novocaine; I found myself unable to articulate my words properly. "Okay." I said, dropping down on the edge of the bed.

"It's a bit late today, so could you and Ryan come in tomorrow to review her chart and make your decision?"

"Okay. Yes. Of course," I managed. I knew I must be sounding like a fumbling idiot, but without a videophone at her disposal, Jeanie could not see that I was adjusting to the physiological changes of my swelling heart and the collapse of my lungs.

After I hung up, I did not know what to do next. I sat there twisting my husband's socks in my hands, reveling in the news. It was a girl, indeed. I tried to recall the now-faded vision of the toddler I had seen running up to me on that day when I had been shelving books. She was now a mere apparition, a body with a blank face. I wished I could picture her more clearly

The following day, we sat in the counseling room at the Welcome House offices, waiting for Jeanie to bring us the baby's folder. We were both on edge. But at least, we did not fight over parking spaces this time.

Finally, in walked Jeanie with a new, shorter hairstyle that made her look older and more professional.

"Okay, here you go," she said, sitting down and moving her chair closer to the table. She unfolded the manila file folder, revealing the baby's photo. I had prepared myself for the eventuality that the photograph might not be flattering, as photos of newborn babies often weren't. As far as I remember, Jake's photos, taken soon after he was born, didn't even remotely resemble what he turned out to look like a month later. Blame the photographer, blame the lighting, blame the birthing process, but newborns always looked shriveled and scrawny when they first came into the world. It was as if their water-soaked skin needed to dry out, stretch and fill in.

Despite my state of mental preparedness, my first reaction to this baby was, *Ugh*. It was a terribly inappropriate response, I realized, but this was simply not a photo one could fall in love with. The baby's eyes were closed and her body was lost in an oversized pink outfit. If our decision about adopting her had been based solely on this photograph, I might have declined. She'll grow into her looks, I told myself. She just needed some baby fat on her. Thankfully, there were pages of descriptive data accompanying the picture.

Jeanie cleared her throat. "I'll just go over some highlights and then I will leave you alone for a bit to think it over." She turned to the first page. "She was born seven days ago by C-section, full term at 3.1 kg. That's approximately 6.8 pounds. It looks like she had some jaundice and was given light therapy. Her general health is good. She was treated at the hospital a couple of days later with a fever, then sent home. She is now in her foster-care home and reportedly doing well."

Ryan was studying the papers while Jeanie continued with her overview. "What's this here?" he asked, pointing to the description of the baby's physical condition. "It says 'Mongolian spot'. What's that?"

"It's a birthmark, a typical Asian birthmark. They're usually located on the back or in the buttocks area. No need to be alarmed. It's purplish, like a bruise. They usually fade with age. You would want to educate any caregivers, so they know it's not a real bruise."

I was not sure why I needed to ask about the birth mother, but I could not visualize the baby and its biological mother as separate entities. Who was she? Why was she giving up her child? Surely, this woman was isolated in her grief on the other side of the world? Did she feel as wretchedly empty now as I had with every failed attempt to conceive? No matter what the circumstances, it must feel deplorably unnatural to give up a child that once squirmed, kicked and hiccupped inside you.

"Just for the sake of curiosity, why was she put up for adoption?" I asked.

Jeanie turned the page, exposing a document called Confidential Background Information. "The mother was twenty-four and unmarried. There was no possibility of a future with the father. She was unemployed. It's fully explained here." She pointed to a section on the background health of the biological parents. "You'll want to refer to the parents' medical history. I'm going to leave you now for a bit. Buzz me when you're ready. Take your time."

Over the summer, Ryan and I had attended a weeklong seminar at the Welcome House offices. It was a comprehensive overview of positive parenting, adoption issues and cultural-diversity awareness. We learned that while Korean society was a progressive one, their general attitude toward unwed mothers was similar to that of the United States forty or fifty years ago. The women were simply shunned, hidden away. Rather than be ostracized by their family and community, unwed mothers were pressured into giving their children up for adoption. That seemed to be the situation with this child.

"What do you think?" asked Ryan, after Jeanie closed the door.

"On paper, she appears healthy and normal. That's what really matters, isn't it?"

We were both still perusing documents, trying to read between the lines for anything suspicious. Nothing alarming surfaced. When most people received their new baby, they became acquainted with the infant through sensory stimulation. They cuddled and breathed in the baby's scent, committing it to memory. I remember scrutinizing every inch of Jake's little body that first day in the hospital, after my recovery and his bath. I had absorbed every inch of him, the discernible shape of his chin, the smallness of his ears, his delicate hands. I remember unswaddling him and surveying his body for birthmarks. I remember counting his toes. And if he had inherited webbed toes or an unsightly strawberry mark, we would still have loved him. He was perfect, because he was ours. With this child, we could only become familiar with her from her description on paper. Someone else's subjective opinion was all that we had to rely on. That's when you realized how critical it was to have trust and faith in your adoption agency. There was no room for skepticism. Trust and faith would ultimately influence our decision. They stood beside each other like the Gemini twins.

We were both hoping the other would make the decision. I did not want to be the first to say yes and persuade Ryan to agree with me. We both wanted the answer to leap from the pages before us and we looked for some sign to show us the way. Feelings of paranoia were clouding my ability to judge the rightness of this decision.

"Ryan, come on. Help me. What do you think?"

He looked at me helplessly for a moment, and then a light bulb of inspiration flashed behind his eyes. "Do you remember when we got married? Remember how I was so sure in my convictions and how you were the one with doubts?"

I nodded. I knew I wanted to be with him, but was distrustful of the idea of marriage, especially with divorce rates at nearly fifty per cent. How did anyone really know if they were marrying the right person? What was right at the moment might not be right five years down the road. I did not want a half-hearted marriage. I was torn over the fact that, perhaps, we were going into this too soon. Maybe, we should have waited another year or two to see if we still felt the same about each other.

Then one day, two weeks before the wedding, I had an epiphany. I realized that I had to live in the moment and not worry about the future. I had to follow my heart for now. And even at the very moment before I walked down the isle, I inhaled and exhaled a deep breath and took the biggest leap of faith in my life. With that, the pressure was gone. It was as though I had conquered my fear.

"I remember," I answered softly.

"Maybe, we have to listen to our hearts and take a leap of faith, just like we did at the time of our marriage."

"So what is your heart telling you?"

He ran his hand through his hair, a nervous gesture I wished he could control, because it made his hair oily. "I think it's yes. Her name keeps drawing me in. Sun he Jung. Jung, as in Carl Jung, the psychologist known for his theories of synchronicity and the principle of equivalence."

I drew back so that I could see him better, and threw him a confused look. "What?" I muttered (as in, "What the hell are you talking about? You're way over my head here!"), "What exactly does all that mean?"

"I'm just saying that, maybe, there is some connection here. The way things have fallen into place for us. Your vision, the dreams you've been having. It's all starting to feel synchronized. Like she was born for us. It just made me think of Jung's theories. That's all."

"And isn't he the one who was thought to be mentally ill when he came up with his ideas?" I asked, trying to recall bits of information from my long ago college psychology classes.

"Being crazy is all relative. It depends on who is judging the crazy person." I sensed now that Ryan felt defensive, because I was challenging him. "Look, you asked for my opinion. I got nothin' else."

We lapsed into silence, absorbed in our own reflective thoughts. Could it be as simple as a name, especially, one given randomly by the social worker? Could it all really be a series of random events coming together, becoming synchronized, as Ryan put it? I looked at the baby's picture once more. "A leap of faith sounds plausible," I said, more to myself than to him. I paused. The more I thought about it, the more the word, "faith", kept flashing inside my head. A voice seemed to say, *do it, do it, do it.* "Okay."

Through the glass wall of the room, I spotted Jeanie and waved her in.

"Ready?" she asked.

"Yes," replied Ryan.

"We accept," I said. Then slowly, but surely, a great sense of relief washed over me and I felt cleansed. Sun he Jung, born in a land far, far away was going to journey to the United States, the "land of opportunity", and become our daughter.

Just like that.

Welcome House Social Services
Pearl S. Buck International

October 15, 2004

Ryan and Julia Leary
1400 Hampton Ave
Attleboro, PA 19040

Dear Mr. and Mrs. Leary,
Congratulations on your decision to adopt Sun he Jung from Seoul,
S. Korea. We have forwarded your child's documents to the office
of Immigration and Naturalization. Your documents have also been
sent to Hill Children's Services in Seoul.

Your visa approval for Sun he Jung's travel should be processed
soon.
Please notify us immediately when it comes, so we can make travel
arrangements for your daughter.

A well-baby report will be arriving in approximately one month.
Her estimated date of arrival in the United States is February
2005.

As always, please feel free to contact us if you have any questions or
concerns.
Sincerely,

Karen Roberts
Karen Roberts

Adoption Coordinator
Welcome House

CHAPTER THIRTY

There was a sense of expectation in the frosty air, the anticipation of new beginnings that came with the New Year. A fresh start. A do-over. It was a time for the absolution of misdeeds and for the initiation of positive changes. It was the one time of year when even seemingly incurable pessimists harbored hopes of a fresh awakening, when people were supremely confident that bringing about changes was easy and that they could lose those extra twenty pounds or finally quit smoking with little effort. Whatever be their cause, the energy in the air was intoxicating for everyone. I was not immune.

It could have been the excitement of facing a new year, the lack of raging hormones or simply the elation over having a new baby in the house soon, but I'd decided that a grand resolution was in order to address my problem with handling money—my not being able to either manage it or save it. I thought about that little secret stash I had tapped off the grocery bill and it occurred to me that if we ran short of money to pay bills because of me, I was only stealing from myself. That was not how I had planned it, when I started hiding money.

One day, while Ryan was having mini-strokes over paying the bills, I started to drown in guilt. A little effort on my part could ease his pain, I thought. For all I knew, I might actually be killing him. Stress had been proven to do awful things to one's health, and I was causing so much financial stress. I realized I had to stop. Going cold turkey might be too traumatic. I needed to wean myself away gently from my spending habits. I would just have to let up, a little at a time. I would start with the gift cards. No more of those, unless I actually did need to buy a gift for someone else. I supposed I could try harder to stay within the budget that Ryan had set up. In fact, I no longer felt I needed things the way I once had. Was it possible that I had become a crazed shopper to distract myself from my own grief? That was it! I was clearly numbing my pain by creating a comfort zone of self-indulgence.

So that was my New Year's resolution: less frivolous spending to ensure that I did not end up killing my husband. He was a decent guy. And despite some quirky habits, I did love him. He was not perfect, certainly, but he was perfect for me. I vowed to stick to my resolution. It was an attainable goal, not an unrealistic one like trying to lose twenty pounds or exercising more.

Our daughter was coming in February. Nothing was going to stop Airplane Day from happening. She was to arrive by escort at any one of the following airports: JFK, Newark or Philadelphia International. The decision to have her escorted to us was the best possible option. Some prospective parents felt it necessary to travel to the baby's native country, become acquainted with the local culture and make the journey back home with the child. We, however, did not feel that it would be productive to take Jake out of school for the entire processing period of two or three weeks. And we certainly would not be able to leave him home for that long either. Also, if Ryan were to take that much time off from work, his pay would be docked. We felt that more would be gained from the experience, if we waited until she was older before taking her to her birthplace for a cultural-discovery visit.

She, she, she. I wished I could stop referring to her as a "she". We couldn't seem to come up with a suitable name for the baby. I had always been partial to traditional English or Irish names such as Kathryn or Erin. I had always pictured a daughter of mine being called Kaitlyn or Lisa. But nothing seemed to fit. I was reluctant to give her an Americanized name. I wanted her to have a perfectly fitting name. Her name had to be neutral and non-ethnic. I kept looking at that awful "leap of faith" photo, hoping it would inspire me. What is your name, baby girl, I thought. What is your name?

Since our placement match with Baby Sun he Jung, Ryan and I had been trying to keep ourselves busy with preparations. In November, we had sent formal announcements to friends and family to avoid having to field endless questions about the imminent adoption over and over again. The response to our news had been overwhelmingly supportive and gracious. Some people called personally. Others sent cards conveying their congratulations and a few passed on notes in their Christmas cards. I knew we had terrific friends. It was comforting to know that the people who mattered most to us already approved of and accepted our baby.

The only person I hesitated sending our announcement to was my mother. For some reason, it was important that I tell her in person. I wasn't sure why I was so apprehensive about the idea of telling her, except for the fact that considering my past history with my mother, things could go either way. Depending on her mood, her response could be either positive or so negative, that she might spit out every nasty thought that came to mind.

The opportunity to speak to her in person presented itself when my Aunt Sara called in November to inform me that my mother had not been feeling well. I caught up with her by calling her on her cell phone, just as a friend was driving her to her primary doctor's office, twenty minutes Southeast of Wilmington, North Carolina. Mother had moved to North Carolina after being ousted from her last teaching position at Penn State's Fayette campus. Naturally, I suspected that her drinking had been the cause of her dismissal, but she insisted that she could no longer tolerate the northern winters and had always dreamed of living near the beach. So she had accepted yet another teaching position at the University of North Carolina at its Wilmington branch. My mother's gypsy lifestyle was hard to keep up with. My address book was full of her residential addresses and phone numbers that I had noted down over the years and subsequently scratched out. There was a distinctive pattern to the way she uprooted herself from one place and set herself down in another. She averaged a move every five years or so. I knew, at least, that she had not left us simply because she had found a better place. I could see now that she was still trying to find it.

So back in November, when the last leaves were falling, I had boarded a flight for the obligatory visit. Somehow, my mother had always had a hold on me. I did not go to her out of some desperate concern for her health. Nor was it a deep and abiding love that drew me to her. I went purely and, inexplicably, out of a sense of guilt.

I packed lightly, not intending to stay more than a day or two. For all my guilt, I also resented having to leave my family to make time for her. After steeling myself in the salty ocean breeze that swept the main entrance of Bayview General, I trudged in through its revolving doors.

I found Mother sleeping in Room 402. I stood in the doorway, motionless and barely breathing, trying to familiarize myself with this woman who had supposedly given me life. It had been a year since I last saw her. Lying there, wearing no make-up and connected to a complex network of tubes, she seemed so old. She was only fifty-nine years old, but could easily have been mistaken for seventy or more. Her hair was whiter than I remembered, having gone from bottle blond to gray. Her wrinkles were deeper, but it was the sallowness of her skin that shocked me. It was the color of sickness, the color of a disease steadily eroding its host body.

"Mother?" I croaked softly. Calling her "Mother" always felt so alien and insincere.

Slowly, her eyes opened. Recognition dawned. "Who called you here?" she asked, as if my visit had somehow offended her. Even her voice seemed to have aged. Or was it, perhaps, the cigarettes she smoked incessantly?

I dropped my overloaded travel purse on the floor near the radiator. "It's good to see you too," I retorted defiantly, stung by the singular lack of welcome in her voice.

Sensing my tone, she huffed, "What I meant was, why are you here? Am I dying? Is that why you came?"

My legs were still stiff from the flight and I chose to remain on my feet. "No, Mother, I came to visit. I heard from Aunt Sara that you had been admitted."

"Sara should mind her own business. I'm fine. I'll be out of here soon." With great effort, she shifted her weight. "Where's my grandson? Did you bring him to see me?"

I loved the possessiveness her words hinted at when she referred to Jake, as if they shared some kind of emotional bond. In reality, she had barely spent enough time with her grandson for him to know her. "Jake has school, Mother. It was not a good time to travel with him. Besides, I wasn't sure what kind of condition I would find you in. This is not a place to bring a child."

She did not answer.

"So what happened? Why are you here?" I prompted.

"Oh, it's nothing, just a little virus," she replied dismissively. "I went to my primary doctor for some antibiotics and now I'm being held hostage for tests."

"Right."

"Please don't give me that patronizing look the way your father used to. I haven't had a drink in over a month, I'll have you know. But I would kill for a cigarette right now."

My meter with Mother ran out after forty-five minutes. It was all I could bear for the moment. She was obviously cranky from alcohol and nicotine withdrawal. That much I understood, but her presence was so cantankerously negative, that I could feel myself sinking with her. I made an excuse of needing to check into my hotel and make a few phone calls and promised to be back later in the day. But not before I'd had a chat with her doctor.

I cornered Dr. Piccard at the nurses' station, interrupting his flirtation with a young brunette. After my brief and unpleasant visit with mother, my own nerves were frayed. I introduced myself to the doctor and cut to the chase. "My mother won't tell me the truth about why she's here. I saw drainage tubes coming out of her, so I'm pretty sure it's not a virus, as she claims."

He cleared his throat and put on his serious-doctor face. "Well, she has ascites, which means her liver is inflamed and there is fluid retention in the abdominal cavity. We have her on diuretics while we're draining the fluid."

"Does she have cirrhosis?"

"Not quite. She's hepatitic. If she does not lay off the alcohol, she could well be on her way." The cute nurse he had been flirting with walked past us with a chart in her hand, leaving behind a trail of perfume. Dr. Piccard's lustful eyes followed her.

"She's battled it her whole adult life."

"Yes, well...It's going to kill her, if she doesn't abstain and get treatment."

"She's already going through withdrawal. She claimed she hasn't had a drink in a month, but I don't believe her. She does that sometimes. Takes months off. What's more, she's missing her nicotine. Look, I only have a couple of days here. Isn't there something you could give her to calm her? She's irritable and downright mean. I can't talk to her when she's like this."

He seemed to understand my needs. He smiled and said, "I'll see what I can do." I hoped he meant, "I'll see what kind of mood-enhancing drugs I can give her." My Visa card treated me to an oceanfront room at the Surfside Resort. Because of the reduced off-season rates, I could afford a luxury hotel. Too bad, I did not have one of my "gift cards" to make this purchase. But I had, so far, managed to keep my pledge of abstaining from unnecessary spending. This charge had been approved by Ryan. It was only a twenty-minute drive from Surfside to Bayview Hospital. I felt that if I had to come here, I might as well take advantage of the beach and squeeze in a walk or two as well.

The Carolinas were a favorite vacation spot for Ryan and me. We'd had neither the time nor the money in the past three years to get away for any length of time. So our "beach fixes" had been day trips to the Jersey shore. It had not been the same as going to the Carolinas. North Carolina water was warmer and cleaner. Being near the ocean and inhaling the salty air was therapeutic. I could understand why my mother had moved here. Perhaps, she was slowing down. Maybe, this move would be good for her.

When I checked back with her later in the evening, she was still irritable. She complained about my brother, Jeff, never coming to see her. It did not apparently matter that he was bound by the military and had, lately, been going back and forth to Iraq, risking his life in covert missions. When he was home in Florida, he trained other pilots, getting them ready for their tours. I assured Mother that Jeff's absence was not intentional; no one saw much of him. He was as emotionally remote as he was physically distant.

I approached the next morning with as much positive energy as I could muster, starting with a three-mile walk along the beach. I walked back along Beach Avenue and stopped at a flower shop, hoping that taking some for Mother would improve her mood. Browsing through the selection, I realized that I didn't even know the kind of flowers my mother liked. There were so many little facts about her I was not privy to. Was it tulips, roses, peonies or hydrangeas? I had not a clue. I decided on a pre-arranged assortment, full of color. Surely, there had to be one flower that was her favorite in the bunch? But my eye kept traveling to a small bunch of white lilies. They were understated, yet, elegant. I bought them for myself. I'd always had this obsessive compulsion to place something personal in my hotel rooms wherever I stayed. Usually, I brought a candle or lavender linen spray, anything to make the room feel like mine, if only for a night. I liked the olfactory stimulation of a scented room. It was calming.

I placed the lilies on the table near the window and stepped back to admire them. Lilies. Lily. Lily. The name kept following me around the room. It haunted me in the shower. Lily. Lily. When I came out of the shower to look for my clothes, I studied the flowers more carefully. What if we named our daughter Lily? That was it: the simple, understated and non-ethnic name I had been searching for. Lily Leary. Perfect. I had once read that many celebrity names were alliterated, so they would be easier for people to recall. I knew Ryan would be easy to convince, because he was completely stumped for a girl's name.

During the entire drive to the hospital, I repeated the name aloud, needing to imprint the feel and sound on my psyche, like an infatuated teenager who scribbles her boyfriend's name all through her notebook. If I were not driving, I would have been doing the same.

This morning, I found Mother sitting up, working on a crossword puzzle.

"Feeling better?" I asked, breezing into the room.

"I slept well." She tilted her head and peered over her reading glasses, studying the flowers as I placed them on the nightstand. "I like yellow roses," she said.

"What?" Here we go again, I thought, more surly attitude. Can't you just be grateful that I brought you flowers?

She removed her glasses. "Yellow roses are my favorite," she explained. "But thank you. You didn't know that, did you?"

"No, Mother, there's a multitude of things I don't know about you." I sat on the edge of the bed. "There are just as many things you don't know about me either."

Like our impending adoption.

"I have tried my best to keep up, to keep myself informed," my mother retorted. "I have never missed your birthday or Christmas, have I? I may not have raised you, but that does not mean that I did not want to know you."

"Right. Because that's all there is to being a parent. Right Mother?" There was an uncomfortable silence between us. Even talking about the old standby—the weather—was not an option.

She sighed, "Okay, let me have it."

Innocently, I asked, "What?"

"Let's hear it. You obviously have something to say to me. Get it out so you'll feel better."

"I don't want to argue with you."

"You still don't get why I left, do you?"

"That isn't what's weighing on my mind right now." Or was it? "I know, I know. You were never meant to be the day-to-day mother. Maybe, you should have never had children. Being a mother isn't natural to every female. I get it, Mother. But it is natural to me. That's why it hurts so much, when I see what you have missed in your life. You said you left to get well, to spend some time in a recovery program. But look at you. Here you are again."

Defiantly, she said, "I am not here because I was drunk."

"But you are here because of your years of drinking. You have alcoholic hepatitis. Do you realize how serious that is? Cirrhosis is next. If you want to live, you have to stop drinking for good. Do you want to live? Maybe, you don't. Maybe, you have always had a wish not to be part of this world."

I moved away and stood gazing out the window at the parking lot below. I couldn't help but notice a couple taking home a new baby. They were everywhere.

"You don't know how hard it is." She eased herself into the pillow. "You don't know how many times I have given it up." Again, that awkward silence filled the room. "Julia, I..." she stopped. "Your father did a good job raising you. If he had been the one to leave and you were left with me, you would have been so screwed up. Please believe me, I was not being selfish." This was one of the many ways in which she assured me that she had done what she thought was best for my brother and me. It was her way of saying that love had prompted her decision.

"I know," I conceded softly.

We moved past the blame and launched into small talk about family members. Talking about others was safe territory. This was almost always the routine we went through, updating each other on the lives of other people. I realized that I made her apologize to me almost every time I saw her, especially, after long absences. It was as if I needed the reassurance. I did not particularly like the idea of needing her reassurances. I wanted to be more mature than that. I was always the child looking for approval and acceptance where I would never get it.

Sometime later, Dr. Piccard came in. He scrawled something on her chart and said. "Well. There is no reason to keep you here any longer. The swelling has gone down. I'll have the nurse remove your tubes and you can go home."

"But why did she black out?" I asked the doctor.

"There was excess fluid in the cranial cavity as well. Acute encephalitis. Just enough to cause dizziness and mixed signals." He closed the chart he signed off on and folded his arms across his chest. "Now, Ms. Connolly," he said. "I am releasing you only on one condition. That you register with a treatment program. I can recommend an excellent outpatient facility in Maryville."

"You think I haven't heard this before?" Mother snarled.

"I don't doubt that you have. But this center, Wedgewood Oaks, has a very good record. It's not your typical AA meeting. It is a holistic healing center. Their detox program combines the best of conventional methods with acupuncture, hypnosis, nutritional support and behavior modification."

CHAPTER THIRTY-ONE

I don't know how he managed it, but Dr. Piccard persuaded mother into agreeing to the Wedgewood Oaks program. She fussed and argued that it would do no good for an old woman like her. Well, of course it wouldn't with an attitude like that, but the doctor remained firm and impervious to her arguments.

And there I was, the dutiful daughter, driving her there for her initial boot-camp induction. She was to complete a seven-day nutritional detox program and acquaint herself with the rules and the routine. After that, she would be released as an outpatient, which would require her to attend three days a week for blood-screening and behavioral-modification meetings.

After leaving the hospital, I took her home at her request to shower, pack and organize her one-week absence from classes. I wished I could have said that we went to her house, painted our toenails and talked late into the night. But it was just another of my Mom fantasies. She would never be that kind of mother. So we spent that night in separate residences.

There was so much I needed to discuss with her, but no moment ever seemed the right one to bring things up. Finally, on the drive to Maryville, I blurted it out.

"We are adopting a child soon." I held my breath, waiting for her response.

"Why?" was all she said.

Not the answer I had been hoping for.

"Because I cannot seem to have another child of my own and I want to raise another."

"Don't you think one child is enough?"

I rolled my eyes at her. "No, Mother, I don't."

"What about your career? Don't you want to work again? Isn't it time you got your Master's degree? You aren't getting any younger, you know. You're thirty-four and you still haven't gotten your career going."

Like you, you mean. "I couldn't care less about my career. Unlike you, I enjoy parenting." She could not say anything to that remark. Why did I feel like I was dodging bullets? "By the way, this child is Korean."

"Korean? Why do you want one of those children?"

"One of *those?*" I mocked.

"What I mean is, aren't there enough orphaned children right here in the United States?"

Of course, I realized that my mother was ignorant of the research and effort that we had put into this decision. But damn if her tone and arrogant questions didn't get under my skin! I was not going to get, "Oh, that's lovely, dear," from *my* mother.

"We have already signed on the dotted line. She will be arriving in February. You're invited to the big hoopla—the welcome-to-the-family party we're having then…if you would like to come, that is." I could not believe I had invited her. It had come from nowhere, but I was sure it was a safe bet that she would not make it.

"I don't see why you would want a child of a different race, is all. Don't you want a child that has some resemblance to you?"

My chest constricted in defense of my waiting daughter. "I look like you, Mother. Does that make us closer or the better for it?" I was now gripping the steering wheel so hard that my knuckles had whitened.

"You should really think it out, is all I'm saying."

Enough! You think I haven't thought this out? I've spent five years of my life being tortured by it and thinking it through!

A full five minutes of silence elapsed, during which I silently cursed my mother for all her shortcomings. I was infuriated with her yet again. It had always been like this. She invariably got in the last word, while I fumed silently and chewed on the inside of my mouth. Well, not this time.

I jerked the rental car over into the empty parking lot of a nightclub and turned off the engine. I climbed out, slammed my car door and paced furiously, organizing the rush of thoughts in my head.

Mother sat regally in the car with her chin jutting out in indignation. "Julia, get in the car."

"No."

"Julia, are you angry because I did not tell you what you wanted to hear? You tend to romanticize things you think are noble. You tend to jump on board without really thinking things through."

How would you even know? What do you even know about me, really?

Her comment stopped my pacing. I stood with my hands on my hips, simmering and trying to recognize the alien creature who sat in my rental car. She was the one who did not see life like the rest of us. She was the one who needed to think things through.

I squinted, aiming to project my most vicious look, the one that usually came out only during PMS week. "You think I haven't thought this through? You know what, Mother? You have no idea of the physical and emotional hell I have been through in the past three years. I have been through the stages of grief more times than I can count. I nearly died during a simple laparoscopic procedure. I had such severe adverse side effects from taking fertility medication, that I thought I had lupus. I spent thousands of dollars and all I got for my money was mounting credit-card debts, for the doctors could not find anything wrong that they could fix in order to get me pregnant." My arms were flailing wildly as I paced back and forth near the open car window. "My heart has felt empty for so long. And where were you? Were you there to comfort me? I know you knew about my time in the hospital and about my miscarriage. Because Aunt Sara would make sure you knew. Did you call to check on me? Hell, no! Were you there to offer moral support? No. Not you."

Mother got out of the car. "Julia...," she started, but I did not hear her.

"I had this ridiculous fantasy that my big news would bring

us closer, that if I confided in you, maybe, you would be supportive. But why would you be so now, when you never have been? You know what? I just realized that you will always be just a fantasy. You didn't leave us because you were too ill to take care of us. You left because you were selfish, and you still are. It's all about you. You're sick, all right, but I'm not so sure it's alcoholism. It's some sort of social disorder that prevents you from fully being a part of the world."

"I don't have to listen to this."

But I had already made her listen, because she was my captive audience. No more biting my tongue, afraid of displeasing my mother. Had she herself ever been concerned about displeasing me? Not at all.

"Take me to that place and you can leave." She stressed "that place" as if it were rancid meat she had to choke down. There was a tremor in her voice.

I was huffing and puffing so hard, my nostrils were flaring. It was the same look I'd seen in her many times, and I detested the similarity. I did not want to resemble her in the least. "Fine!" I shouted. "I'm done. And I don't need your approval or support any more. I know that this adoption is the right thing to do."

"Fine," she said.

Determined to have the last word, I gritted my teeth and said, "Fine!" again.

I left Mother clutching her suitcase at the curb of Wedgewood Oaks. I was relieved that she did not want me to walk her in and see her get settled. Though I would have, had she asked. We did not go through the protracted emotional goodbye. No loving embrace. She stood there frozen, refusing to make the first move. The stand-in mothers in my life had taught me to be the better person. I could not just leave like this. I had to initiate some sort of kindness between us. I rolled my eyes and moved in for a quick hug. "Goodbye, Mother," I said. "I'll call you in a few days."

We were two women, uncomfortable with each other and anxious to part. I left North Carolina and headed home to my family where I belonged, where I felt loved. During the flight, I replayed Mother's words in my head, just as I always had, searching for hidden meanings, trying to read between the lines.

An enormous woman swathed in green polyester waddled down the aisle as I prayed, please, God, don't let her sit next to me. I did not hold her size against her. But airplane seats discriminated against size-challenged individuals and it was completely unfair to those sitting next to them. Instead of the oversized woman, I got a middle-aged one who fidgeted with her rosary. At take-off, she grabbed my arm and muttered a prayer for our safety. It was a bit awkward, but I did not pull away. No sense in stopping someone when she was praying for you. Odd, how a total stranger could reach out to you, but your own mother could not.

Mother and I had been through many arguments and disagreements over the years. Little opportunities would come up and I would just have to interject, "Like you would know, Mother." Or "How would you know about that? You weren't there." A few years ago, she had asked me during a conversation if I remembered my sixteenth birthday. I had replied that I remembered her not being there. Even though she did spend the weekend with me the day after, she had not been there for the party my father had thrown for me.

Our latest tiff, however, was a little more serious than those we had had in the past. She would speak to me again, but it would probably take her a while to gather her nerve. Even though I had gotten some things off my chest, as Dr. Snyder had encouraged me to, I did not feel vindicated. Instead, I felt like an orphan. I felt just as orphaned as Sun he/ Lily was. Suddenly, I felt a deep sense of rightness in bringing Lily into my home. What was that word Ryan had used? Synchronicity. If you really paid attention, you could almost connect all the dots of your life and make everything fit. Could it be, that to be emotionally prepared to adopt, I had to have a non-functional mother, followed by infertility then one conception failure after another?

But wait. If I were truly meant to adopt, why was the matter of finding the money to finance the adoption so fraught with difficulties? Why hadn't I just won the lottery or something? Oh, I was so tired from the effort of figuring things out! It was too much work, really. I vowed to just sit back and learn to let things fall where they might. Just let life flow. Who was I kidding? I simply was not wired that way.

PRE-FLIGHT CHILD REPORT

Escort: rsk

Case No: K 2004-955 Date of Report: 25 January 2005
Child Name: Jung, Sun he   Race/ Sex: Korean Female
Birthdate: 9-27-04 Weight: 16 lbs.

Eating Habits: Takes 140 cc of milk every 3 hours, with good sucking.

Places both hands on bottle firmly, while feeding.

Sleeping Habits:	Sleeps from between 9 p.m. and 10 p.m. until 7 a.m., but wakes 2-3 times for feeding. Takes 2 naps a day for 2-3 hours each. Sleeps lying on her side. Doesn't fret when sleeping.
Toilet:	Has good stool once a day. Several wet diapers.
Speech:	Turns head toward the source of sound. Babbles well. Smiles and laughs aloud, when stimulated.
Ability:	Turns over. Looks at TV. Reaches for toys and other objects. Carries things to mouth.
Personality:	Is not shy with strangers. Likes to be held and to be outdoors. Likes to take baths. Cries, if left alone. Sun he is a cute and lovable baby. I love you!

General Health: Excellent for travel
Temperature : Normal
Teeth: 0
Exposure to Disease: None

Lee, Sin Ju MD

CHAPTER THIRTY-TWO

I was trapped in a sweltering hot room. To make it even worse, hot air was blasting its way in through the vents. I went from door to door, window to window, desperately seeking an opening. All were either nailed shut or painted over and permanently sealed. My mouth was as dry as sawdust. My tongue stuck to the roof of my mouth. And the heat kept blowing in my face. A warbled ring sounded in the background.

I woke up to find myself lying on the couch smothered in a blanket. Perched like a cat on the back of the couch was Taco. He was leaning over me. His catatonic stare alone was enough to rouse me. The phone rang again, but I figured I would let the machine answer it. The hot air in my dream had actually been Taco expelling his breath in my face. He sat there looking at me, his tongue dangling over his jaw like a piece of ham. For such a tiny dog, it was a disproportionately large tongue. I must have fallen asleep while reading. Part of my nesting agenda was to squeeze in the reading of some classics. Reading in itself was a luxury. To manage it with a child around was very difficult. After Jake had left for school, I had headed to the couch to cuddle in a blanket and begin *Lady Chatterley's Lover* by D. H. Lawrence. I had been only twelve pages into the novel when I must have dozed off. All that rambling by Lawrence on how Connie and her sister cavorted with German boys had become monotonous. The phone rang a fourth time and the machine picked up. A click and a pause.

"Hi, Julia. It's Jeanie. I have some exciting news for you. I..."

I jumped up so fast, the blood rushed to my head and for a second I saw those little floating silver stars. "I'm here," I answered, my mouth dry, and clicked off the machine.

"Oh. How are you?"

"I'm good. What's up?"

"Like I said, good news. Your daughter will be arriving next week. We just received a fax, and provided she is healthy pre-flight, she will be on her way. Julia, are you there?"

I could not breathe. It was like I was in full scuba gear and my tank had just run out. Oh, wow. "But I'm not ready," I managed to say. "There's so much to do. It was supposed to be February," I rambled on, as if I were actually going to argue about my long-awaited baby coming earlier than planned. But I had not shopped yet. I did not have supplies. Her bedroom was painted and carpeted and the crib was up, but beyond that, I had nothing ready. Neither diapers nor wipes nor blankets nor bottles.

One rainy day, when Jake was four, I had torn through all of his old baby gear in a tearful rage and given everything away. It had become too painful to see it cluttering our home and taking up space on the third floor. I had needed to cast out the constant reminders that my baby had grown up and I might be finished with babydom forever. Soon afterward I had regretted my hasty rampage. The only items not subjected to my wrath were the crib and some special outfits I could not bring myself to part with. Of course, I still had Jake's wooden high chair, but only because it had once been my husband's and happened to be another of his priceless heirlooms.

After I hung up the phone with Jeanie, I lingered in the new baby's room, trying to absorb the reality of actually having her in my home. In only a week's time, she would occupy this room. In the past months, I had spent several weeks transforming the office into a baby's room. Having been through the experience of decorating a child's room before, I had decided not to confine myself to a theme for this one. With Jake, I'd learned that children grew up very fast and the relevance of baby décor didn't last long enough to be worth the trouble. So this time, I started with a mature girl theme that Lily would grow into. I painted the walls yellow and papered the bottom half in a lavender and yellow floral print. The furniture was white. The carpet was ivory. The rest of the room would be accessorized in yellow and lavender. I scanned the room, making a mental note of all the things I needed. When we had accepted the match in October, I was sure that the period of waiting until her arrival would be an agonizingly slow one. That time would stand still, the way it did when you were a child waiting for Christmas to come. Now it seemed that time had suddenly evaporated.

It was in this adrenaline rush that I slightly regretted not attending the adoption Lamaze class suggested by Lauren. I figured that if the first Lamaze class for Jake's birth had done absolutely no good, why would this one? I wanted drugs then and, to be perfectly honest, I wanted them now—just a little something to take the edge off and help me sleep for the following week, because surely, I would be too tightly wound to get adequate rest.

Phone calls and arrangements needed to be made. Naturally, I started with Ryan.

"Hello," he answered on the third ring, speaking from his school office. I pictured him sitting there next to the phone, but consciously waiting for the third ring before picking up the receiver.

"Want some good news?"

"I could use some. It's been a tough morning."

"Our Lily is arriving next week."

"Wow. That's earlier than we planned. What airport?"

"Philly," I replied, already knowing that Ryan would be relieved to learn that. He had been dreading having to go JFK or Newark and deal with the extra hassle of city traffic.

"Jeanie is going to call back in a couple of days with exact flight info," I told him. "I'm going to see if we can rent one of those club vans so we can all fit in one vehicle."

When Ally had given birth to her third son, her mother, sister, best friend, husband and two older boys were in the delivery room with her to witness the blessed event and immortalize it on camera. As miraculous as new life was, I could never allow a room full of gawkers to watch me discharge a human being from the most private part of my body. But since Lily was entering our life via Philadelphia International Airport, Ryan and I figured it would be a neat opportunity to have a crowd consisting of family members to welcome her. So far, we had ten people on board to welcome Lily.

I phoned Alex at work to share the good news. I mentioned that I was on my way out to go shopping for supplies.

"No, wait," she said. "I uh…well…It was supposed to be a surprise. Lauren and I had a shower planned for you in two weeks. I'll see if I can move it up. Don't buy anything yet."

"It's awfully generous of you, but I can't just sit and twiddle my thumbs. I have to do something. I can't sit still." The nesting syndrome was in full gear now.

"So go clean your house or something."

"I've done that already." Since I had not formally worked this school year, my house had been much better organized. I had even begun to spoil my husband with fabulous meals that sometimes took half the day to prepare.

"So go clean *my* house then." Even though she was joking, Alex was half-serious. It was amazing how a baby could take over a home. When you left for the hospital, your house was orderly and immaculate. A post-baby house was nothing but chaos, especially, if you were back to work full-time and juggling a sexy new boyfriend.

Alex and Bart had become an official item after the birth of Jessica. He had started seriously courting her the day he visited her in the hospital. He told her later that he had fallen in love with two women and couldn't part with either one. He was, of course, talking about both Alex and her baby, Jessica. Bart had been a fairly permanent fixture ever since, so much so that it had considerably reduced the time I got to spend with my friend. I suspected there was little time for Alex to suffer from post-partum depression with Adonis Bart waiting in the wings. She had to be the only woman I knew who could not wait for the six-week healing period to be over so that she and Bart could consummate their relationship.

Bart was a natural father, and the resemblance between him and Jessica was a little uncanny. He was so taken with her that anyone— especially, Dave—would have assumed he was the biological father.

Good old Dave. At least, he had moved on with another girl, but one that definitely ranked much lower than Alex on the beauty scale. Ryan and I had met Dave's new girlfriend, Gina, at this year's school Christmas party. To be honest, I'd been convinced she was a crack addict. She was gaunt, with dark circles around her eyes. Her hair was thin and straggly and in need of a deep VO5 conditioning. Yes, in the war of ex-spousal new love, Alex had won the grand prize. Bart was just too good to be true and that fact made my cynicism tentacles twitch a bit. I wasn't used to fabulous-looking guys being so down to earth. But here he was, and I just could not trust it. I thought I made him nervous, because the last few times I had been around Bart, I had acquired just enough of a beer buzz to question his intentions.

We were gathered at Alex's house, one blustery Saturday evening, for pizza and beer. I was sitting with Bart and Jessica at the kitchen island, when I leaned in and said, "So Bart. You are a legal citizen, aren't you?" I knew his parents were directly from Greece, but wondered if Bart might be in need of a Green Card.

"Yes, I was born here. Were you?" He winked.

Thrown off-guard by his question, I answered, "Well, of course." What did he mean by that? "You know, Alex swears she never wants to get married again. How do you feel about that?" I asked a little insistently.

"The important thing is being together, sharing your life. Who says we have to be married?"

Smooth reply. He must have anticipated my question and rehearsed his answer.

Trying to gauge whether or not I thought his reply was rehearsed, I said, "What if she's just using you for sex?"

"I like sex," he smiled seductively.

Duh! What guy didn't?

"Okay, dumb question on my part." I thought for a minute about what I could ask him that would provide an insight into his psyche. "What if you were marooned on a desert island for a month?

No, marooned indefinitely, what three things would you absolutely need to have with you?"

He took a long swallow of beer, waited for it to go down and said, "Easy. One, my toothbrush." There it was. I knew he was stuck on himself. Wouldn't want to risk losing one of those pearly white teeth, would ya, Bart? "...and Alex and Jessica here," he lifted Jessica up and kissed her head, "would get me through."

Awwww. That's so sweet!

"I said *things*. Alex and Jessica are *people*. Why would you want them to be marooned, anyway?" It seemed a little selfish to want your girlfriend and her child to suffer with you.

With a smirk, he rolled his eyes and continued to play along. "Okay, my toothbrush. An apple tree, because I hate coconut and I wouldn't want to get scurvy. And a GPS tracking band, so that the coastguard could find me and I could get off the damn island as soon as possible."

GPS? That was smart. It was like saying, if you had three wishes, one of them would be to have one hundred more wishes. He was smooth.

Alex came over to take Jessica from Bart. "Julia, stop trying to intimidate my boyfriend. I'm keeping him, whether you like it or not," she chided.

"I never said I didn't like Bart. I'm just trying to see beneath the surface, is all. I figure your eyes are so clouded over with romance right now, that you might be missing a few things." I turned back to Bart. "Come on, Barty boy, everyone has a dark side. What's yours?"

From the corner of my eye, I saw Alex flash me a scolding look before she went off to change Jessica. I knew that Bart's family was quite wealthy and as a lawyer, he made a comfortable salary. So I wondered just how much he valued money.

"How do you feel about pre-nuptial agreements? Would you make your wife-to-be sign one?"

"Basically, people get pre-nups because they feel insecure. It implies that they don't really trust the person they intend to marry.

If you're sure it's the right person, you don't need one. A marriage is a legal partnership; the wife should not be reduced to a mere portion of the marital wealth."

Julia, close your mouth now. Pick your chin up off the floor. Obviously, he is not a divorce lawyer. Was I hearing voices?

Inside my head, I was screaming, "Yahoo!" And I refrained from shouting, "He's a keeper, Alex!" I did, after all, have gracious manners.

I held my hands up, as if to say, truce. "Okay, you win. For now. You seem to be a stand-up guy, but watch your back, buddy. I'm watching you." With that, my left butt cheek could no longer contain itself and I slipped off the counter stool. I quickly straightened to show that I was fully in control of my faculties.

CHAPTER THIRTY-THREE

A s usual, I had a closet full of clothes and nothing to wear. It was finally Airplane Day or Gotcha Day, as some adoptive parents called it. As we were preparing for Lily's arrival, I held up a periwinkle blouse and a red shirt to go with my black trousers. What did one wear to meet a new child?

I turned to fashion-ignorant Ryan for help. "Which shirt says Loving Mom?"

"Neither," he offered, fastening his belt.

"Then I have nothing to wear. Everything is awful." Frustrated, I slumped on the bed.

"Julia, a four-month-old baby will not care what you are wearing."

I nodded forlornly in agreement. "What if the plane crashes?" I was edgy from getting roughly two hours of sleep the night before. The adrenaline was gushing through my veins.

"Stop. Don't think like that. It couldn't be a better day for flying. Nothing is going to happen."

"Are you ready for a crying, screaming baby? Because I'm not. What if she's so scared that she just cries all the time? What if she never bonds with us?"

Receiving a child that could not bond was my ultimate fear. It happened all the time, perhaps, more so with older children, but it happened.

Ryan came and sat next to me, shoulder to shoulder. "I'm nervous too. But it'll be fine. You know there'll be a period of adjustment. It'll take a few days."

I bounced up, noticing the time. "We should get going now. It's 12 p.m.," I said, getting more and more anxious.

"She's not due until four. And since when are planes ever early?"

"But there is always some sort of construction delay on 95."

"If it makes you feel better, we'll leave by two-thirty."

It did not make me feel better. Why couldn't he just humor me a little and leave early? God forbid we'd be late for this most important event. His cavalier attitude reminded me of the time I had gone into labor with Jake. Since it was a Saturday, we had thought we would go out for breakfast. As I was standing at the ATM machine, my water had broken. Actually, it had gushed. We turned around and went back home to call the doctor and get my overnight bag. I had been instructed not to eat anything and to head to the hospital. I was ready to leave in five minutes. But Ryan insisted that he needed to eat something. Not just something. He had started cooking sausage and making oatmeal. When I asked him what the hell he was doing and couldn't he just grab a cereal bar, he had claimed he needed some protein to keep his strength up. *His* strength?

"You do realize that I will be the one laboring for like forty-eight hours and I am not allowed to eat," I had said. He was not persuaded. Then the genius decided to have broccoli quiche for dinner that night at the hospital. So the next morning, when I was finally in the throes of violent labor after the Pitocin kicked in, Ryan was off praying to the porcelain toilet god, because his bowels were exploding. Bad time for him to forget about his stress-induced nervous intestinal problem.

This time around, he had enough sense to forgo eating broccoli quiche. He had been on a strict bread diet all day. The only person not nervous in this house was Jake. He was so thrilled to be getting a baby sister. I was thrilled for him and grateful for his positive attitude. He emphatically believed that all his years of praying for a sister or a brother had paid off. He was not even bothered by the fact that he wouldn't be getting bunk beds to share with a brother. His excitement was probably heightened by the fact that he had got a day off from school and a truckload of new-big-brother gifts from various people. Lately, Jake had been hounding me for his own camera. So we had given him one to take candid photos of Lily's arrival and he couldn't wait to be Joe Photographer for the day.

After getting through airport security clearance to welcome our daughter at the gate, Jeanie met us at Gate 3B. We had made it to Philadelphia International Airport in precisely thirty-eight minutes, with no construction delays on I 95. The sky was crystal clear. Though the sun made it seem as though it were warmer, it was actually 39 degrees outside. Well, maybe, no one else thought it was warm, but I was perspiring and shedding my layers. Since tons of pictures would be taken that day, I had concluded that I should wear a color that flattered me. I had, therefore, chosen the periwinkle blouse.

At ten minutes to four, with the plane on time, I quickly ran down the corridor to the bathroom. I did not want any distractions, once she came off the plane. I knew that the moment I had this long-awaited child in my arms, I wouldn't want to put her down for a bathroom visit.

With just a minute to go, my stomach turned over, as the monitor announced that United Flight 1237 had landed and was taxiing to the terminal. Everyone in our group—my in-laws, Ryan's brother, Dan, his wife, their two children, Alex, my father, Ryan, Jake and I—descended upon the window to watch the plane crawl to the jetway door. We were told that the babies on the flight would be the last ones off the plane to prevent the other passengers from getting caught in the chaos.

What chaos? How much chaos could there be? There was hardly anyone here! There were two other families waiting to receive babies from this flight, but they were not from our agency. Nor, unlike us, did they have an army of family members waiting to greet their adopted babies. It made me wonder if we hadn't, perhaps, gone overboard with our preparations for celebration. But no one had declined our offer to be with us on this momentous occasion. The entire waiting area was fairly empty, which made things a little more comfortable for us. We had plenty of elbow room and quality air space, even though I felt like I could not breathe.

Finally, the plane was at the gate. No passengers, however, were emerging from the plane. Suddenly, paramedics were running down the hallway with one of those rolling beds. They rushed to the jetway door and disappeared. The few people in the waiting area huddled in silence. Then rumors began circulating that someone on the plane had suffered a heart attack during landing. Passengers had to remain seated until the man was stabilized.

Oh, for the love of God, I thought. All these months of endless waiting and now that just a few feet separated me from our baby, someone had to have a heart attack and delay it even more!

The sound of time ticked away in my head, as I began gnawing at my nails. Ten minutes passed. Then twenty minutes went by. Finally, the door opened and an elderly man was wheeled out, escorted by two male paramedics. Then one by one, disheveled passengers disembarked. It seemed to be the geriatric flight because most of the passengers were at least over sixty years old. Then, suddenly, there came a collective "Awwwh!" from the small crowd. I looked up and saw the first escort and baby emerge. Baby No. 1 was bright-eyed with curiosity as she scanned the crowd, looking; it seemed, for her new mother.

She was not Lily.

The second baby appeared. He was sleeping, totally unaware of his fate.

Finally, the third escort appeared through the gate, and there she was! Lily was the one with the big, fat cheeks and jug ears that stuck out from under her red Aunt Jemima hat. She was wearing a red flowered jumper. Yep, that was definitely Lily. Amazing, how I could recognize her from that single newborn photograph. My stomach fluttered.

Then the room started to swirl, and out of nowhere, the waiting area filled with bodies and flashing cameras. Ryan and I had requested our group to act as our photographers, because we did not want to be distracted from the actual event by being burdened with the responsibility of managing a camera. Apparently, they had taken our request very seriously. The flash of cameras was blinding. I caught a glimpse of my father juggling a video camera, a digital camera and a 35 millimeter. He had three camera cases strapped around his shoulders and neck.

Jeanie had given us instructions on protocol. We were not to crowd around the escorts. The social workers would greet them first and check identification. The babies were wearing hospital armbands with the adoptive parents' names on them. I thought that was a pretty clever idea and the band would be a neat little keepsake for the baby book. After the babies had been identified, they would be handed over to us.

So I waited patiently and nervously at the same time.

But no one else seemed to be following the rules.

Why was I the only one adhering to the rules here? Suddenly, I, one of the adoptive mothers, was pushed outside the circle of greeting relatives. An eight-foot-tall brick wall of a man, wielding a paparazzi-style camera, blocked my view. Who are you? I thought. And where did all of these people come from? And, furthermore, why was I standing here doing nothing about it? I was frozen in place. It seemed that if I wanted to meet my new daughter, I would have to fight my way in.

Ryan reached around the big, burly guy and grabbed my arm to pull me into the circle. The escorts were in the process of unstrapping the body slings that carried the babies. Jake was there in the melee, snapping pictures like a pro, working the crowd. Being small made it easy for him to slip through. Before I knew what was happening, Lily had been placed in my arms, and good Lord, she was a pork chop! She was wide-eyed and soulfully took in all the people smiling at her. Her chipmunk cheeks were rosy red, with a slight rash. She looked nothing like I had imagined. My images of her were now a blur. She was fat in the way a baby should be. To my delight and great comfort, she had a chubby, contented little face.

In that surreal instant, there was only one thing of which I was completely sure. This process had actually taken so much longer than a few months or even a few years. A feeling of completion came over me, and I knew that I had waited my whole life for that moment to arrive. It was a truly defining moment in time. I locked eyes with my father and saw the wetness welling up in his. He looked so proud.

Then time fell into a lapse. For a second or two, I felt I was looking at myself in a photograph. Or, rather, it was like seeing it all as a dream, an out-of-body experience. All the voices in the room became one unified humming sound. As cameras continued to flash, I was overwhelmed by emotion and hot tears streaked my face.

When in my life, had I ever cried for joy? I was not wired for happy tears. I regretted inviting so many people to come and witness this experience. I now felt it was too intimate to share with everyone. I was emotionally naked, and it was unsettling to be so with such an audience. Feeling my knees about to buckle, I moved to a chair and dropped into it. I handed Lily to Ryan who had sat down next to me.

Somehow, you manage to get through difficult moments in life. I likened this experience to the fifteen-minute speech I had dreaded making in ninth grade, when my shyness and feelings of insecurity were at their height. I remembered how I had seen swirling stars and nearly fainted from that experience. But I had, somehow, been able to step outside myself and pretend that no one else was around. And that was what I made myself do again, while Ryan and I acquainted ourselves with our new daughter. Jake snuggled beside us, as we examined her in the same way that all new parents do.

Jeanie came over with papers for us to sign. For all I knew, I might have been co-signing a bank loan! Then she handed over Lily's carry-on bag and started pulling items out of it to show us. First, she presented baby formula in single-serve packets. "She is on a milk-based formula," she told us.

"That's odd. For some reason, I thought it would be soy," Ryan commented.

Jeanie pulled out some papers. "Here is her pre-flight health report, and instructions on the type of routine she has been following."

Instructions? Where were my instructions for Jake? One advantage of taking on a second child was that I felt so much more confident this time around. There were two outfits in the bag, her passport and Green Card, a teething toy and bottles. For her first birthday, her foster mother had chosen a beautifully embroidered and jeweled Hanbok in dark pink to wear. Then Jeanie pulled out the most priceless thing of all. "Here are some photographs that her foster family took of her."

Did I say priceless? It had never occurred to me that the foster family might send us photos that documented Lily's life up to this point. I was so grateful for the pictures, because they seemed to fill in the four months I had missed. Even though I knew we were fortunate to get her so young, I still felt that I had missed out on a large part of her infancy.

We arrived home an hour later to balloons and banners welcoming Lily. A veritable food court had been set up in my kitchen. Soon afterward, the party cherubs, Ally and Lauren, arrived. Bart, who was sitting with Jessica, had even met Alex at my house.

As the celebration continued downstairs, I disappeared upstairs for some quiet moments with Lily. I gave her a quick bath, counted all of her toes and examined the birthmark on her lower back. It did indeed resemble a purplish bruise. I spoke softly to her, so she could get used to the sound of my voice. As I was dressing her, it dawned on me that her eyes were keenly focused on me. That was a good sign, wasn't it? In fact, she had looked from me to Ryan, all the way home from the airport.

We'd been informed that newly-adopted babies often demonstrated specific signs of grieving when they entered their strangely different-smelling world. Oddly enough, they didn't, always cry. Sometimes, they turned inward and found comfort in some repetitive movement. Or if all the new stimuli became too much, they might avoid direct eye contact for several days. The easiest way for a baby to deal with loss or separation anxiety was to sleep more than usual. I could certainly relate to that. But Lily had stayed awake during the entire ride home and as she sat between Ryan and me, she never stopped gazing at us. She was still intently observing me and making little grunting noises as I dressed her.

I gathered Lily and held her close. Sitting in the rocking chair, I cuddled her while she eagerly sucked on her bottle and watched me. "I hope you're happy here, Lily," I whispered. "I promise to take good care of you. I'm sorry your birth mother had to give you up. But I'm glad we get to raise you." Then I kissed her gently on the forehead.

CODY & HEFNER, LLP
ATTORNEYS AT LAW

250 PENNSYLVANIA AVENUE, DOYLESTOWN PA 19008
215 555 8115 OR 800 555 8116

January 30, 2005

Mr. and Mrs. Leary
1400 Hampton Ave
Attleboro, PA 19040

RE: Lily Jung Leary (Sun he Jung)
Our File No. 33110

Dear Mr. and Mrs. Leary,
Please accept our sincere congratulations upon the legal adoption of your child, Lily Jung Leary. This is, indeed, a joyous occasion for you and your family and we are happy to have been a part of these proceedings.

We will forward to you two certified copies of the adoption decree and a certificate of adoption as soon as they are received by us. These documents will be sent to us by the Court in about four weeks after the adoption.

We will also apply to the Pennsylvania Division of Vital Statistics to register a birth certificate for your child. This is generally completed in about six weeks. It will be forwarded to you upon receipt.

We thank you for the cooperation you gave us throughout these proceedings and extend to you and your family our very best wishes.

Very truly yours,

Frank R. Steadler

Frank R. Steadler
For Cody & Hefner, LLP

CHAPTER THIRTY-FOUR

In like a lion, out like a lamb was the euphemism for the month of March. How true, how true! We had started off with violent, stormy weather and we were now thankfully creeping our way toward the calmer second half of the month. This was ideal for Alex and Bart who were getting married. They had planned a simple, yet elegant occasion for close friends and family. We were gathered at Pen Ryn Mansion on the Delaware River. I was with Alex and her sister, Maryanne, in the bridal suite, waiting for the rings to arrive. Bart was supposed to bring them, but in his haste, had left them at home, sitting atop the dresser. His brother had been sent to retrieve them. Something always seemed to go awry on such occasions? So, there we were, waiting again and getting anxious. Alex and I had spent a lot of time waiting for things to happen. But this time, it was not for a needle in the ass or a catheter full of sperm up the love canal. This kind of waiting was full of promise.

Alex was reading a story to Jessica to keep her still, so she did not ruffle her hair or dress before the service. "You're so calm," I said admiringly. I think I was more nervous than she was.

"What's not to be calm about? It's right, this time. This is the person I should have married all along." How comforting it must be to know that with conviction. So many people seemed to get married, not really knowing for sure if it was right. "So, how's the sexy therapist, these days?" she asked, teasing me about my schoolgirl crush on Dr. Snyder.

"He's fine, I guess. I haven't seen him in several months. And for your information, I'm over him."

Dr. Snyder had turned out to have flaws like everyone else. He had been unceremoniously removed from the pedestal on which I had temporarily placed him, when I started noticing intolerable quirks in him like his habit of sucking air through his teeth, emitting a sound that, to me, was like fingernails grating on a chalkboard. I had also observed that he had very small, almost feminine hands. Once this had imprinted itself on my brain, it became impossible for me to stay focused on our conversations. I could not help thinking about the oddity of his disproportions. He was otherwise very masculine. It occurred to me then, that strong, manly hands were high on my priority list. How had I sat across from him for so many months and not noticed his hands?

Alex's aunt stuck her head in the door. "We're ready."

Alex looked radiant with the glow that pregnant women seem to give off, once the morning sickness subsides. Just a hint of her new pregnancy teased the pale lilac of her wedding gown. Nothing about this wedding was overtly traditional. She walked herself down the aisle, carrying Jessica on her hip. It was not just a marriage ceremony, but the creation of a family. Bart pledged his love for and acceptance of Jessica as his own and vowed to be her father in every way. After the wedding rings were exchanged, Bart slipped a specially-made ring on Jessica's tiny finger and she smiled on cue. His legal adoption of her would take place the following month in Doylestown family court.

"I will never get married again," Alexandria had vowed a year ago. A year had made a huge difference. It was either that or the fact that she was pregnant again that had overturned her never-marry-again mantra. Strangely, no extra-curricular fertility treatments were needed this time around. Alex had been surprised to find herself pregnant the old-fashioned way.

When the all-day morning sickness first began, she had been so sure she had cancer that she had not confided in anyone. After all, she was losing weight, had no appetite and had been abusing her body for years with chemicals to over stimulate her ovaries. The fear of cancer had always been lurking in the background. When she finally went to her family doctor for an exam, he smirked and ordered a pregnancy blood test. To this, she had balked emphatically, "No. I am not pregnant! There is no way that I could be pregnant. I'm infertile." She had subscribed to the belief that once infertile, always infertile. Maybe, she had just needed the right partner. Maybe, Dave was simply never meant to be the father of her children. Maybe, romantic love in all its newness and excitement had rejuvenated a tired body and forced those hormones to pump out extra doses of receptive eggs. Who knew? I only knew that I was somewhat resentful of people telling me, "You're next. Now that you have adopted, the pressure to conceive will be gone and you'll get pregnant again."

That remained to be seen. Medical science had so far failed to provide an answer to my infertility problem. But I knew one thing for sure. As long as I was conscious of wanting to be pregnant, it would surely never happen. Even though I had now achieved emotional stability, thoughts of pregnancy still visited me. I was always aware of the thirteenth or fourteenth day after my period. The routine had become so much a part of my psyche. There was no longer as much negativity associated with my womb any more. For now that I had experienced the joys of adoption, I no longer felt that giving birth was the be-all and end-all of my existence.

Raising a child, not giving birth to it, was what made a parent.

CHAPTER THIRTY-FIVE

It has now been over a year since Lily graced our family. That's the way I phrase it, when well-meaning people tell us what a wonderful thing we've done for her. It is too soon to judge whether or not we did her a favor by taking her from her native country and removing her from her culture. But our daughter has definitely graced us by her presence. Lily is effervescent with happiness, and has been pleasantly easy and lovable. It is she who has saved me, not the other way around. She has saved me from the depths of depression. She has brought joy back into our lives. I can't imagine my life without her. I know that everyone believes their child is the most beautiful in the world, but Lily truly is. Honestly. She is just adorable.

During the first few weeks after her arrival, however, I was full of trepidation and anxiety. For a full two weeks, I had felt as though I were taking care of someone else's child. Then one day, when Jake and I were playing with her on the floor, she burst into giggles. Her laugh was so infectious that Jake and I started laughing with her. I cannot pinpoint the particular moment when I fell in love with her. But this one moment was close to it. Falling in love with Lily was more of a gradual evolution. But this giggling fit was the moment when I first said out loud to her, "I love you."

Then I realized that falling in love with her was not a feeling I had expected to experience. Before she came, I had been confident that I would express my affection and take good care of her. I suppose I had assumed that since she was my adopted child, there would be some kind of distance, a certain detachment, and that loving her would be different from loving Jake. But there on the floor, as we played with her, I felt like the Grinch whose heart had been too small, but had grown three sizes larger that day. I had naively believed that there was only so much love in my heart to go around, that somehow, I was bound by emotional limitations. But it's true what people say: your heart really does grow with love. In no way can Lily ever replace Jake; my heart has simply found more room for her in all its deflated crevices. I have come to understand and accept that I had been misguided in my quest for a baby. It hadn't been my womb that was empty and waiting to be filled up; it had been my heart, all along.

My children are both equally mine. Lily's almond-shaped eyes are perfectly normal next to ours. Our family is unique. We have all come to feel that it is a privilege to be outside the box. I am at the point in my relationship with Lily where I forget she is adopted until someone reminds me. This usually happens in the grocery store, where people notice Lily and me and remark, "Oh, she's so cute! Is she adopted?"

She is Asian and I am Anglo white. Is it not obvious that she isn't my biological child?

But I smile politely and reply, "Yes."

"Which Oriental country is she from?" a woman recently asked, attempting to sound intelligent, but failing miserably.

I stiffened and answered, "South Korea," but I was really thinking, food is Oriental; people are Asian.

Some people are even crass enough to ask me how much she cost. To this, I grit my teeth and reply, "She is priceless" or "She's worth every penny."

We often feel as though we're on public display. On most days, I don't mind having to educate the general public, but it can become tiring. You just want to get through the grocery story unnoticed and as efficiently as possible.

Recently, my mother, of all people, had the nerve to ask me what had happened to Lily's real parents. It made me wonder when she would stop ramming her foot into her mouth. Of course, I knew what she meant. Her comment had not stung the way it might have once. I had rolled my eyes and said politely "Ryan and I are her real parents." My mother did finally make the perfunctory visit last June and was, predictably, diffident with Lily. It was not so much a racial divide, as it was her general unease with young children. So be it.

Out of necessity, I have moved on. I had to move forward where my mother was concerned. I could no longer cling to a past that I could not change. When it finally dawned on me that my mother would never meet my expectations, I stopped needing her approval. I feel profoundly liberated. Now when she makes an insensitive remark, I am able to respond as I would to anyone—in as polite a tone as possible. I have come a long way in dealing with her.

I have learned to accept things as they are, rather than to fight so much to change them. This is what having Lily has taught me: getting her involved a process of events and there was perfection in the process. Had I not been infertile, I'm certain that I would never have adopted a child. I'm sure of it now. Without suffering infertility there would have been no call to action. Concerning my relationship with my mother, I now think that her absence might have been meant to teach me a valuable lesson. Even if the lesson was just the value of a bad example. How *Not* To Be A Mother 101.

Ryan claims that dealing with people's curiosity is part of the deal of adopting. I don't know who he is trying to fool. He becomes just as defensive as I do when people ask stupid questions. She has her daddy wrapped around the proverbial finger, and it is quite hilarious to sit back and observe how he allows himself to be manipulated by his daughter.

My relationship with my husband is another astonishing example of how love can evolve. Early one morning, after Lily had been with us for approximately a month, I awoke to find the two of them sleeping on the recliner in the living room. Lily was comfortably slumbering on Ryan's chest. I remember sitting on the steps for a moment and gazing at the two of them. Seemingly arbitrary moments in life can knock you off your feet and open your eyes to things you were refusing to see. This was just such a moment. This was the moment I fell in love with my husband all over again. I had imagined that we had moved beyond that kind of new love, that we were settled into some kind of comfortable co-existence. But as I sat there, watching them sleep in his grandfather's Lazyboy, I realized how lucky I was to have this particular man as my husband. We were meant for this. I was such an idiot not to have seen the real person before I had gone through this experience. How could I have missed seeing what a solid person he was?

Ryan had never once regarded my inability to conceive as a challenge to his masculinity. Abandoning me for another, more fertile wife was never an option for him. He had methodically produced the required sperm samples without complaint. He had eagerly and openly embraced the idea of adoption and patiently waited for me to go through the motions and be the one to decide. And he is such a doting father with Lily; it would make any mother's heart melt. Isn't that what women really want in their husbands? The presence of an attentive father makes mothering that much easier. Ryan's confidence enhances my own. So much so, that a year later, we are considering the possibility of another adoption. It is challenging trying to decide whether or not we feel complete as a family.

Like an interloper I too crawled upon his lap, entering the enchanted aura that surrounded them. He smiled and shifted to make room for me. Come, join us, his smile had said. He kissed me on the temple and I absorbed their love. I finally understood that in all the time we had been married, I had never truly let my guard down and let myself be loved like this. Maybe, it had something to do with my mother and fears of rejection? I knew now that with Ryan, this instinct to not give fully of myself was both wrong and unnecessary. After all, I had chosen to marry him, knowing that he would be the kind of husband who would see me through thick and thin.

It is strange how life seems to work itself out. Like a broken puzzle full of individual pieces, everything came together in the end. No matter what you plan for yourself, life always appears to operate on Plan B.

Thanks to Lily, I have a new job. It's one of those cathartic jobs that continually aid in my healing process. Owing to my teaching credentials and adoption experience, Welcome House has invited me to present their introduction seminars. Once a month, I get to eat free hors d'oeuvres and tell people about my personal experience with the process of adoption. I am the person who convinces couples to choose Welcome House as their agency. I also co-instruct the parenting seminars, once couples are in the program. The extra money is nice, but I would do this for free. I feel I have learned one of life's great lessons and am eager to pass it on and save others the grief and struggles I went through. My message is simple: just because you cannot give birth to a child does not mean you have to live childless.

On the marriage front, I have decided that just co-existing is not the kind of marriage I want to end up with. I now put much greater effort into our relationship. I give in a little more, but not too much. I can't give up all control. I try harder to recognize that he has needs as well and that this marriage is not all about me. Although, of course, I'd sometimes like it to be! Making love comes more spontaneously, now that we are no longer "trying" to make a baby. It is an enormous relief to not have your mind wrapped around the singular goal of procreation. One bummer about adoption though: you cannot claim a six-week hiatus due to body trauma the way you can when you actually give birth.

Okay, so self-awareness and a resurgence of love are great, but there is still the issue of my husband's incessant need to vocalize his gastrointestinal belches. He had too much champagne at Alex's wedding and was being very crude in the car on our way home. Ryan has a talent for talking though his extended burps. Jake and Lily are giggling in the back seat like it's the funniest act ever. I'll never understand why bodily noises are so funny to men. Thanks to his dad's example, Jake has begun to master the useless skill as well. I roll my eyes and wonder how I am supposed to break Jake of the habit, if Ryan can't control himself?

We have accomplished much, but some things will never change. I, for one, still have a house full of unfinished projects. I am still plotting to destroy that infuriating grandfather clock. Perhaps, someday, I'll make peace with that too.

Not Flesh Of My Flesh

Not Flesh Of My Flesh,
Not Bone Of My Bone,
Yet Still Very Much My Own.
Never Forget
For One Single Minute
That You Grew Not Under My Heart,
But In It.

Author Unknown